JIM AND TAMMY

Charismatic Intrigue Inside PTL

by JOE E. BARNHART

with Steven Winzenburg

PROMETHEUS BOOKS

Buffalo, New York

B
BAKKER

Library of Congress Cataloging-in-Publication Data

Barnhart, Joe E., 1931–
    Jim and Tammy: charismatic intrigue inside PTL
    by Joe Barnhart in collaboration with Stephen Winzenberg.
    cm. Includes index.
ISBN 0-87975-460-5 : $18.95
1. Bakker, Jim. 2. Bakker, Tammy. 3. PTL. 4. Television in religion—
United States. 5. Pentecostalism—United States—History—20th
century. I. Winzenburg, Stephen. II. Title.
BV3785.B3B37

To the writing staff of the *Charlotte Observer*

Contents

Preface

When my first book, *The Billy Graham Religion*, was published fifteen years ago, Jim and Tammy Bakker had only recently moved to evangelist Graham's hometown of Charlotte, North Carolina. The multimillion-dollar water park and building complex called Heritage USA did not exist even as a dream in Bakker's head.

During my studies at the Southern Baptist Theological Seminary in the mid-fifties, Billy Graham had begun to see the vast potential of television. Bishop Fulton J. Sheen was the only Catholic television preacher who regularly commanded national attention on the television screen. The word "Charismatics" as a religious term scarcely existed outside academic circles and scholarly journals. Also in the mid-fifties a man named Sun Myung Moon, growing up a Pentecostal Presbyterian in Korea, initiated his Holy Spirit Association for the Unification of World Christianity and announced that his book *Divine Principle* was revelation from heaven. In Tulsa, Oklahoma, Pentecostal faith healer Oral Roberts had begun to gain visibility and to stir up controversy as he exposed millions of Americans to the raw drama of what he called the healing line. In Muskegon, Michigan, Jim Bakker was still a teenager trying to get a driver's license.

Twenty-five years later, not only would Bakker become a close friend of Oral Roberts and have Billy Graham on his television show, but he would be seen on TV more often than Graham and become one of Roberts's most formidable competitors for the TV religious market.

Acknowledgments

In my fourth book, *The Study of Religion and Its Meaning*, I began exploring the question of religion in its broad aspects, cutting across denominational lines of every kind in order to discover, if possible, the chief problem that all religions held in common. I had much earlier been led to see the flaw in the claim that all religions were really saying the same thing. It became increasingly clear to me that they were often saying quite. different things and that students of religion ought to be sensitive to the rich diversity of belief and experience.

Over the years I have worked closely with colleagues in the American Academy of Religion, the Society for the Scientific Study of Religion, and other organizations that encourage researchers to share their material on American religious movements. To scholars within these organizations I am deeply indebted for their insights into both televangelism and the modern Charismatic movement.

In early 1987 Stephen Winzenburg and I met at the Anatole Hotel in Dallas to participate in a forum sponsored by the Broadcast Education Association. The topic was televangelism. When I was asked to write an interpretative book on PTL and the Bakkers, Winzenburg came immediately to my mind. He had worked for an Assemblies of God radio station in Florida and written an important thesis on an aspect of televangelism. The chapter under his name in this book represents selections from his thesis and from his paper on the future of televangelism. Any flaws of the book are mine and not Mr. Winzenburg's.

Members of the writing staff of the *Charlotte Observer* supplied invaluable facts, insights, and leads regarding the PTL story. Without their years of hard investigative work on the Bakkers and their ministry, my own research and labors would have remained a bony frame at best. Help from citizens of Charlotte, such as Revé and Quentin Perrault and Tommie and John Hasty, saved me months of work. My warmest thanks to them.

Friends at North Texas State University encouraged me in various ways to complete this book. I am especially grateful to Kay Prewitt and Betty Grise, as well as my good-humored colleagues of the Department of Philosophy.

At home my wife and daughter, Mary Ann and Linda, helped me to meet the deadline. Neighbors in Denton, Texas, were supportive, and I am keenly aware of my indebtedness to Linda Lee and Harry and Dorothy VanDyck. Jim and Traute Danielson of Moorhead, Minnesota, supplied needed information for the research. Gratitude goes to my fellow writer, Lawrence Montaigne, for his sense of humor and encouragement when I needed it most. Above all, I would like to thank Edwin M. Eakin, of Eakin Publications, Austin, Texas, for initiating the idea of my writing this book and for agreeing to publish my forthcoming novel on televangelism.

PART I:

An Overview

In 1958 Jim Bakker at the age of eighteen faced the shattering question, "Will I have to go to jail?" Twenty-nine years later he came face to face with the same question.

1

Premonitions:
From Pulpit To Prison?

For over half a century the renowned Harvard psychologist B. F. Skinner carried out intensive research on pigeons, rats, and human beings, including himself. In a recent TV interview he was asked what he did with his time, now that he was retired. With a twinkle in his eye he replied that he watched TV evangelists. Why? He wanted to understand what caused them to behave the way they do.

If Professor Skinner watched the "holy war" among TV evangelists in the spring of 1987, he could not have overlooked similarities between the antagonistic behavior of the evangelists and the behavior of Norway rats biting one another under adverse conditions. Unlike the prophet Elijah, who slaughtered 450 of his competitors, the TV evangelists hired lawyers to do battle for them in the arena of words and ancient laws. The colorful U.S. bankruptcy judge, Rufus Reynolds, one of the nation's best, said of the PTL case: "What I'm trying to do is separate the preachers and let them preach, and let the lawyers lawyer." He might have found it easier to part the Red Sea.

The spring and summer of 1987 took an astonishing turn when Oral Roberts claimed that Jehovah was about to dispatch a band of angels to carry him home unless his supporters mailed in $8 million of their seed-faith. Meantime, evangelist John Ankerberg was preparing to go on Larry King's interview program to charge that Jim Bakker's December 6, 1980, hotel room encounter with young Jessica Hahn was merely the tip of the iceberg. More surprising to some was the U.S. Justice Department's decision to try to decipher Jim Bakker's financial records and go after him the way they went after the Reverend Sun Myung Moon, who eventually landed in prison. Moon appeared as a minor-league batboy when compared with a real professional like Bakker.

In Southern Louisiana the incomparable, swashbuckling TV preacher Jimmy Swaggart stopped speaking in the tongues of angels and bankers long enough to warn Ankerberg to beware of lying brothers who could not be trusted. He was talking about two of his fellow Pentecostal preachers, Jim Bakker and Richard Dortch.

During this period of Jacob's Trouble, some secular humanists were holding their sides and earnestly trying to refrain from breaking out in laughter as they watched the evangelists wash their linen in front of the television cameras. "There but for the grace of circumstances go I," said one secularist as he watched Tammy Faye Bakker weep over losing one of her earthly mansions and her dog's airconditioned house. A devout cynic piped that the only saint in the entire holy war was Tammy's Saint Bernard.

One of the biggest shocks of the televangelism business was the strange deal that Pentecostal TV star Jim Bakker cut with independent fundamentalist Baptist Jerry Falwell. Considerable controversy still brews over what the deal really was, with Bakker and Falwell accusing each other of dealing from the bottom of the deck.

Tolstoy's classic novel *War and Peace* contains a cast of 500 characters. The PTL story has at least that many. Fortunately the number of major characters is only ten to twenty, depending on how these bizarre and yet truly human events are interpreted. The story began in earnest on Independence Day, 1976.

The 1970s

On the Fourth of July, 1976, PTL's president, Jim Bakker, led in dedicating Heritage Village in Charlotte, North Carolina. His "Praise the Lord" show aired on seventy stations and twenty cable TV systems in the United States, Canada, and Mexico. On his thirty-eighth birthday, January 2, 1978, Bakker broke ground for the new PTL complex in Fort Mill, South Carolina, twenty miles south of Charlotte. By then, Bakker had developed the habit of speaking less than truthfully about his financial operations. In the summer of 1978 he announced that Tammy and he had given "every penny" of their life savings to PTL. Only days later he made a $6,000 payment on a houseboat.

Scandal broke out a year later when the *Charlotte Observer* discovered that $350,000 raised by PTL specifically for supplementing programs in South Korea and Brazil and a transmitter in Cyprus had been diverted. Interviews with three PTL vice-presidents revealed that the money went to pay bills at home, including meeting building expenses at Heritage USA. Concerned that his own integrity and reputation would be tarnished if he remained with PTL, Bill Perkins in December 1978 resigned as vice-president over PTL administrative operations.

1980–1984

At the age of twenty-one, Jessica Hahn took a jet from New York to Florida on December 6, 1980, to meet Evangelist John Wesley Fletcher. A friend of Jim Bakker, Fletcher escorted the Pentecostal church secretary to room 538 of the Sheraton Sand Key Resort in Clearwater Beach, Florida. Newspapers and magazines later called the meeting a sexual encounter. If Jessica's depiction is accurate, however, it could have been called a double rape.

The Federal Communications Commission (FCC), in a bitterly contested 4–3 vote on December 8, 1982, decided not to have a public hearing of charges against Bakker's mishandling of funds if he agreed to sell the PTL-owned station in Canton, Ohio. According to the three dissenting FCC members, the four who voted for this proposal, which Bakker himself had advanced, did so under the expectation that PTL would simply go out of business and that the questionable practices would therefore cease. The *Charlotte Observer*, appealing to the federal Freedom of Information Act, tried to gain access to the FCC records on PTL. From 1982 to 1985 the FCC denied the newspaper and other parties the right to review the documents. Some of the FCC members insisted that Bakker be prosecuted for "fraudulent solicitation of funds over the air." All members were concerned that Bakker had given false testimony.

In 1983 a reporter at the *Observer* received an anonymous phone call advising him to keep alert for the name Jessica Hahn. The caller was identified as an evangelist. In the same year, Richard Dortch became PTL's executive director, second in command to Jim Bakker. (Four years later, Dortch would not only lose his job but be defrocked because of his key role in shuttling PTL money to Jessica Hahn.)

Always eager to court the favor of popular TV ministers, President Ronald Reagan sent a letter to Bakker in May of 1984.

Dear Jim:

Over the years you have been a strong and courageous voice in support of family-oriented issues, and have been very effective in helping us get this important message to the American people. I particularly want to express my deep appreciation to you, Tammy, and the PTL partners for all your work in support of the School Prayer Amendment.

God has truly blessed America because our people have had faith that He would help us face the challenges of life. The traditional moral values are as important today as they were when the nation was founded.

Nancy and I wish you the best for continued success with your ministry, and may God bless all of you.

Sincerely,
(Signed Ronald Reagan)

The year 1984 proved to have far-reaching and ultimately chaotic consequences for Jim Bakker and PTL. Early in the year, he unveiled his Lifetime Partnership Plan, a master scheme to entice more than a hundred thousand PTL supporters to contribute at least $1,000 per person. In exchange for their tax-free contributions, Partners would receive a three-night lodging in the Heritage Grand Hotel every year of their lives. The hotel was a part of the dream that included a shopping mall, a cafeteria, and a conference center. Work began early in 1984 on Heritage USA's 500-square-foot Partner Center.

On September 17, Jim Bakker announced plans to begin construction on still another hotel, the Towers Hotel. Roe Messner served as the contractor, and the plan called for completion by the fall of the following year. Because of several miscalculations and difficulties, however, the first hotel, the Grand, did not open until December 1984. The more grandiose Bakker's Lifetime Partners scheme became, the more it seemed to become a magnet attracting problems.

Eventually, the U.S. Postal Service would step in to investigate allegations of fraud.

The *Charlotte Observer* had been on the PTL money trail for many years. In December 1984, however, the newspaper came face to face with what seemed to be an altogether different type of PTL story, one that called for a critical decision. Jessica Hahn had just disclosed to the newspaper the 1980 incident in the Florida hotel room. Only a few weeks earlier, Richard Dortch had pressed Hahn to sign a document recanting the allegations that her lawyer had secretly sent to PTL. But she later said she felt it was wrong to let Bakker get away with what he had done. She wanted him disciplined by the Assemblies of God, the denomination to which both Bakker and she had devoted much of their lives.

1985

On February 7, 1985, Richard Dortch boarded a jet to Southern California to meet with Paul Roper, the law student who had drafted Jessica Hahn's lawsuit and sent it to PTL. Through Roper's mediation, Dortch arranged a trust and payments for Hahn—all totaling $265,000. Building contractor Roe Messner allowed the PTL payments to be funneled through his company, apparently to keep the transaction covert and inconspicuous. Why Dortch thought he could trust Messner with this sensitive information is unclear—except that Messner was PTL's chief creditor and stood to lose millions if the PTL empire collapsed with the disclosure of Bakker's relationship with Hahn in the hotel room. After shuttling the funds by issuing a check for Jessica Hahn via Paul Roper, Messner billed PTL an equivalent amount in construction invoices. A considerable portion of the money went to cover legal and other expenses. In March 1985, Jessica received $10,045 in interest from what newspapers and magazines later described as the hush money. Hahn and her legal representative looked upon the payments as compensation for emotional damage to her.

November 13 brought more potential disaster. The IRS issued its examination report of PTL's 1981–83 tax returns, which claimed that PTL had operated partly for Bakker's private benefit. The report threatened to revoke PTL's tax-exempt status for 1981–83, and the IRS began opening subsequent years to scrutiny.

November was indeed a woeful month for PTL. After a three-year delay, the FCC finally released its 4,500 pages of documents amassed during the 1979–82 investigation of Bakker and PTL. Local papers kept PTL in the headlines into January 1986, as they combed through the documents.

1986

Evangelist Jimmy Swaggart, having obtained damaging information about Bakker's sexual misadventures, went to the Assemblies of God denominational officials on July 30, 1986, and presented his information about Bakker. This bad news, plus mounting evidence of Bakker's unorthodox financial methods, came together like two weather fronts. Bakker sensed the growing turbulence. Already he had begun paying himself, Tammy, and certain close associates inordinately large sums of bonus money. Later, critics charged that he loaded himself with money because he knew he would have to abandon ship before another year.

Two attorneys, Charles Chapel and Michael Wigton, withdrew from PTL counsel on September 9, 1986. No longer wishing to represent PTL before the IRS, the attorneys explained their reasons in their six-page letter marked "Privileged Attorney-Client Communication, Personal and Confidential." The contents reveal that the excessive pay for PTL executives and the failure to give the governing board power to make decisions severely threatened the tax-exempt status of PTL.

Minutes of PTL's 1986 board meetings revealed that many of the board members were at best confused about the exorbitant bonuses going to the Bakkers and their aides.

Tammy Faye Bakker told a January 1986 PTL audience that someone had just donated a car for a PTL auction. The auctioneer identified it as a Mazda RX7. Contrary to Tammy's suggestion, the $17,000 sports car was not donated; the owner was the Bakkers' daughter.

Near Christmas of 1986, PTL pulled out of the Evangelical Council for Financial Accountability. Jerry Falwell had already withdrawn, and Swaggart had never joined in the first place. Of the top ten evangelists, Billy Graham alone retained membership in good standing. In the year 1986 the Bakkers had collected $1.9 million for themselves. Jim Bakker's executive assistant David Taggart ran up $263,000 in credit-card charges during the same year. In addition, $110,000 in cash advances and loans to Taggart were turned into a 1986 bonus. Bakker's personal secretary, Shirley Fulbright, received a bonus of $80,000 in the same manner.

1987

Tammy Faye Bakker began the new year with a resolution to kick her drug habit. She left her Tega Cay, South Carolina, home to enter Eisenhower Medical Center near Palm Springs on January 13 to be treated for pneumonia and drug dependency.

In January, Jerry Falwell went to Bangor, Maine, to take temporary charge of the ministry of a fundamentalist Baptist church whose pastor had just resigned after revealing his secret adultery. Falwell recommended one of his men as interim pastor of the church, thus allowing Falwell to remain at his "Old Fashioned Gospel Hour" ministry in Virginia.

The month of March rushed in on the Bakkers like a tornado. On the seventeenth, the highly controversial meeting between Jerry Falwell and Jim Bakker took place in Palm Springs. Tammy was present for twenty to thirty minutes for the crucial meeting in which both the Bakkers and Falwell made one of the most important decisions of their lives. Two days later, Jim Bakker publicly announced that he had temporarily entrusted his ministry to Jerry Falwell. He confessed his single encounter with Jessica Hahn in the Florida hotel room. Bakker's chief deputy, Richard Dortch, became PTL president and TV show host to replace Bakker. Falwell, as chairman of the board, became the top executive.

On March 20, Jimmy Swaggart met with Hahn's legal representative, Paul Roper, in Palm Springs to discuss Bakker's lifestyle. Evangelist John Ankerberg and John Stewart were also present at the meeting. The *Charlotte Observer* referred to Roper as the self-appointed watchdog of Pentecostals. Like Swaggart, he was an ordained minister.

Unaware of the meeting in Palm Springs, Falwell publicly called Bakker a good man who both erred and concealed his sin. He claimed he agreed to take over PTL to help Bakker and the organization. On March 23, Bakker charged on TV that he went to Falwell, a fundamentalist Baptist, for help because a fellow Pentecostal evangelist was threatening a hostile takeover of PTL. The next day, Jim and Tammy secluded themselves in Palm Springs, over 2,000 miles from PTL headquarters. New York attorney Roy Grutman, having publicized earlier the hostile takeover claim, reaffirmed that Jimmy Swaggart had plotted the overthrow of PTL. Swaggart denied any role in such a plot.

The spring of 1987 proved to be a hot season for televangelism. Jim and Tammy appeared on the April covers of *Newsweek* and *US News & World Report*. A photograph of Swaggart, with his finger pointing toward heaven, appeared on *Time's* cover. "Unholy Row," the *Time* headline said.

On Monday, April 6, a former PTL board member, Ernie Franzone, registered a complaint with the Assemblies of God, which is the Pentecostal denomination that ordained Bakker, Swaggart, and Dortch. The complaint proved to be the first major hint of a possible battle between the Charismatics and Jerry Falwell's more stolid fundamentalists. According to Charismatic Franzone, PTL attorney Roy Grutman had pressured PTL board members to resign, thus freeing Falwell to appoint a new board to his own liking.

Franzone went on to charge that attorney Grutman claimed to have absolute proof that the Assemblies of God planned to take control of PTL and then put Jimmy Swaggart in charge. (Swaggart and Bakker had crossed swords earlier.) Regretting his resignation from PTL, Franzone said that Grutman told members of the old board that they might be subject to legal action not covered by insurance, implying that it might be a good time for them to make a quick exit.

The *Charlotte Observer* reported on April 18 that the Bakkers received a total of $4.8 million between January 1984 and March 1987. Falwell announced that he was shocked at the money paid top PTL executives. On April 22, three former PTL board members disclosed that they did not know at the time how much Bakker was paid. None remembered authorizing the $1.1 million in bonuses that Bakker received during his last fifteen months at PTL.

A day later, Jim Bakker sent Falwell a long telegram asking him to turn the PTL ministry over to the Charismatics. Bakker hinted of a holy war if his request went unheeded.

On April 24, Baptist TV minister John Ankerberg of Chattanooga, Tennessee, leveled stunning charges that Jim Bakker had had multiple sexual encounters beyond the single incident with Jessica Hahn.

On April 25, the relentless Charlotte newspaper revealed that the opening of the new $26 million Heritage Towers Hotel at Heritage Village USA, south of Charlotte, would be delayed because of financial problems—even though nearly $49 million had already been raised for the hotel through PTL.

According to the August 3, 1987, issue of *Time* magazine, PTL under Jim Bakker had at one time forty-seven bank accounts and seventeen vice-presidents, with financial control divided into four separate departments. Executive turnover was constant. Only Bakker and his closest aides enjoyed anything close to an overview of the money flow. In the final months of the Bakker era, PTL pulled in a monthly average of $4.2 million but spent $7.2 million, leaving a *monthly* deficit of $3 million. Dallasite Harry Hargrave, PTL's new chief operating officer selected by Falwell, found the financial records left by Bakker to be a labyrinth. According to a July 5, 1987, report by the *Charlotte Observer*, more than $70 million was raised through partnerships for the Towers Hotel project, whereas only $12 million actually went toward the hotel's construction.

In the last week of April, Falwell announced on "Face the Nation" that Bakker would never return to PTL so long as he, Falwell, remained as PTL's chairman of the board. Later, he made it clear that he would conceal nothing about PTL's financial history—even if it meant sending Jim Bakker to prison.

Pink slips were issued to the inner circle of Jim Bakker's executive aides after the board meeting on April 28. Richard Dortch, David Taggart, Shirley Fulbright, and many others were asked to leave "in a cost-cutting move." Dortch was said to have exited quietly through a side door after hearing the board's bad news. He was, however, retained as a $13,500 per month consultant through late July 1987. Jessica Hahn's payments were cut off in March of the same year.

Jim and Tammy Faye Bakker's May appearance on Ted Koppel's "Nightline" gave the program its all-time peak in ratings. On May 6, Bakker and Dortch ceased to be ordained ministers of the Assemblies of God by a 13-0 vote of the Executive Presbytery.

Belligerent exchanges between Falwell and Bakker intensified during May and June, Jim charging that Jerry came "with the motive to steal Heritage USA." Claiming that he had only twenty-five minutes to make a decision at the Palm Springs meeting in March,

Bakker said he had asked Falwell to become merely a caretaker of his ministry.

Calling on supporters to save PTL from sinking financially in May and June, Jerry Falwell raised the millions he had hoped for. Like Oral Roberts, he called for a miracle, and he believed it had happened. Three weeks later, however, Falwell acknowledged that PTL owed its creditors a total of $72 million. The miracle to save the ministry now would have to be Chapter 11 of the U.S. Bankruptcy Code. Reading the handwriting on the wall, the board members turned to God and Chapter 11 for a period of grace to carry them through the remainder of the volcanic year.

In mid-June Falwell and his chief executive officer, Jerry Nims, portrayed Bakker and his followers as a cult. Falwell even spoke of a "sort of 'blood covenant.' " Don Hardister, bodyguard to Jim Bakker, resigned from Bakker's service but discredited the wild talk of a blood cult, calling the charge a misunderstanding. All during May and June new accounts of the Bakkers' lavish lifestyle surfaced. Then the story of Richard Dortch began to take focus, revealing that the man who had talked much of heaven seemed preoccupied with the material possessions of earth.

June proved to be an exciting month for the faithful, with Oral Roberts speaking of raising the dead and sharing the limelight with Jesus Christ on the latter's second return to earth. While not exactly Christ coming from heaven, white-haired Melvin Belli, one of America's best and most theatrical attorneys, left San Francisco to make a Sunday, June 21, appearance in Tega Cay, South Carolina. His purpose was to do business with his new clients, Jim and Tammy. The big-chested lawyer comforted the Bakkers, calling them good people, and portrayed Falwell as an "old wart hog."

In Los Angeles, the cigar-smoking evangelist Eugene Scott, who caters to late-night TV viewers, seemed amused at the battles among his fellow evangelists. He created a parody of the conflict, referring to Falwell as "Jerry the Fat" and in general viewing his brethren as something less than colleagues in sublimity.

On August 17 the federal grand jury began investigating the PTL records. Rufus Reynolds, the experienced bankruptcy judge, was placed in charge. Not content to sit in a room and listen to auditors and lawyers, he went incognito to Heritage USA, where he talked to members of the workaday staff. Knowing that he would not greatly

please either side, he resolved to find a way to put PTL back on
its feet.

Inquiring into PTL and the Bakkers may be compared to studying
life in the oceans and seas. Life at a hundred fathoms differs significantly
from life near the ocean's surface. It is profoundly different on the
ocean floor. Much of what has been reported of the life of the Bakkers
and PTL is at the surface, as it were. But there is yet another life
fathoms deeper.

There is no doubt that Jim and Tammy Bakker ushered in a
new style of religious TV programing. They mingled old-time Pentecostal religion with the latest electronic communication techniques
and the new Gospel of Wealth to create the unique "Jim and Tammy
Show." Jim started off in the entertainment business, disc jockeying
at high-school dances. A little over two decades later he became a
religious entertainer-evangelist second to none in popularity and fund-
raising ability.

Tammy Faye Bakker came from the frigid country of northern
Minnesota. In contrast to the outhouse of her childhood, the Grand
Hotel executive suite in sunny South Carolina where she and Jim
sometimes slept in the 1980s had gold-plated bathroom faucets. In
strictly worldly terms, Jim and Tammy had made it to the top. On
the surface, they were the American dream come true.

At the age of eighteen, Jim borrowed his father's car on a Sunday
night to go cruising with his blonde girlfriend named Sandy. The
car radio played his favorites: Little Richard, Buddy Holly, Ritchie
Valens, and Fats Domino. When Jim returned and parked the car,
someone shouted over Fats Domino's "Blueberry Hill": "Jim, you've
just run over somebody!"

When he stepped out of the car and saw what he had done,
Jim began to cry. He had unknowingly run his father's car over
a little boy named Jimmy Summerfield and ruptured one of his lungs.
The child, playing on a snowbank, had slid unnoticed under the car.

The doctors and nurses at the emergency room worked quickly,
trying to save the boy. During the night Jim was terrified that he
would go to jail for killing a child. He got religion and vowed to
give up disc jockeying at school dances. Not until the following morning
did his mother inform him that the child's life had been saved. Over
the following months, Jim began to believe that he was called to

preach the gospel. Convinced that the restoration of little Jimmy from his brush with death was a supernatural miracle, Jim Bakker surmised that his call to the ministry and the child's near-death experience were somehow intricately bound together in the divine scheme of things.

Twenty-nine years later, in the summer of 1987, Jim Bakker again had to face the grim question, "Will I have to go to jail?" This time, it was not an accident that prompted the question but accusations of a long trail of misdeeds committed knowingly and with calculated design.

For Jim and Tammy Bakker, one of the first experiences of the misuse of money in the name of God took place when they were in their early twenties. They were the victims. A missionary whom Tammy calls John Doe (but whom Jim identifies as Dr. Samuel Coldstone) came to preach a revival at the Minneapolis church where the Bakkers were members. "He was a fantastic preacher and God really moved through him," Tammy remembers. He told exciting stories of his evangelistic work in South America. Describing in vivid detail his idea of sailing up and down the Amazon in a fancy yacht once owned by Hollywood star Errol Flynn, Samuel Coldstone succeeded in filling the young and impressionable Bakker couple with dreams of converting thousands of natives on the banks of the Amazon. Coldstone succeeded also in collecting thousands of dollars for his South American ministry, and the Bakkers persuaded him to take them with him in his new missionary venture. He agreed but stipulated that they would have to raise money for their own support.

After giving away all their household belongings, Jim and Tammy went on the road, preaching in revival meetings in churches as a means of raising money for the missionary trip to the Amazon. The revival crusades took them for the first time from Minnesota and Michigan to North Carolina, which to the Bakkers was like going to a foreign country. Amid their success in raising money to become missionaries, Jim and Tammy came face to face with reality. There was no Errol Flynn yacht and no South American ministry. Coldstone had vanished. In Tammy's words, "John Doe was a fake! Most of what he said was lies, and he had spent the monies he collected on himself."[1]

The Bakkers were left with the money they had collected for

their missionary adventure in South America. After praying about it, they wrote letters to churches that had given them money and explained that they were going to use the money to help them become evangelists in America. Then they bought a white Valiant as their first car for the revival circuit.

The Bakkers began their evangelistic ministry with an incredible innocence about them. The Pentecostal Bible college they attended served to keep kids like them insulated, naive, and as ignorant of the world as possible. When Tammy was preparing for her wedding, Jim's boss, Lena, had to say to Tammy, "No, no, honey, you can't get married in red." Today, Jim and Tammy have no pictures of their wedding because the camera broke. They have no pictures of their honeymoon because they had no honeymoon.

As a boy, Jim grew up in an orange house that looked like an oversized citrus. Whenever anyone drove him home from school he always asked to be dropped off several blocks away. He wanted no one to see the eyesore that was his house. Early in life he developed deep-seated feelings of inferiority. Looking back at his youth, he wrote:

> I was a Charismatic before the term was invented—when people who received the infilling of the Holy Spirit were Pentecostals. When I was a child it wasn't popular or even socially acceptable to be Pentecostal. Most of these "fanatics and holy rollers" conducted their services in brush arbors, rag tents, cow sheds, store buildings and little tabernacles— all on the wrong side of town.[2]

Uncanny irony pervades the Jim and Tammy story. In 1980 Tammy paraphrased the account of King David and Bathsheba with such clarity that it appears that she was drawing a parallel between David's fall and Jim Bakker's fall. King David called on his general, Joab, to help him cover up his sin. (Jim a few years later called on Richard Dortch for help in covering up his one-time sexual tryst with Jessica Hahn.) David's sin, Tammy pointed out, "was leading to more and more sin, and David's fear of getting caught was leading him into more trouble."[3] Tammy went on to say that God had sent the prophet Nathan to confront David and to help him stop his downward spiral. (She could never bring herself to think that Charles Shepard's reports in the *Charlotte Observer* might help save Jim from continuing on his downward path.)

As if anticipating the spiraling fall of her husband and herself, Tammy turned to the truly tragic Hebrew story of King Saul: "Power, wealth, and success became Saul's gods, and his power went to his head. . . . Imagine realizing that God's favor was no longer on him— the God who had raised him up and given him power and blessings and honor was no longer close to him."[4] Tammy wrote these words in 1980, the same year she became romantically involved with Nashville recording artist Gary S. Paxton.

The electricity between Gary and Tammy developed slowly and for a while went unnoticed. Gary's wife suspected nothing until a friend phoned to warn her of something developing between her husband and Tammy. He was not someone to whom Tammy would initially have been attracted had she been single. He wore long hair and beads and had the reputation of a man who had yielded to the pleasures of drugs, alcohol, and many women. His songs "Alley-Oop," "Monster Mash," and "Honeymoon Feeling" had risen to the top of the record charts. When he first met Tammy and Jim, he had been a born-again Christian for only a short while.

In time, Tammy had good reason to be sincerely grateful to Gary Paxton. They prayed together and worked hard together, Gary giving his time to help Tammy set her songs in correct keys. He wrote "songs for Jesus" that Tammy would include in her first LP recording in Nashville. "Our spirits bore witness to this man," Tammy wrote in 1978, bubbling with genuine gratitude. By working patiently with her on her singing, Gary gave Tammy a confidence she had never before known. He wrote songs that would fit her voice. In Tammy's words, "Gary opened our eyes to another world and expanded our spiritual vision."[5]

There is every reason to believe that the bonds of care and affection between Tammy and Gary were genuine. And there is every reason to believe that the friendship between Tammy and Gary's wife Karen rang true. Karen Paxton came to understand just how emotionally dangerous falling in love could be. At long last she grasped the truth that her husband and Tammy, stepping over the line, had wandered into an emotional mine field. An explosion was inevitable.

The millions of dollars, the expensive cars, and the luxurious houses that the Bakkers possessed for their personal use seemed conspicuously out of step with much of what they had preached. The chasm between their practice and their preaching appeared so wide that many of their followers began to charge the Bakkers with blatant hypocrisy if not cynicism.

As late as 1983 Jim wrote that the cheating, dishonest tax collector named Zacchaeus "gave back what he had taken wrongfully and shared what he had left with the poor." In the spring of 1987, however, after Jerry Falwell had replaced Bakker at the PTL helm, Jim asked the new PTL board for $300,000 every year for the rest of his life, and Tammy asked for $100,000 annually plus a maid. Not a word was said about returning some of the money to those who had given it. Falwell, whose gross income in 1986 was $435,000, fired back with a demand that the Bakkers demonstrate true repentance.

When asked on TV about the apparent gap between his preaching and his practice, Jim Bakker's reply surprised many who were not familiar with his preaching. Jim brazenly claimed to see no gap because, he said, he had always preached the gospel of *prosperity*. In short, the Bakkers preached what they practiced, quoting in the meantime 3 John 2: "Beloved, I wish above all things that thou mayest prosper and be in good health, even as thy soul prospereth" (KJV).

2

Testing the Faith
From the Cliff's Edge

History has a way of repeating itself. In early November 1973 Jim Bakker in California was president of Trinity Broadcasting Systems (TBS) when the board asked for his resignation. According to Jim, the board wanted to place TBS under one denomination whereas he wanted to keep it interdenominational. "I left that studio that day . . . broke, unemployed and a failure."[1] Getting back on his feet required time and a willingness to borrow money. But borrowing money had already become a necessity in Jim Bakker's life. Even though Tammy came from an exceedingly poor family, Jim had had to borrow fifty dollars from her in order to make a down payment on her engagement ring. They were married on April Fool's Day, 1961.

Though the Bakkers have persisted in charging that Jerry Falwell took over their ministry by the use of deception, Jim himself became personally involved in something of a takeover of PTL in 1974 in Charlotte, North Carolina. Jim and Tammy had begun having suspicions about the handling of money at PTL. Although Jim had developed into a specialist in raising big bucks, creditors were calling in demanding to know why they had not been paid. Jim claims that he confronted Stu Miller, who along with his wife Carol was the corporation's business manager, and said, "I know something is wrong."

Bristling, Stu replied, "There's nothing wrong. Carol and I have everything under control."

Not long after that exchange of words, Carol on a cold morning in Charlotte slipped on a sheet of ice and broke her ankle. While she was in the hospital, Jim took the opportunity to search through her files on the business side of PTL. What he discovered alarmed him. The bills were not being paid. In the words of Tammy, "He discovered poor management and went to the board of directors."[2]

At first the board did not believe Jim, which prompted him to invite the board members to examine the records for themselves. They soon came around to Jim's way of thinking. The bills were clearly not being paid. "God began to convict me," Jim later wrote, "that I was raising money for Christian television and yet I really didn't take responsibility in saying how the money was spent."[3] The PTL board members felt they had no option but to ask Stu and Carol Miller to leave. It was at this time that, in Tammy's words, "Jim took over all phases of the operation."[4]

Jim and Tammy have often referred to their ministry as a roller coaster. Among personality types, Jim Bakker would have to be classified as a risk taker. As a Pentecostal, he believes that the deity gives him very specific directions in virtually every area of his life. Knowing that PTL could not cover a check to one of the many creditors that as PTL head he had vowed to pay, Bakker had the check delivered nevertheless. That was on a Friday. By Monday, enough money came in by mail to cover it. Convinced that Monday's miracle could be repeated within a week, Bakker had another check delivered on the following Friday even though there were insufficient funds in PTL's account. Again the money arrived just in time to make good the check. "Our pint-size faith grew larger with every instance," Jim explained in 1986. "The Lord knew we needed a larger faith for what lay ahead."[5]

Jim compared his ministry to cliff divers at a noted resort in Mexico. He vividly described the breathless swan dive that carries the diver past jagged rocks jutting out from the cliff's side. Life in this daring feat literally depends on split-second timing. The headlong leap must take place while the cove below is empty of water. If it is filled at the moment the leap is initiated, the diver will plunge to his death because the tide's ebb will have carried the water away before the diver's arrival. This means that the leap from the cliff's edge must be made while the cove is empty, so that the diver's hands and head will meet the incoming tide and a surging wave will absorb the bulletlike impact of his body.

Jim's point was that he has often leaped from a financial cliff's edge when the cove below was empty. Each plunge was an act of faith. This financial high dive had become a high-risk way of life for Jim to test either his faith or himself, trusting that the tide (the money) would flow in just in time to save him. Apparently, the need to test himself and his faith has intensified over the years, leading him to take increasingly risky financial plunges. Like a compulsive gambler, he seemed to be telling himself and his followers that with God at his side he could not lose. In the words of Tammy's favorite passage of scripture, "All things work together for good to them that love God, to them who are called according to his purpose" (Romans 8:28 KJV).

Several years after writing those first two checks against an insufficient bank account, Jim's faith either shriveled or encountered something it could not handle. PTL was no longer thousands of dollars in debt. It was millions of dollars in debt. And there was no miracle to save Jim and Tammy. There was only Jerry Falwell breathing judgment and calling for repentance while listing on national TV the sins of the flesh that Jim had allegedly committed.

What happens that causes these so-called ministers of putative spiritual needs to turn into brazen materialists? It is a question that keeps nagging even the most dispassionate observer of the PTL crisis and the Bakkers' deposal. There is an important partial answer that might at first be disturbing to some until they realize that the idea has already occurred to them at least vaguely. The suggestion, very simply, is that words like *spiritual, gospel, Christian,* and even *Jesus* have no established common meaning among Christians. Under the heading of "Christian" can be found a bewildering diversity of interpretations and definitions as to what it is. What seems to one group to be wholly out of Christian character will seem to another quite in character. Until this fact is faced with forthrightness and persistency, little progess can be made in gaining an in-depth understanding of televangelism.

Oral Roberts writes that in the 1940s he "began to be consumed with a passion either to have a ministry "like Jesus" or to get out of the ministry."[6] What he meant by "like Jesus" is clearly not what a large number of Christians mean. Over the centuries, Jesus has become something of a Rorschach or ink-blot test. When individuals report what they observe in the ink blots, they are not so much observing something about the ink blots as revealing something about themselves. What evangelists say about Jesus usually reveals more information about themselves than about someone who lived in the first century.

Oral Roberts, for example, may assume that if Jesus were transported in the flesh from the first century to America today, he would be dressed in expensive suits, driving luxurious automobiles, wearing solid gold bracelets and expensive diamond rings, living in an expensive house—so long as Jesus appeared on TV and said a few hundred words in favor of financial prosperity, pronounced the sick cured, proved himself to be (like Oral or Jim) among the smoothest fund-raisers who ever walked on the face of the earth, and urged everyone in his audience to send in a check at least once a month.

There are books portraying Jesus as the world's greatest salesman. Some second-century Christians, by contrast, saw Jesus primarily as one who laid down his life for others. In those days, those who wanted to be like Jesus cherished the idea of their own martyrdom. Today, TV preacher Jimmy Swaggart sees Jesus as coming in clouds of glory, his eyes as a flame of fire and out of his mouth coming a sharp, two-edged sword. Consequently, Swaggart likes to look his audience straight in the eye and send out a stern message as sharp as a two-edged sword.

Those who charge that the wealthy televangelists are not "like Jesus" fail, therefore, to grasp that among Christians there exists no universally accepted description of Jesus. Some see him in terms of his turning the other cheek, giving someone in need the coat off his back, and having no home of his own where he could lay his head. Most people who claim to want to be like Jesus will first select certain characteristics that fit with their own values and will then label those characteristics as those of the real Jesus.

How did it happen with Bakker? How did a follower of Jesus Christ end up with a walk-in closet longer than many suburban homes? The probable answer is that a drastic change took place in Jim and Tammy's image of who Jesus Christ was. But if that is the case, how did their image of Jesus change?

It started back in the 1960s, when Pastor Russell Olson told the Bakkers that they should not travel by bus from Minneapolis to Burlington, North Carolina.

"What'll I do?" young Jim asked.

"I think the Lord can take care of this," Olson said to his young assistant and then reached into his pocket, presenting Jim and Tammy with the money to fly first-class to North Carolina.

Pastor Olson knew how poor the Bakkers were and how very hard they had worked in his church. They truly deserved a treat. A harmless first-class ticket was something special they would remember all their lives. It was a generous gesture from Olson's warm heart. But it may have left the Bakkers with the impression that the Lord had given his approval of going "first-class." More than one TV evangelist has announced that "nothing is too good for God," or "God always travels first-class." The name on the ticket, however, is never God or Jesus, but the evangelist's name. God is the supremely rich Daddy; therefore, nothing is too good for his children, especially those who are ordained.

But this kind of logic and its special premises did not develop overnight in the minds of the Bakkers. There is no clear-cut evidence to show that they consciously set out to pile up a treasure of this world's goods. There is, however, reason to believe that the goal of being "big time" and climbing to the top in the realm of material possessions became a part of their character before they were in their thirties. It was as fundamental as their sense of being called to evangelism. Indeed, it was so fundamental that gradually and steadily it became entwined with their sense of divine calling.

There was another factor: stardom. For whatever reason, Jim Bakker became early in his life an outstanding and absolutely remarkable fund-raiser for religious TV programs. Pat Robertson recognized that the finanicial success of his own Christian Broadcasting Network was largely due to Jim Bakker's phenomenal ability to solicit checks from TV viewers. Both Jim and Tammy had the Charismatic's ability to shed tears on television, a talent that Pat clearly lacked.

Jim and Tammy could not help sensing that in their own genre and circle they were on the way toward becoming TV stars. Their puppet show was a sensation with children. As a religious talk-show host, Jim was winsome and professional. Tammy's combination of vulnerability and boldness made her an interesting one-woman show for a lot of Christians about whom no one seemed to care. In short, Jim and Tammy were soon a part of show business. And along with this image of being in the entertainment business (mingling it smoothly with the evangelism business) came the image of living in the Garden of Success. The question of how the Garden of Success became the Garden of Excess cannot be answered, except superficially, without exploring Jim and Tammy's roots in Pentecostalism.

PART II:

Roots

3

Growing Up in
the Pentecostal Womb

As children, both Jim and Tammy were deeply disturbed by the question of how they came to be born into the Pentecostal world. Long before reaching adulthood, children are likely to wonder who they would be had they been born into another family and neighborhood. To children, this question is both intriguing and disturbing, and it reveals to them how utterly dependent they are upon the circumstances of birth. A culture cannot be inherited through genes, but it is everything the child learns or receives from the family and community in which he happens to grow up. The Pentecostal faith creates a unique subculture which shaped the personalities of Jim and Tammy Bakker.

At the age of ten, Tammy Faye La Valley lay on the floor of a Pentecostal church and spoke in tongues, which may sound unintelligible to outsiders. Among Pentecostals, this is still regarded as one of the peak experiences of human life. An anthropologist would recognize it at once as a rite of passage that normally transforms the Pentecostal believer into a full-fledged insider.

Unfortunately, Tammy's passage was almost muted because her mother was divorced. Among the Assemblies of God in the 1940s and 1950s, divorce was spelled with a scarlet D. Despite the putative experience of the baptism of the Holy Ghost (outwardly manifested in speaking in tongues), Tammy was denied the full status of being an insider at her Pentecostal church because of her mother's abasement. As little Tammy Faye saw it, her mother was denied rightful participation in her church despite the woman's musical talents. "I couldn't

27

understand how they could take her money but wouldn't let her play the piano."

Not that Tammy's family had a lot of money. Only after Jim and Tammy had married did Jim learn how poor the family was. Months elapsed after the wedding before Tammy in tears found the courage to inform her husband that she was from a family of eight children. He had assumed his wife to be an only child. Never having met Tammy's brothers, sisters, or parents, Jim decided to journey with her to her home in International Falls, Minnesota, nestled on the Canadian border. To his astonishment, he learned that his bride's home had only an outdoor privy—in an area where temperatures could reach forty below zero in the winter. Since the house had no worldly luxury such as a bathtub, Tammy offered Jim two large galvanized tubs filled with steaming water, one to wash in, the other to rinse in.

Tammy still remembers feeling like an outsider in her childhood. She suffered what sociologists call status anxiety. The people of her local church seemed to the impressionable Tammy to be mean-spirited toward her mother, who was not even welcome at the church altar. Anyone divorced and remarried was treated as one who had committed the unforgivable sin. "To the church," Tammy said, "my mother was just a harlot."

Many people have remarked that the more-than-generous application of cosmetics to Tammy's face gives her the appearance of the stereotypical harlot. A psychoanalyst might suggest that Tammy's admitted cosmetic excess is an unconscious identification with her mother-viewed-as-a-harlot. The more significant point is that from childhood Tammy viewed herself as unjustly alienated from her church community. To compound her sense of estrangement, her church was itself regarded by the community as a congregation of emotionally unstable "Holy Rollers."

It is a testimony to young Tammy's powers of abstraction that she succeeded in distinguishing the ritual and drama of her church from its flawed human members. It was the ritual itself—the emotional Pentecostal service—that gave meaning and personal status to the vulnerable pre-teen girl's life: "I'll never forget the sight of my precious little brothers and sisters kneeling at the altar, their little hands raised, tears streaming down their little faces, saying, 'Jesus, Jesus, Jesus.' " According to Tammy the adult, it was the baptism of the Holy Spirit that allowed her to keep her sanity. By submitting to this ritual, Tammy in effect compelled the church to collectively grant her a positive social status. This happened despite the misgivings that individual members had regarding her mother and, by association, regarding Tammy. It is not surprising that the child clung with desperation to the ritual. It was perhaps all she had that allowed her to stake her claim and thereby become *somebody* in her church.

A modern Charles Dickens could write a profoundly moving novel based on Tammy La Valley's childhood. She was a small girl; as an adult she now stands only four foot eleven. An inordinate amount of fear plagued her childhood. Even after becoming an adult, she became convinced she had committed the unpardonable sin of blasphemy against the Holy Ghost. The stark terror that this conviction inspires cannot be fully felt by those who have not grown up in either the Pentecostal or the fundamentalist environment. Both the Russian novelist Nikolai Gogol and the English poet William Cowper suffered from the conviction that they had committed this sin against the Holy Ghost.

Those who did not grow up as Pentecostals are sometimes prone to ask, "Why didn't Jim and Tammy simply step out of it?" The answer is complicated. In the first place, an individual's cultural conditioning is not like an overcoat that can be easily removed and cast aside.

One of the most astute twentieth-century anthropologists, E. E. Evans-Pritchard, spent years observing the people of the Zande culture in Africa. In great detail he described what he labeled as their "mystical way of thinking," which included belief in the power of witch doctors and the efficacy of certain magic medicines. He observed that members of the Zande society were quite capable of doubting some of the claims about the powers of witch doctors and magical medicines. What they were not capable of, however, was abandoning the entire mystical way of thinking. Why was this so? In part, the answer is that they had been indoctrinated in no other way of thinking.

Evans-Pritchard refers to the Zande mystical way of thinking as a web of belief:

> In this web of belief every strand depends on every other strand, and a Zande cannot get outside its meshes because that is the only world he knows. The web is not an external

structure in which he is enclosed. It is the texture of his thought
and he cannot think that his thought is wrong.[1]

So it was with the Bakkers. In his May 1987 interview with
Jim and Tammy, Ted Koppel urged them not to wrap themselves
in the Bible when answering his questions. Both Jim and Tammy
replied that they knew no other way to reply.

The Bakkers have been submerged and are drenched in Pentecostal
language, and it should not be surprising that they would employ their
own language and modes of thinking rather than wholly secular modes.

Ted Koppel made little in-depth progress in interviewing the
Bakkers on "Nightline" because he could not enter fully into the
Pentecostal mystical way of thinking and speaking. By insisting that
Jim and Tammy speak exclusively in the categories that he recognized,
the incomparable Koppel gained an important advantage in the
exchange but lost an opportunity to enlighten his audience on the
subtleties of the Pentecostal web of belief.

Growing up as a strict Pentecostal female meant that Tammy
did not wear jewelry or cosmetics. Not until after marrying Jim did
she venture to wear lipstick daily. Before the marriage, Jim referred
to Tammy as "my little holiness girl." Years later Tammy wrote:

> It seemed as though holiness was a list of what you could
> or could not do. . . . For example, your hair had to be worn
> in a certain way. Your blouses all had to have long sleeves.
> There was no mixed bathing. Your skirts and dresses had
> to be a certain length. Earrings, lipstick, powder, fingernail
> polish, rings, jewelry—these were all forbidden.[2]

The girls at Tammy's church were taught that any female who wore
makeup was not a Christian.

I had a pleasant conversation with a young man who worked
at Heritage USA, located about twenty miles south of Charlotte,
North Carolina. His grandfather had been his Pentecostal pastor.
"My mother wore no makeup," he told me, "until she was thirty-
five. She was forty when she first had her ears pierced." The young
man went on to say that he had been engaged to a young woman
who in his judgment wore too much makeup. She refused to comply

with his request to use considerably less. The disagreement ended
in the dissolution of the engagement. The young man's grandfather
had earlier been forced to resign from his West Virginia pastorate
when as a widower he married a woman who had been divorced
for six years.

Even wigs were once regarded by Pentecostals as sinful. When
Tammy first asked Jim for a wig, he replied, "What makes you think
of wearing those sinful things? Of course you can't have a wig." In
his late thirties Jim Bakker was able to look back at his childhood
and make the following chilling observation:

> I used to be literally terrified of God. When I was just a
> small child, someone put up a large black and white picture
> of a human eye in my Sunday School classroom—it must
> have been three feet across. To me, the eye was God himself,
> and he was looking directly at me. . . .
>
> No one ever made me understand that God wanted to
> help me, not punish me. . . . And over the years I've dis-
> covered that lots of other people had a similar experience
> in their first concept of God.[3]

Like Jim, Tammy remained a devotee of the Pentecostal faith.
But as the years progressed she stretched its boundaries. She not
only ceased asking her husband's permission to buy this and that
("The head of the woman is the man," 1 Corinthians 11:3), but began
wearing both "a little eye makeup" and a string of beads. "It seemed
that everything that I did brought fear into Jim, and then it backlashed
in me and brought fear into my heart."[4]

Like Tammy, Jim had grown up with the conviction that women
should "adorn themselves in modest apparel, with shamefacedness
and sobriety; not with braided hair, or gold, or pearls, or costly array"
(1 Timothy 2:9). Through her television ministry, Tammy Bakker
has unquestionably opened wide the door to a new freedom for Pentecostal and Holiness Christian women, freedom to dress more or less
as their neighbors did. At PTL's Heritage Village USA, "mixed bathing" is permitted in the pools inside and outside the hotel. Swimsuits are no longer forbidden, though generations ago the wearing
of swimsuits was denounced from virtually every Pentecostal and
Holiness pulpit as vile and wicked. Immodest attire is redefined in

terms of the scantiness of the swimsuit. It is the evangelist Jimmy Lee Swaggart, not Jim or Tammy Bakker, who warned Pentecostals against mixed bathing and wearing swimsuits regardless of the size.

In the spring of 1987 a vast audience of Pentecostal and Holiness Christians applauded Swaggart's denunciation of the film industry and most television programs, especially soap operas. Before the emergence of television in the early fifties, Pentecostals and Holiness believers regarded it as sinful to attend the movies. Tammy shares her own childhood experience regarding the movies:

> One time my mother and father were going to see the movie *The Ten Commandments.* I told mother if she went to that movie I'd leave home and never return. I thought it would keep her from backsliding. They went, and I cried and cried. I saw my very first movie after I was married. I'll never forget it. It was *White Christmas,* with Bing Crosby.[5]

Jerry Lee Lewis, Jimmy Lee Swaggart, and Mickey Gilley grew up as cousins in the Southern Louisiana town of Ferriday, located on the west bank of the Mississippi. Jerry Lee and Jimmy Lee were more like brothers than cousins. Music and Holy Ghost religion became the succor and substance of their young lives. Like his older brother, who had been run down by a car and killed, Jerry Lee had the fire of music in his bones and marrow. Jimmy Lee Swaggart, whose younger brother had died of pneumonia, burned with another fire, a religious zeal fanned by the little white Assemblies of God church and by his grandmother, Ada Swaggart.

Ada had been to a Pentecostal camp meeting in Snake Ridge, and upon returning home she spoke in tongues and told stories of "miracles and works of wonder." Sitting in Ada's home on Mississippi Avenue, Jimmy Lee felt the thrill of sanctification and of the baptism of the Holy Ghost. At the church, traveling evangelist J. M. Cason stirred the congregation, inspiring Mamie Lewis to jump and shout in the aisle while her younger sister, Minnie Bell Swaggart, howled in praise and ecstasy. Mamie's sister-in-law, Irene Gilley, kneeling before Brother Cason at the altar, shouted to heaven in an "unknown tongue," and Minnie Bell's husband, Willie Leon, suddenly sprang to his feet, crying and shouting. Falling to his knees, Evangelist Cason wept and praised heaven as women lost in the Holy Ghost rolled in the aisle and men stomped their feet and spun around amid the noise of tongues roaring like swarms of locusts.

Later that summer, Jimmy Lee became so filled with what he was sure was the Holy Ghost that he could speak no English for several days. By contrast, cousin Jerry Lee Lewis was so filled with music that he could not get enough of it. The music that he would eventually play and sing across America and Europe was branded by his Pentecostal relatives as the devil's music. Sometimes Jerry Lee became almost convinced that he had received the gift of music only by selling his soul to the devil.

Strange things were happening to the three young cousins who together had played music, gone swimming in Lake Concordia across the railroad tracks, licked ice cream cones at Vogt's Drugstore, and listened to the preaching and shouting inside the little white Pentecostal church. Jimmy Lee Swaggart quit going to the picture show with Mickey and Jerry Lee. "Don't go to this place," a voice said to him. "I have chosen you as a vessel to be in my service."[6]

Assemblies of God preachers inveighed against tobacco, liquor, movies, dance halls, gambling, mixed swimming, and life insurance. Believing as they did in the imminent return of Christ to earth, many of the faithful looked upon life insurance as a clear sign of unbelief. Jimmy Swaggart's branch of Pentecostalism did not believe in drinking diluted strychnine or handling rattlesnakes to prove their faith (as suggested in the strange ending of the King James Version of the Gospel of Mark). In the mountains of East Tennessee, there were Pentecostals who did dare to pit their faith against snake fangs and to drink deadly drinks. Some Pentecostals lost their lives, and a few lost their faith. In handling snakes, Pentecostal women proved that they were equal to men in faith and courage, or in whatever drove those Pentecostals to such holy/unholy extremes.

If Pentecostals were strict about women's dress codes and cosmetics, they were radical in their views on women preachers. While other Christians suffered bitter internal battles over whether to ordain women, Pentecostals were ordaining women and had been doing so for decades. Even ultraconservative Jimmy Swaggart chided fundamentalist Baptists for their refusal to ordain women. The single most important scriptural proof text employed by Pentecostals to support the ordaining of women is Acts 2:17–18:

And it shall come to pass in the last days, saith God, I will
pour out of my Spirit upon all flesh; and your sons and
daughters shall prophesy, and your young men shall see visions,
and your old men shall dream dreams: And on my servants
and on my handmaidens I will pour out in those days of
my Spirit; and they shall prophesy.[7]

Partly because of their belief that women are open to the highest
Pentecostal religious experience of the baptism of the Spirit, the
Assemblies of God recognized from the start of their movement in
1914 the freedom of women to receive the "gifts of prophecy, tongues,
healing, and discernment of spirits." Leaders of the Charismatic
movement, self-consciously aware of having an impact on religion
in America in the 1980s, insist that the gifts of the Spirit are available
to both men and women in what they see as a mounting battle between
supernatural cosmic forces.

Pat Robertson, with whom the Bakkers once worked at CBN,
claims that through supernatural gifts bestowed by the Holy Spirit,
"human beings may be able to harness the force of storms, or overcome
the power of mighty oceans, or sidestep lethal bolts of lightning."[8]
Robertson is convinced that a powerful storm coming in off the Atlantic
would have demolished his Virginia TV station had not the answered
prayers of Charismatics turned the storm north toward New York.

Taking their cue from 1 Corinthians 12, today's Charismatics
and Pentecostals insist that the dispensation of supernatural "gifts"
did not end with the death of the first-century Christian apostles
but continues to this day. The word *charismatic* derives from an
ancient Greek word that means *gift* or *bestowed favor*. Believers like
Jimmy Swaggart and the Bakkers are the heirs of a model that compels
them to view the universe as a perpetual battle that has risen in
intensity in recent years. Despite their invectives against Charles
Darwin's theory of evolution, the Pentecostals exhibit a kind of Christian Darwinism that portrays life as endless conflict and fierce competition. But whereas Charles Darwin spoke of *natural* selection, the
Pentecostals speak of *supernatural* election and damnation. For them,
the universe is populated with supernatural powers and cosmic personal
forces in fierce competition with one another.

Modern secular men and women sometimes find it exceedingly
difficult to believe that anyone in the DNA-and-space age could view

the universe in this way. Even though modern-day men and women of industrialized nations dress more or less alike and process their money through similar banking and investment institutions, they often perceive the world in drastically different ways. At one end of the continuum is the secular outlook that regards angels, demons, and gods to be nothing but fiction. At the other end is the worldview of people like Jim and Tammy Bakker, who can scarcely carry on a sixty-second conversation on any topic without making reference to God, Satan, demons, Jesus, or supernatural miracles. "There are two forces in the world—God and Satan," Tammy wrote. "We are in the middle."

It is not that Charismatics deny the existence of the material world of jet planes, trees, molecules, and genes. Rather, they look upon it as a mere tool in the hands of the real and ultimate powers of the universe, namely, invisible personal beings that are divided into two camps, one devoted to doing good, the other devoted to doing nothing but evil. The scientific approach to the natural world is largely beyond the understanding and interest of the new Pentecostals. If they talk about science at all, they usually mean technology.

For the past three centuries the impact of science on Christianity has been steady and relentless. Witches were phased out so that most Christians of the eighteenth and nineteenth centuries lived as if such underworld creatures no longer existed. Angels have been relegated to limited roles in Christmas plays and manger scenes. Pentecostal leaders today rarely claim to have been visited by angels. At Heritage USA exists a strange scene of a simulated mine that is worked by bearded dwarfs, something that vacationers might expect to see at Disney World. What is unique about the Heritage USA dwarfs, however, is the little white wings attached at their shoulder blades. The entire setting is one of make-believe designed for children, classifying angels alongside Grumpy, Dopey, Sneezy, and Snow White's other friends.

Supernatural wonderworks and miracles have fared a little better than angels in the past three centuries, even though one school of evangelical Christianity succeeded in convincing a number of Christian leaders that the "dispensation of miracles" ended near the close of the first century, presumably when the last book of the Bible was completed.

Not all Christians, however, have accepted this stern verdict. Many have settled for a compromise, which allows for miracles upon rare and usually highly critical occasions; God may step in with a miracle when all else has failed. The new Pentecostals, by contrast, have opened the floodgates so that for them miracles abound everywhere. Pentecostals who take their faith seriously are expected to testify to several miracles in their lives. To go through life without being able to report even one spectacular miracle would relegate a Pentecostal believer to a very low spiritual status.

The existence and role of demons among Christians has enjoyed a bizarre and checkered history. One Christian tradition insists that while Satan and his underlings once infested the entire universe, they have been largely contained and effectively divested of power. A large number of Christians in practice live as if demons either do not exist or are too anemic to cause trouble. Among the new Pentecostals and Charismatics, however, Satan and demons are given major parts in the salvation drama.

When Tammy Bakker talks at length about fear in the lives of believers, the word *Satan* dominates the conversation. Tammy speaks of Satan as a personal being who is untiring in his efforts to ruin her life: "Satan must really laugh sometimes at how we act. I bet he really licks his chops when he sees we don't understand God's great love." If she is frightened in a storm or in a jet plane, Tammy always ascribes to Satan a major role in generating the fear in her. "There are millions of little fears that confront us. Satan loves to attack in the small areas of our lives. He can't take our salvation, but he tries to take our joy. He's no dummy; he's a bully who's trying to ruin our victory in Jesus."[9]

Fundamentalists share with Pentecostals and Charismatics the belief in an activated underworld of demons under the rule of the Chief Mobster, Satan. One fundamentalist with a doctorate in theology recently testified in a legal deposition that UFOs not only exist, but are piloted by demons. Pat Robertson is convinced that in 1977 citrus grower Norvell Hayes saved his orange groves from fire by ordering the devil to take his hands off the orange trees. His neighbors lost trees; but according to Robertson, Hayes's trees were spared by supernatural intervention.[10] Robertson's speculations are based on what lawyers call special pleading, that is, focusing on incidents that support his theory but sweeping under the rug the numerous incidents that contradict it.

In the Pentecostal culture of Jim Bakker's youth, pastors and traveling evangelists regularly reported instructions that, they claimed, came directly from heaven through them. Today evangelist Jimmy Swaggart often says to his audiences, "The Lord told me to say this to you." Fundamentalists among Baptists and other Protestants, however, are more likely to speak of "the Lord's leadership" or to use toned-down words such as "guidance" or "the moving of the Spirit." Traditional Protestantism ranks the words of the Bible higher than any communique from heaven that a fellow believer might profess to receive.

In many ways Pentecostal language is steeped in exaggeration and extravagance. When ministers can look people in the eye and say, "The Lord said thus and so to me," it becomes difficult for both them and their fellow believers to question the message. Presumably, the appropriate response among Pentecostals to a communique from God is obedience, not raised eyebrows and doubt. It is not surprising, therefore, that the surpreme temptation of Pentecostal and Charismatic evangelists is to presume a one-to-one correlation between their human words and the words of the deity. The Pentecostal culture not only encourages evangelists to yield to this temptation, but provides them an entire script for intimidating anyone who questions them. The script states that anyone who questions what the evangelists designate as a prophecy or word of knowledge is the instrument of Satan.

Pentecostal evangelists have as a consequence become both the bearers and the victims of Pentecostal culture. Evangelists who allow their prophecies and pronouncements to be questioned are regarded by fellow Pentecostals not as rational human beings seeking to improve their ideas by exposing them to the criticisms and opinions of others, but as spiritual weaklings. They are viewed as lacking in authority. A kind of religious macho is expected of the evangelists.

In her November 1987 interview with *Playboy,* Jessica Hahn expressed the macho expectation succinctly: "And they're *fierce.* Especially these guys, they're real tough in their preaching. And I thought, God—that authority when they get into preaching." Stated in another way, the Pentecostal culture encourages its evangelists to develop the habit of regarding criticism as an attack on God. The idea of a friendly critic is overshadowed by the belief that critics are enemies. The final step is to regard criticism and critics as devil-inspired.

A comparison between evangelist Billy Graham (a Southern Baptist) and evangelist Jim Bakker proves enlightening. The *Charlotte Observer* discovered the existence of $22 million in a world mission fund of the Billy Graham Evangelistic Association. One reporter from the newspaper revealed that Graham was invited downtown to talk with members of the newsroom. He accepted the invitation and was informed that the newspaper knew of his plans to use money from the world mission fund to build a Bible school in Asheville, North Carolina. Graham was informed also that the newspaper would have to report that the money for the college had been solicited as money for world missions and not for a school in Asheville. Instead of denouncing the newspaper as the tool of Satan, Graham thanked the newspaper people and instructed his own staff to cancel the school project.

By contrast, Bakker used the *Observer* as a foil by which to portray PTL as God's righteous citadel undergoing a ruthless attack by vicious news reporters. Unlike Graham, Bakker refused to face up to the fact that the newspaper articles about him might be more than a diabolical plot in the service of the Antichrist.

The battle between the Bakkers and the Charlotte newspaper began at least as early as 1977. Rather than profit from the newspaper's criticisms by mending their ways and correcting their flaws, the Bakkers used them to make a profit. In the long run they paid a heavy price in more than one way for their eagerness to portray criticism as a satanic assault.

4

Seven Years at CBN

In 1978 the PTL Satellite Network was launched as the first to beam twenty-four hours of Christian programing daily to all of North America. Many believers regard this as the Bakkers' crowning achievement. The earlier story of Jim and Tammy at Pat Robertson's Christian Broadcasting Network is, however, more intriguing than the 1978 PTL Satellite triumph.

It was in 1965 that Jim and Tammy were invited to join CBN in Portsmouth, Virginia. They had been married for four years and had no children. Since the Bakkers were on the road most of the time, Jim thought it wrong to try to raise children in such unsettling conditions. Both Jim and Tammy related well to children, as the success of their traveling puppet show proved. It was in fact their vital rapport with children that interested Bill Garthwaite, a producer at CBN, in trying to entice them to start a program for children on CBN television. Realizing that they knew little about television production, the Bakkers seemed ambivalent about going on TV. With Garthwaite's encouragement and help, they nevertheless agreed to produce a special children's puppet show.

Feeling excited about a show that Tammy and he had just done, Jim received a call through the station's switchboard. To his dismay, the woman calling in did not reinforce him but criticized him severely, telling him to get rid of the "silly puppets" before they brought an end to his entire ministry. With the air let out of his balloon so soon after his debut, Jim temporarily lost interest in television. But the Pentecostal woman who had called in to criticize did not intend to discourage the Bakkers. Jim Bakker was a spellbinder in the pulpit, and the caller felt that a man with Jim's gift of preaching should not waste his talent by entertaining children with puppets. The woman did not understand that in America evangelism and entertainment have frequently joined hands, a good example being evangelist Billy Sunday's one-man show during the roaring twenties.

Pat Robertson sent letters in the mid-sixties urging Jim to join him at CBN. Jim sent a "no thanks" letter, which prompted Pat to write him to talk about it when they were in the Virginia Tidewater area again.

Today, Pat Robertson's television building contains four studios filled with the latest state-of-the-art technical equipment. Gerard Thomas Straub, who was once CBN's television producer, spoke with authority when he said, "Beyond a doubt, the [CBN] television facilities are the best in the world and are the envy of every television operations manager in the country. Two of the studios are bigger than anything I ever worked in at all three networks."[1] There are at least a dozen cameras, costing $100,000 each. Thanks to direct-mail marketing over the years, Pat has created a technological wonder with a $20-million price tag. Special seminars tailored to wealthy supporters are regularly given by Pat Robertson's ministry—much like Oral Roberts's—with lavish banquets and special pitches orchestrated to separate the wealthy from some of their wealth. While waiting for the Second Coming, Pat resides in a luxurious home estimated at over $350,000 and pays a landscaping bill that might have caused Jesse James to wish he had become a Baptist preacher like his father, after making a few opulent adjustments.[2]

For a while at least, one of the CBN executives became convinced that God had chosen CBN to catch the Second Coming of Christ on television. In the meantime, a CBN crew journeyed to Turkey in hopes of reporting that a team of searchers had located Noah's Ark. They returned to Portsmouth with no convincing videotapes.

When Jim Bakker visited CBN studios in the mid-sixties, however, he saw none of the splendor and glitter. Instead of a palatial lobby with dual staircases, marble floors, Persian rugs, a huge crystal chandelier dedicated to Jesus, and a marble sculpture depicting the disciples at Pentecost, Jim saw only a shabby, rundown studio in a poor section of town. In those days, Robertson did not speak of someday trucking in a large wooden cross to suspend from the domed ceiling. Rather, he spoke of his vision of broadcasting the gospel throughout the world. Sitting in a dusty parking lot off Spratley Street, the two visionaries prayed together and swapped miracle stories until Jim looked Pat in the eye.

"Pat, we'll come and work for you on one condition."

"What's that?"

"We'll do a children's program, but I also want to do a late-night talk show one day."

This dream of a talk show had been Jim's for a long time. It was now time to begin transforming the dream into reality.

The "700 Club" talk show that brought Pat Robertson his initial fame was conceived and originated by Jim Bakker, the show's first host. Tammy accurately calls Jim the dreamer in the family. After watching Johnny Carson on TV, Jim began tinkering with the idea of a Christian talk show. A creative genius knows what to borrow and what to add for his own purposes.

According to Tammy, there was constant conflict at CBN, in-fighting to see who would sit at Robertson's right and who at his left. Tammy described him as the kind of person she both intensely liked and intensely disliked. He had been good to Jim, recognizing Jim's talent from the start. The Bakkers had sometimes confided in him, for he was older and had been to college and law school.

Having started in innocence, Tammy was by now a discerning woman. She saw Pat as vulnerable to people who, by playing on his weaknesses, could manipulate him. She resented the way he brought in new shows that had nothing to do with the Christianity that Pat and Jim professed. She resented it because CBN had promised that it would remain a 100-percent-Christian station. What Tammy did not understand at the time was that once a station reaches a certain organizational level, it develops a life having needs of its own, especially the need for money to fuel the engine. Compromises had to be made with "the world" in order to keep CBN alive.

Robertson lost almost $6,000 trying to track down a widow thought to be on the verge of handing $1 million over to CBN. Jim was the only one at CBN who had the courage to go to Pat to say that the effort to track down the rich widow was not the Christian thing to do. In true Charismatic form, however, Jim prefaced his words with the claim that his message to Pat was from the deity.

Eventually, Tammy began to think that Jim's "other woman" was CBN. At six in the morning he served as the radio show emcee and at night on the "700 Club," which sometimes carried into the morning hours. Sandwiched in between was the "Jim and Tammy Show." Preparing for these programs was hectic. Tammy began to feel left out. "We've got to start having some fun," Tammy said to her weary husband. He agreed and they made arrangements to go out that evening. Before evening came, the radio station manager asked Jim to work the late radio shift because the staff was typically short-handed.

"I'm sorry, Jay, I've promised to take Tammy out. I've been up to my ears in work and we haven't been out together for months."

"Well, you still have to do it."

Jim shook his head, repeating that he couldn't. According to Jim's account, that was the way the conversation ended, with Jim simply assuming that Jay would either find someone else or do the shift himself. Jim claims that he did not at the time know that Jay had asked and been turned down by all the other announcers.[3] Tammy's version of the story adds one interesting detail left out by Jim. She says that Jay warned, "Okay, Jim, if you don't work tonight you are fired."[4]

On their way home from dinner that Saturday night, Jim turned on the radio to WXRI and received nothing but silence. When no one had arrived to take over at the station, the announcer from the previous shift had shut down the transmitter and left, locking the door behind him.

At Pat Robertson's office the next day, all the blame fell on Jim Bakker. Pat insisted that there was a chain of command at CBN and that if Jim's disobedience were overlooked, discipline could not be upheld. Pat knew, however, that Jim was his prize fund-raiser. In the spirit of good business and compromise, he fined Jim $100.

Jim resented the injustice and said, "Pat, I've been here long enough that if you feel I need disciplining in front of the whole organization, I guess I'm finished here."

Over a week later Jim returned to the studio to finish packing. Pat called him into his office and shut the door.

"Jim, I want you to come back."

Jim said that God didn't really want him to leave, which prompted Pat to pull two fifty-dollar bills from his pocket. "I'll pay your fine, Jim."

Jim declined, paid his own fine, and went back to work, this time closer to Pat than ever before.

While working as a born-again believer at CBN, production manager Gerry Straub had an unforgettable experience, an account of which he recorded on audiotape on February 21, 1979.

It was an astounding day. Straub recorded that a project known as G.S.P.—God's Special Project—would temporaily remain top secret. A high executive at CBN entered Straub's office and began revealing a project that was in his mind so big and scary that he said he could talk about it to absolutely no one except Straub. The executive appeared nervous, as if perhaps it might not be wise to tell even Straub about the secret. The secret was: "I believe that the Lord was telling me to get ready to televise—to capture—the Second Coming."

The project was so overwhelming to the CBN executive that he kept trying to dismiss it from his mind. When it refused to be suppressed, he concluded that the project was a command from God to get the cameras ready. Later, after leaving CBN, Gerry Straub made the following observation:

> As I listened to the tape I had two reactions. First, I couldn't believe I had forgotten this bizarre incident; second, I was frightened to hear myself speak in such a fundamentalist style. . . . The tape jarred my sleeping memory. At the time I was listening to this man confess his secret thoughts, I had no idea what to make of it. I instinctively doubted that God would tell anyone to televise the Second Coming of Jesus, but I was touched by his sincerity.[5]

At Straub's suggestion, the CBN executive agreed to bring a third man from CBN in on the secret project. Caught up in their vision, they were sure that special cameras would be required to capture the greatest show on earth. They wondered where on earth they would place the cameras. Jerusalem, of course. But would not the radiance of Christ be too bright for the cameras? Yes. Adjustments would have to be made. The three men spoke calmly about the details, convinced by now that God had brought them to CBN for this holy purpose.

The third man saw nothing incredible in any part of the discussion. In fact, he spoke of using his time wisely during the thousand-year earthly reign of Christ and his followers after the Rapture. In the millennium he would produce a film on the life of Moses.[6]

Jim and Tammy Bakker were not a part of the vision of capturing the Second Coming of Christ on CBN television, but they breathed regularly and deeply the air of Pat Robertson's twilight-zone Christianity. While working at what can only be described as a frantic pace for Pat and CBN, Jim Bakker developed ulcers and suffered what Tammy called a nervous breakdown. While everyone around CBN was talking about miraculous cures (Pat proclaiming the healing of everything from receding gums to breast cancer), Jim was falling apart. He had to give up taking showers because the water felt like pins pricking him. For a month he secluded himself in the back bedroom and, Bible in hand, begged God to save him from losing his mind totally.

The management at CBN sent word to the Bakkers that Jim would receive no more salary while he was at home sick. It was as if a faithful soldier of the Charismatics had been wounded and left to die in a ditch. After a friend went to intercede for Jim, management reversed its decision. Tammy alone carried the "Jim and Tammy Show" for that fearful month. Jim's condition seemed incurable. He could digest nothing but cream, and he wanted no visitors in the house because he could scarcely endure their walking on the floor. Tammy could not touch him. She could only watch him weep night after night, begging God not to let him go completely insane.

Eventually, Jim learned what had caused his illness. He had forgotten that he was a mortal of flesh and blood who needed rest and a sensible diet. They had lived in the CBN twilight world of wonders for so long that they had forgotten the natural world that ordinary mortals have to heed and come to terms with.

Jim's health soon began to improve. In fact, things were going too well for an adventure-seeking risk-taker like Jim Bakker. He had a reasonably good salary, national TV exposure for his ministry, a beautiful house, and good friends in Virginia. In November 1972 he went to Pat Robertson. "God wants me to leave CBN," he said.

Even though Pat said he would not argue with God, he did tell Jim that the board had just voted him a salary increase. But Jim knew he had to leave. The parting between the two Charismatics was friendly. They had maintained respect for each other over the past seven years. On the last night at CBN, Jim realized that he was again an outsider.

According to Tammy, the Bakkers had barely pulled out of town when some of the CBN staff in an apparent surge of jealousy completely destroyed the set that had been used on the "Jim and Tammy Show." The set had cost thousands of dollars. Others of the staff watched in tears and disbelief at the orgy of rage. The head of Susie Muppet, a favorite puppet in the Bakkers' show, was axed and torn to pieces. The videotapes of the "Jim and Tammy Show" for children were erased—at least seven years of videotapes wiped out forever, despite the fact that they could have been rerun for years to come. It was as if there was a need to eradicate the very memory of the Bakkers from CBN.[7]

After starting the "700 Club" for Pat Robertson's CBN and eventually leaving CBN in November 1972, Jim and Tammy proved themselves once again to be innovative entrepreneurs. In 1973 they started the "Praise the Lord" show for Paul Crouch's Trinity Broadcasting Network in Southern California. Before the year ended, the two Pentecostal preachers, Paul Crouch and Jim Bakker, agreed to disagree about TBN. The Bakkers moved to North Carolina, where they became traveling evangelists. Within months, the Bakkers initiated a new television ministry in Charlotte, North Carolina. From California they brought with them the initials "PTL."

Almost from the initiation, the PTL Network in North Carolina was set in conflict with itself, reflecting the two sides of Jim Bakker's character. On the one hand, he held to the ideal of financial accountability and became convinced that the couple in charge of financial integrity had failed to live up to that high ideal. On the other hand, Jim Bakker seemed unable to keep from skating out on thin ice economically by giving in to poor business procedures and yielding to what appears to have been an almost eerie need to take irrational risks as a method for proving his faith.

By 1977 the *Charlotte Observer* was calling attention to Bakker's unorthodox and unnecessary style of handling money. In 1979 the Federal Communications Commission charged PTL with soliciting money for one project but secretly using it for another. Bakker launched an attack on the FCC, claiming that Satan was using the FCC to try to "stop God from sending revival to this generation." In 1974 and 1975 a rumor spread among TV preachers that the atheist Madalyn Murray O'Hair had petitioned the FCC to prohibit all religious broadcasting. Even though there was no substance to the rumor, Bakker used it as a club on the FCC and to portray the FCC as a tool of Satan's drive to censor religious broadcasting. As Jeffrey K. Hadden and Charles E. Swann noted in *Prime Time Preachers*, by the end of 1980 the FCC was flooded with twelve million pieces of mail protesting O'Hair's nonexistent petition to shut down televangelism.

A lot of water has flowed under the bridge since the November day in 1972 that the Bakkers departed from CBN. In response to the Bakkers' battle with Falwell over PTL and Heritage USA in the spring of 1987, Pat Robertson tried at first to divorce himself from televangelism. At times he calls himself a businessman; at other times he identifies himself as a news analyst after the order of Walter Lippmann and William F. Buckley, Jr.—which Pat clearly is not.

In the holy war of 1987, Oral Roberts came early to Jim Bakker's defense and publicly attacked Jimmy Swaggart's criticisms of the Bakkers. By contrast, Pat Robertson's burning ambition to become president of the United States made it absolutely essential for him to stay out of the battle that had absorbed the energies of several generals of televangelism, including Jerry Falwell, John Ankerberg, Oral Roberts, and Jimmy Swaggart. There is little doubt that Pat Robertson's hopes of becoming a major voice in American politics were severely crippled by the Bakker incident. Robertson had set out on a long campaign to try to lay most of the problems of America at the doorstep of what he labeled secular humanism. But the Bakker incident reminded even his most devoted disciples that human greed and weakness of the flesh did not originate with, and are not even peculiar to, secular humanists. The boast that television evangelists were the agents appointed to bring America back to God—that is, to the evangelists' peculiar version of God—seemed suddenly hollow, self-serving, and pretentious.

5

War Among the Pentecostal Big Guns

The one preacher who until early 1988 spoke via television to the largest audience in the world was Jimmy Swaggart of Baton Rouge, Louisiana. New York lawyer Roy Grutman called him the Sir Laurence Olivier of modern evangelists. Like Oral Roberts and Jim Bakker, singer-preacher Swaggart has deep Pentecostal roots. Faith healing, speaking in tongues, and prophesying in the Holy Ghost were the staples of his religious upbringing. After reaching middle age and traveling to other continents, however, he discovered that people not of his particular subculture could speak in tongues, too, and make bold claims of miraculous cures and works of wonder.

In the spring and summer of 1987, the increasingly desperate attempts of Oral and Richard Roberts to raise money by promising miracles and works of wonder embarrassed Swaggart. Gifted with the kind of self-confidence that often comes with never truly understanding a view of the world different from one's own, Swaggart has recently been thrown into something of an intellectual corner. He is currently trying to do what a number of other Christians have already done, namely, rethink the thorny question of miracles.

Swaggart's self-image and public image did not, however, readily free him to assume the role of a student of religion. He saw himself as a divinely appointed evangelist, and he was perpetually told by his admirers and many employees that he was supernaturally gifted with extraordinary discernment—"to see things that maybe no one else can see." Given this self-image, it becomes difficult for him to

47

'think of himself as a student of religion. He does, of course, refer
to himself more narrowly as "a student of the Word," by which he
means the Bible. Even in this sense, however, his study is typically
the folk biblicism found primarily in the South. That is, he approaches
the rich and diverse literary strands of the Bible as if they were a
self-contained theological document. The idea of examining the Bible
as a network of streams that are fed by ancient sources outside the
Bible itself is largely foreign to him. He is virtually closed off to
the world of scholarship that examines biblical materials in the broader
context of cultural sources and comparative literature. Consequently,
Swaggart is left with accounting for competitors like Jim Bakker
and Oral Roberts in a way that many modern Christians and Jews
no longer accept.

When he saw Oral Roberts pour holy water over a pocketbook
to demonstrate how to obtain a miracle, Swaggart became incensed
and labeled Oral's money-raising gimmick as chicanery. A large
number of Christians, Jews, and naturalists in America would readily
agree with this judgment. Not content to see Oral and his son Richard
as mere tricksters and practitioners of flimflam, however, Swaggart
turned to another hypothesis to explain Oral's behavior. He insisted
with his well-known bluntness that Oral Roberts was a false prophet.
Not only that, he referred to the pseudo-miracles and wonderworks
that Oral performed as the work of evil supernatural spirits. "There
is something in those men [Roberts and Bakker] that makes people
follow them. And it's spirits. And it's not the Holy Spirit," Swaggart
warned. "Lying spirits, homosexual spirits that are in these men—
and that's what these people follow. They don't recognize the true
spirits, and [therefore] evil spirits come. . . . Brother, it's a power,
I want you to know; and that's why people follow [them]."

Even though Oral Roberts switched over to the Methodist church
in 1968 amid considerable opposition and controversy, he remains
entirely Pentecostal in his theology and outlook. Most conservative
and liberal Methodists are unsympathetic to his faith-healing claims.
Ironically, the minister who brought Roberts into the Methodist fold
was Finis Crutchfield, who died with AIDS in May 1987. Crutchfield
was written up in the October 1987 issue of *Texas Monthly* as "The
Gay Bishop," and had been known as Jimbo in the gay bars of Houston
and New Orleans.

After listening to his admirers extol him as a preacher possessing supernatural power to see things that others cannot see, Jimmy Swaggart had to face the puzzling question of why ordinary taxi drivers, housewives, and car salesmen who are not Christians could see that PTL and Oral Roberts were "ripping off the public." More disconcerting to the usually self-confident Swaggart was the fact that the ordinary person on the street had no problem in seeing through Oral Roberts's flamboyant claim that God was going to kill him if the $8 million failed to come in. "Why is it that a large segment of the body of Christ didn't know?" Swaggart asked with a puzzled look. He realized that the logic of his premises had led him to the awkward conclusion that hundreds of thousands of his fellow Pentecostals had less discernment into what was going on than their atheist neighbors and other non-Pentecostals.

It might seem that Swaggart would have given serious attention to the thesis that perhaps there was something about the Pentecostal view of the world that made Pentecostal people highly susceptible to being hoodwinked in certain pockets of their lives. Instead, Swaggart plunged deeper into the Pentecostal worldview to resolve his mental turbulence triggered by the public ridicule concerning Jim Bakker and Oral Roberts.

Almost half a year after the story of Oral's television plea for $8 million broke in the news, Oral appeared on "Larry King Live" and said that it was all a misunderstanding. The news media, he charged, misconstrued his meaning. The truth according to Oral Roberts is that God, speaking in English, informed him that he had failed to follow previous instructions: "You have not done what I have told you to do."

According to Roberts, even though the American Medical Association had granted the medical school of Oral Roberts University a charter for producing medical missionaries, not one of the school's graduates had gone to the mission field. "I told you to take medical missions to the ends of the earth, and you've not done it. I'm going to give you a year to turn the medical school around" the Lord allegedly said to Oral, who replied that he had tried to obey.

"I will not reward you for trying. I reward you for doing," the Lord persisted, adding that he wanted Oral to "scholarship all the medical students, so for each year of scholarship they'll go to the mission field." Oral claims that the Lord was clearly stating that if he failed to turn the medical school around within a year, God would call him home. "Your work is finished."

The $8 million, Roberts claims, represented the amount needed for medical school scholarships. He insists that God did not hold him hostage or threaten to kill him. On the surface, at least, it appears that Richard Roberts must have misunderstood his father too; on TV he asked for money because he did not want his father to be taken away. It would seem odd that one so skilled as Richard Roberts in receiving unequivocal messages from heaven would fail to understand his own earthly father in Tulsa, unless Oral failed to communicate clearly in the first place. Even after hearing Oral's attempt to clear up the confusion, Larry King with good reason asked, "Weren't you saying, 'If I don't get this I'm going to die?' "

Oral's answer was a yes and no.

According to one late summer 1987 poll, Billy Graham was still held in high esteem by the majority of Americans. Below Graham, in order, were Robert Schuller, Pat Robertson, Jimmy Swaggart, Jerry Falwell, Oral Roberts, and Jim Bakker at the bottom.[1] Swaggart could not rest content with saying that Bakker and Roberts were charlatans and hustlers. He had to find still another theory to help distance himself from them.

Few people can evoke Swaggart's ire more than fellow Pentecostal Jim Bakker. "What made people give hundreds of millions of dollars to PTL," Swaggart asked his TV audience, "when you could turn on the TV set and it was as obvious as a bull elephant charging down the road as to what it was? And yet they supported it and would get angry with you if you said one word about it. Why?"

During one of his preaching tours in Brazil, Swaggart saw a number of people burning candles on a mountainside and heard them speaking in tongues. Since they were not of his religion, he faced the problem of accounting for behavior which closely resembled Pentecostal behavior but which enjoyed no connection with Pentecostal theology. He discovered, in short, that speaking in tongues could easily be duplicated outside his own faith. Rather than rest content with the observation that speaking in tongues is practiced in several subcultures around the world and that almost anyone can effortlessly learn how to do it within a matter of minutes, Swaggart was driven to find a more sinister explanation of the Brazilian non-Pentecostals who spoke in tongues. Having from childhood been led to think that speaking in tongues could be accounted for only as a stupendous and wondrous supernatural gift, he was compelled by his premises to face a disturbing dilemma. On the one hand, he had the option of concluding that believers in other religions who spoke in tongues were merely jabbering harmless nonsense even though they erroneously thought they were speaking a supernatural language. This approach was not attractive to a Pentecostal preacher like Swaggart, however, because it proved to be a double-edged sword. If a non-supernatural explanation could be applied to one religious group's speaking in tongues, it might apply across the board to all, including Swaggart's.

On the other hand, if the assumption were made that the gift of tongues represents a supernatural gift, then what could be said about the Brazilians? Unable to believe that they, too, spoke under the influence of the Holy Spirit, he concluded that they were "followers of Satan" and that their gift found its source in "the powers of darkness."

Pentecostal preachers freely use the phrase "false religion." To their credit, they have moved beyond the naive position that all religious claims are equally credible (or equally incredible). People who profess this naive position seem to think that political and religious tolerance of other people requires them to anesthetize their powers of critical judgment when religious claims are set forth.

Almost everyone who thinks about religious claims will conclude that some are very likely unwarranted or erroneous. Furthermore, most adults are capable of judging that some beliefs, religious or otherwise, can create considerable harm if acted upon. Pentecostal preachers like Swaggart go one step further to pass *moral* judgment on every person who holds to what Pentecostals regard as erroneous religious beliefs. According to Pentecostals, it is impossible to be merely in error. Individuals are judged to be *wickedly* in error. In short, according to Pentecostal theology, it is a sin to hold to mistaken opinions in the area of religion. Why? Because individuals are believed to have arrived at erroneous religious opinions by submitting to the influence of a deceiving evil spirit. For Pentecostals, behind every erroneous opinion in religion can be found a sinister spirit of the underworld inspiring it. Since Pentecostals think the theory of evolution is false, they are compelled to add that most biologists, zoologists, botanists, and anthropologists are inspired by Satan and the invisible spirits working under his command. Buddhists, Catholics, Hindus, and all other non-Pentecostals not only are in error, but are judged to be living under the sinister control of Satan and his army of evil spirits.

Some Pentecostal preachers are willing to concede that honest error is possible in the areas of minor importance. But the more significant the error is, the more the preachers are prone to look upon the believers in error as wicked. Swaggart assured his "Larry King Live" audience that he could never pass judgment on anyone's heart or motives. In the evangelist's mind, it is one thing to say that a person has foul motives, and it is another thing to say that he or she is tied in with demons from hell. To be told that one has pure motives but that one's false views are symptomatic of being in league with Satan is scarcely a distinction designed to create an atmosphere of mutual respect between disputants.

Since erroneous views are judged by Pentecostals to be the result of consorting with sinister spirits, true views are judged to be the result of coming under the control of the right spirits or Spirit.

Jimmy Lee Swaggart in one of his evangelistic crusades indicated that the Holy Spirit taught him to play the piano. He portrayed his boyhood piano teacher as something of a pathetic man because he conspicuously lacked the "gift" for playing. The question naturally arises as to who taught Jerry Lee Lewis, a truly remarkable piano player whose ability eventually surpassed that of his cousin Jimmy Lee. The truth seems to be that even in his boyhood Jerry Lee Lewis spent long hours at the piano. He became preoccupied with finding new and better records to listen to, and he sought out musicians in Southern Louisiana from whom he could learn and who could serve as his models. In short, he worked long and hard at what later became his profession. In many ways Lewis was obsessed with music and came under its power and control the same way other significant musicians come under the control of the intricate patterns and sounds called music.

The old-line Pentecostal way of thinking, however, was prone to substitute the word "possession" for "obsession." Musical ability then became something of a supernatural possession or gift, the hard work that went into practicing sometimes being forgotten. In ancient times poets and musicians were thought of as individuals possessed by a spirit or god named Muse. To be inspired by this spirit was to be "in-spirited."

Today evangelist Jimmy Lee Swaggart is prone to look upon

his cousin Jerry Lee Lewis's playing of the piano as supernatural in origin. Given this assumption, Swaggart is plagued with the question as to whether the Holy Ghost inspired Jerry Lee to play rock music. Since the evangelist thinks rock music is satanic, he has to conclude that Jerry Lee's playing is from an evil supernatural spirit of hell. Even if it was the Holy Spirit who originally taught Jerry Lee to play the piano sensationally, the spirit of Satan has taken over and is now the chief fount of Jerry Lee's music. The fact that Jerry Lee can play hymns or gospel music now and then does not impress Swaggart, since according to the Pentecostal theory, Satan can imitate the Holy Spirit in a number of ways.

Given the Pentecostal and Charismatic belief that the universe is densely populated with supernatural spirits and that supernatural miracles flow freely, it should come as no surprise that many believers would send Jim Bakker and Oral Roberts millions of dollars each year. Jimmy Swaggart needed no Muse to lead him to see that those believers simply wanted to get in on what they thought was a good deal. "Something good is going to happen to you." "Expect a miracle." Those words roll off the lips of Oral and Richard Roberts almost daily.

No profound understanding of Pentecostals and Charismatics is possible without a grasp of their belief that diseases and most human hardships are brought on by supernatural evil spirits. If believers can be convinced that faith is necessary to counter the malevolent influence of these spirits, they will unquestionably wish to know how to put their faith into operation. Jim Bakker and Oral Roberts successfully convinced a number of people to classify sending in money as an act of faith. Money mailed in became seed-faith.

During the years of the Roman Empire, people offered sacrifices and made contributions of various sorts to their gods as a way of making premium payments on insurance policies. Or, more accurately, they paid "protection money" to priests who had convinced them that the payments would fend off disasters and calamities that the mobsters of the spiritual underground threatened to bring about. Oral Roberts and Jim Bakker introduced a new program of what might be called the spiritual sweepstakes to accompany the old protection plan of ancient Rome. The new program could not have worked with Pentecostals before World War II because they had little money for this kind of gambling.

Oral Roberts and Jim Bakker are in many ways the product of two ingredients coming together in the latter half of the twentieth century. Those ingredients are (1) the new affluence among Pentecostals and Charismatics and (2) the old Pentecostal belief that much if not most of everyday life is controlled by good and bad spirits of the supernatural realm. The sweepstakes program is simply the practice of laying down money (seed-faith) in the expectation of someday hitting it big. A large portion of Jim Bakker's PTL shows featured testimonials given by "winners" in life's lottery. In fact, using their belief in a God who has all power to do what He wills, Bakker, Oral Roberts, and Robert Tilton of Dallas have gone so far as to guarantee that everyone will be a "winner."

Jimmy Swaggart grew increasingly angry with Bakker and Roberts for making outlandish promises in the name of Jesus that, in Swaggart's view, they had no right to make. He did not hesitate to refer to their tactic of raising money as "deceitful," and he advanced the additional thesis that Bakker and Roberts had fallen under the spell of evil supernatural spirits. It is important to see that the deceit and excesses of Bakker and Roberts did not lead Swaggart to question the colossal assumption that preachers are able to work miracles by the influence of supernatural spirits. Rather, the question for Swaggart was that of keeping in contact with the right spirits and avoiding the evil spirits.

Before the *Charlotte Observer* unveiled the story of PTL's money going to pay Jessica Hahn, Oral Roberts appeared on the grounds of Heritage USA and proclaimed that he felt the presence of God as never before and prophesied that Jim Bakker was going to be bigger than ever. In mid-August, 1987, Swaggart on TV denounced Oral Roberts (referring to him as "the man who sent out holy water") and called him a "false prophet." Instead of saying merely that Oral had missed his prediction or had made a gigantic error of judgment, Swaggart once again tried to connect Roberts with the invisible underworld that Pentecostals think is working overtime in "these last days." Pentecostals do a lot of supernatural prophesying, but when one of them falls on his face, he is treated as wicked for having gone presumably to the wrong source for his prophecy.

6

The Two Selves of
Jim Bakker

The human species is not the only species to dream when asleep. It is apparently the only species whose members can generate an imaginary, invisible world and try to live in it. Some people become lost in this world to the point of being able to function only marginally in the publicly observable empirical world.

Perhaps one of the first experiments in trying to interact with a fantasy world comes in the form of children's imaginary playmates. And perhaps the interaction with gods and spirits that some people profess to enjoy is an offshoot of the imaginary playmate phenomenon. It may even be that the imaginary playmate is the first step in the development of genuine multiple personality. Most humans do not become multiple persons, although some appear to be two or more selves at times.

Jim Bakker is one of those who appears to have become a dual self, although not full-fledged multiple persons. Instead of portraying him as possessed by putative demons, the dual-self thesis regards all of Bakker's behavior as fully human. The double life that he has led is the life of a divided self, one in conflict with the other. It is possible for one human to function as two selves, since a self is a unique cluster of covert or private experiences and a repertoire of behaviors that can be observed by others. It appears that Bakker's managing self (Jim the Adult) either was unaware of a major dimension or self of his overall life or was aware of it and tried to conceal it from others.

Bakker pled ignorance of what was going on inside the business department of his ministry. He claimed that the board ran the business behind the scenes while he did his job out front. If anything is clear in the PTL house of mirrors, however, it is that some key members of the board did not know what was going on as much as they ought to have known and that Bakker took steps to keep them uninformed.

The word *integrity* has come to mean honesty or incorruptibility. Its more elementary meaning has to do with integrating the aspects of the self into a whole so that no one aspect goes off on its own as an unmonitored outlaw. The charge has been made that Bakker had shown himself to be a man without integrity. In the elementary sense of the word, Bakker had probably not thoroughly integrated himself. A "self" or dimension of him ran relatively wild and free. This could be called Jim the Spontaneous Boy.

No one is fully integrated. Each individual is only an approximation of wholeness. It appears that Jim the Adult lost the skill of observing or monitoring some of the critical behavior of Jim the Spontaneous Boy. It is too simple to portray Bakker either as a cynic or as a demon-possessed man whose only god was mammon and whose religion was basically show business. The *Charlotte Observer* reporter Charles Shepard is more to the point: Jim Bakker was and is a complicated and fascinating man. Thinking of Bakker as two selves would account for much of his duplicity and contradictory behavior.

As a reporter and staff writer for the *Charlotte Observer,* Frye Gaillard had spoken with Bakker on several occasions and written articles about him with profound insight. Gaillard recalled Oral Roberts's visit to PTL in 1980, when in a sermon he compared Jim Bakker to the little boy who in innocent trust gave Jesus his loaves and fishes to feed the multitudes. "What Jesus needs," Roberts said, "is the little boy, the little girl, in all of us."

When the innocent Jim with the sincere, boyish demeanor is blended with the mature Jim the Adult (who understands the powerful potential of television), an effective talk-show host emerges. Yet there are still two distinct sides to his personality: the creative and the self-indulgent. When spontaneous creativity fails to acquire discipline, it becomes increasingly self-indulgent, heedless of rational counsel, and impulsive. If we have no control over others or over their money, our impulsiveness will often be regarded as harmless or even as refreshing and charming. The man-boy called Jim Bakker had charmed his way into millions of Christian homes. Radiating a boyish aura of wonder, he had spun dreams and visions before the cameras and invited his "Partners" to step onto the magic carpet with him. And in many cases he turned the dreams into brilliant reality.

Roger Flessing, who left PTL in disillusionment despite his long-time friendship and close working relationship with Bakker, had an insight into Bakker that Frye Gaillard thought worth quoting: "There is no question about the innocence and sincerity of Jim Bakker's faith. But there is another childlike quality that is not as good—the quality of indulging his whims, and not accepting responsibility for problems he creates."[1]

We can identify with Bakker's unresolved ambivalence about the inner child, who is an aspect of each of us. The Bible from which Bakker draws resolution and courage is itself ambivalent about the complicated relationship between our childhood and our adulthood. Jesus is reported to have said, "Truly, I say to you, unless you turn and become like children, you will never enter the kingdom of heaven." Paul told the Christians at Corinth, "When I was a child, I spoke like a child, I thought like a child, I reasoned like a child; but when I became a man, I gave up childish ways." On the one hand, creative genius can be destroyed by childishness. On the other hand, without childlike playfulness, wide-eyed wonder, and relentless optimism, creativity will turn sour.

Bakker's books read like the adventure tales of a wonder-seeking boy. Like most children, Jim almost always believes that "you can make it," as he states in the title of one of his books. His strong and persistent belief in miracles, in part, proved to be both the secret of his success as a fund-raiser and the source of his woes. On the positive side, he stepped into the lives of his viewers and blew on the sparks of hope and adventure in their hearts, telling them wonderful stories and turning the sparks into flames of new expectations. He was the Music Man of Charismatic believers. Even though he could not teach them to play real instruments, he could make music play inside their heads and fill them with dreams and visions that lifted them out of their routine lives. And sometimes—at great material cost—he could make his dream their dream and turn it into reality.

Bakker's "PTL Club" can be compared to modern romance novels. "Category romance" novels are written according to a strict formula, and it appears that Charismatic talk shows have a somewhat similar formula. Publishing companies send out guidelines to which writers must pay strict attention. A similar tip sheet of Charismatic talk shows would instruct the aspiring host to feature struggle-and-success stories and accounts of miracles or sensational transformations. There must also be a villain, an archenemy who threatens but cannot ultimately destroy the believer who remains faithful.

Like the romance novel, the Christian talk show tells the audience that things are going to work out. It offers hope. And in the case of a growing number of TV Charismatics, it promises materialistic miracles and worldly success as partial reward for faithfulness.

While recovering from an illness in a hospital, Ruth Graham found great comfort in reading Barbara Cartland's romance novels. "Mrs. Billy Graham," writes Cartland, "said recently when she was in [the] hospital and so ill, the only thing that stopped her from suffering pain was reading my books. You become so immersed in them. And they do take one's mind off everything else. When people are ill . . . they don't want tension, ugliness, misery, or pornography. They want love and beauty. . . . You know everything is going to end happily, so you go to sleep in the arms of the hero and get well quickly!"[2]

On the "PTL Club" talk show, Jim and Tammy often spoke of "people who hurt." One purpose of the program was to give the viewers at least temporary escape from their pain, telling them they could rest with assurance, safe in the arms of Jesus.

As in a good romance novel, the Bakkers provided entertainment and an ongoing story. The story line of the PTL show had become, of course, the life of Jim and Tammy, with minor characters brought in daily to enrich the story.

As any student of romance novels knows, the tastes of romance readers vary. Some want intense adventure—suspense romance. Others want romance and mystery—velvet-glove romance. And still others want the story to be steamy and sexually explicit. On their "PTL Club," the Bakkers had always been aware of the competition for a limited audience—a genre audience. To their special blend of TV entertainment and evangelism they added the elements of suspense and even a touch of sexuality in the form of stories of adultery, estrangement, and reconciliation. Themes of marriage and divorce became a part of PTL entertainment, so that the Jim-and-Tammy story has taken on the characteristics of the daytime soap opera, just as some of the new romance novels have moved closer to the soap-opera genre.

What the "PTL Club" has not emphasized is the equivalent to Gothic-horror romance novels. Viewers interested in cosmic horror tales turn to Pat Robertson's "700 Club" reruns for macabre scenarios of the apocalypse drawn from two of the all-time favorites of horror literature, the Book of Revelation and the Book of Daniel.

Like most boys, Jim the Spontaneous Boy had flirted with magic all his life. It is in magic that the self-indulgent side of childhood is likely to gain strong reinforcement. Stated more accurately, belief in magic is the carry-over of self-indulgent childishness into later life. It is the inability to admit that the dream of one's own omnipotence is a delusion. Fundamentally, it is a refusal to recognize that to be human is to be a finite creature. Magic is also the spontaneous child's revolt against work. In its most undisciplined form, it is the self-indulgent, spoiled child demanding life on a silver platter. It not only expects miracles, it demands them.

When Charismatic Christianity came to the forefront in America as a social movement in the 1970s and 1980s, the belief in all sorts of occult phenomena was also on the move: Jean Dixon's and Edgar Cayce's prophecies, astrology with its competing charts, near-death experiences, gem healing, faith healing, exorcism, psychic surgery, astral travel, and an outpouring of supernatural claims originating in Southern California, America's cornucopia of phantasmagories. Charismatics and fundamentalists saw all these phenomena as signs of the times, as Satan's revving up for the greatest shootout in human history as described in the Book of Revelation. The Charismatic demand for more and more miracles and the occult search for magic seem to be attempts to increase human power and influence in the universe. In some ways, the modern longing for magic and miracles is the tribute that the ambitious but relatively powerless of the world pay to technology's power. In the world of technology, people are usually required to go through a difficult learning and training process before the new power becomes their possession. And even if the training process is completed, there is no guarantee that they will be able to do anything with it. The competition for jobs is keen and the openings are comparatively few. With belief in miracles, however, they can always feel that they can make an impact on the world.

Like all TV evangelists, Jim Bakker had mingled the belief in miracles with reality. He asked his viewers to send up their prayers to heaven but to send their checks and credit card numbers to him. Jerry Falwell rejoiced over the "May Miracle," when the desperately needed millions came in to PTL at the close of May 1987. But the miracle did not last, and Falwell's board had to declare bankruptcy for June in the hope that they could bring in more real money, not hocus-pocus, over a long period of time.

The apparent two selves of Jim Bakker reflect in some respects the fact that he tried to run his life by the laws of nature and the rules of society on the one hand, and the whims of the world of miracles and magic on the other hand. The problems in Bakker's own life erupted when these two worlds came into direct conflict. When his Charismatic advisors tried to get him to face reality, they were in effect telling him that in the real world there are consequences that not even prayers, faith, and incantations can resolve. One of Jim's books is entitled *Move That Mountain.* The battle over the "PTL Club" and Heritage USA came about when a mountain of piled-up debts and obligations refused to be moved by Jim Bakker's faith alone.

Apparently, Bakker failed to consider that Falwell would also prove to be something of an immovable mountain. Bakker used the news media to attack Falwell, characterizing him as a liar and a power-hungry villain bent on taking over his ministry and personal possessions. Meantime, Falwell, who was no stranger to the practical world of media manipulation, publicly vowed his brotherly love for the Bakkers. The battle had begun, each calling down both judgment and heavenly reinforcement while pinning their faith on lawyers and judges. In the process, the two evangelists have created one of the most interesting church-state legal problems that the nation has ever been forced to face.

A vivid example of Bakker's conflict between Jim the Adult and the self-indulgent side of Jim the Boy is found in Bakker's reaction to Kevin Wittum, a teenager only twenty-nine inches long. Because of a rare bone disease, Kevin could neither walk nor sit up. Bakker seemed so profoundly moved that he promised to build a specially equipped house at Heritage USA. Because he had to be carried everywhere he went, Kevin requested an elevator in the house. Even though Kevin's House, as it came to be called, cost $1.5 million (and is valued in some estimates at $3 million), seventeen-year-old Kevin had to be carried up the steps, for there was still no elevator. While Bakker had given supporters the impression that several handicapped children would live in the house, in June 1987 Kevin was the only handicapped occupant.

In some ways Kevin's House was symbolic of Jim Bakker's style. Although a man of deep compassion and vision, Bakker's overall follow-up on his decisions proved to be less than inspired and unconscionably wasteful. He seemed to believe that a highly successful fundraiser of his ability must work within the context of either a crisis or a new project, but he never tried to make the case that disorderly and mystifying management procedures were essential to fund-raising.

Controversy over Kevin's House began before it was built. According to officials of York County, South Carolina, and several PTL employees, PTL submitted building plans that ignored requirements for group-care facilities. PTL appeared uncooperative and refused to meet certain standards despite the fact that Bakker raised $3 million for the house that cost $1.5 million.[3]

In August 1987 the new PTL administration told Kevin's parents that they had to leave the controversial house. "A place will be made for Kevin if he desires one there," said Jerry Nims, who was PTL's chief executive officer until he resigned late in 1987.[4]

PART III:

A Financial Roller Coaster

7

The Fatted Calf

The opulence that Jim and Tammy Bakker enjoyed in recent years would boggle even J. R. Ewing's mind. They moved into and out of several dream houses within a span of six years. In 1981 they occupied their Tega Cay, South Carolina, parsonage, which was valued at $1.3 million in 1985. Purchased with PTL money, this Lake Wylie house sported a two-level tree house that was furnished, carpeted, and air-conditioned. Life on Lake Wylie became a world of its own, with some of the Bakkers' PTL friends living in nearby luxurious lakeside homes that they expected to be deeded to them by the great horn of plenty, PTL.

Having fallen in love with Florida, Jim and Tammy felt they needed an ocean-front dwelling. Again PTL provided, contributing $375,000 for a condominium and $202,566 for furniture and fixtures, with the floor-to-ceiling mirrors costing $22,000. The house was purchased by David Taggart, Jim Bakker's personal aide. After selling this home for $506,000, PTL paid out $449,000 for a chalet in the Coachella Valley of Palm Desert, California, in 1984. Ninety-nine PTL employees had just been laid off as the result of a recent "efficiency study." Three years later, the Palm Desert home was sold.

The Bakkers bought a $148,500 home in Gatlinburg, Tennessee, on the edge of the Great Smoky Mountain National Park, one of the lush areas of the United States. For improvements to this mountainside home, $90,000 had also been set aside, $35,000 going into the stone, wrought-iron, and chain-link fence to guarantee Jim his privacy on the two-acres with a panoramic view of the mountains. When Jerry Falwell's PTL administrators recovered from the shock of the Bakkers' opulence, they tried to retrieve some of the $87,000 security system, a jeep, and $15,000 worth of furniture from the Gatlinburg home for the May 23, 1987, auction held at Heritage Village Church. In the previous year Jim had toured PTL offices and selected furniture for his new Tennessee home. But these items could not be sold at the auction because a Tennessee judge barred PTL employees from trespassing. Roe Messner, the principal construction contractor for Heritage Village USA, claimed that Jim and Tammy were deeding their mountain home to him in payment for $275,000 worth of additional improvements he had done on the house that originally cost $148,500.

Not wanting to risk being put out on the street, Jim and Tammy bought also a Palm Springs, California, home on February 20, 1987. Always believing in having either money or investments for a rainy day, the Bakkers paid $600,000 for the home of five bedrooms and five baths. Sitting on one acre of park-like grounds, this red-roofed hacienda once belonged to a member of the Florsheim family. It has a caretaker's cottage, a forty-six-foot pool, a cabana, and a sauna. The house was bought under the name F.S.C.O. Trust, whose name was formed by taking the middle initial of each member of the Bakker family: F for Tammy Faye, S for daughter Tammy Sue, C for son James Charles, and O for James O. Since the home was equipped with technology for videotaping and transmitting via satellite, there was some speculation that the Bakkers had plans to use it as a base to start a new televised ministry.

On July 28, 1987, the Bakkers got into their white Cadillac convertible and left their hacienda behind to return to their home in the Tennessee mountains. Following the Cadillac was a rental truck containing their belongings. Originally they had listed the Palm Springs house at $700,000; in July they lowered the price to $650,000 and sold it later in the summer.

Jim's office at PTL headquarters contained a Jacuzzi bath that the staff dubbed the "Floozie Jacuzzi." Luxury permeated every sector of the Bakkers' work and living space. The forty-foot closet with the cut-glass chandelier in the presidential suite of the Grand Hotel became the brunt of jokes and public outrage. At the May auction, the toilet and sink fixtures, shaped like swans, sold for $825, since they were 14-karat gold-plated. Jim's Franklin coupe brought $27,000, and the seven-foot brass and copper giraffe from Jim's office brought $2,900. PTL lost money on the Habitat in Tammy's dressing room, which originally cost $11,678 but sold for only $1,700. A Habitat is a showerlike stall that can simulate different environments with the touch of a button—from sun to rain to a warm breeze. The little air-conditioned "condo" for Tammy's Saint Bernard sold for $4,500. The buyer returned it to PTL to sell again, but on the resale it pulled in a mere $600.[1]

Other blessings that had descended upon the Bakkers were (1) a fifty-eight-foot houseboat, with a queen-size bed and a bar, (2) a $60,000 Rolls-Royce that was displayed in plexiglass atop one of the Heritage Village hotels, (3) a 1939 Rolls-Royce that Jim was having restored by his Christian brother Garry Cannon (Jim still owed $12,000, but Cannon intended to finish the restoration, sell the car, and donate the proceeds to the Heritage Village Church Missionary Fellowship),[2] (4) two $60,000 560SEL Mercedes purchased in December 1987, one for Jim, the other for Tammy, and (5) a $17,000 Mazda RX7, which magically appeared, with the use of PTL funds, after the Bakkers' daughter Tammy Sue saw the car in a dealer showroom and indicated an interest in it. Despite having neither a driver's license nor a learner's permit, Tammy Sue drove the car. It was this car that Tammy Faye auctioned off during one of PTL's televised fund-raising drives, claiming it was donated by an outsider.

Dr. Robert Manzano, a former world missions director for PTL, charged that Jim used PTL funds to give Tammy Faye a $2,500 mink coat. There was speculation that she did not purchase the coat at K-Mart or TJ Maxx, despite Tammy's insistence that she shopped at discount stores. Tammy could be called a compulsive shopper, as evidenced in the backlog of unworn dresses with price tags un-removed that give her large closet the appearance of a department store.

Jim was even more extravagant than his wife in the quality and quantity of his self-indulgence. His high-priced aide David Taggart often accompanied him on shopping trips to help him make selections. One of Jim's favorite haberdasheries was Dallas's Galleria store called Beylerian, where suits ranged in price from $650 to $1,400. In 1985 he bought $3,000 worth of suits and accessories at Beylerian. When indecisive about the color of shirt he wanted, he solved the problem by buying six shirts, each a different color. He had been known to purchase ten to twenty suits in one outing.

Considerable complaint was raised about Jim's employing bodyguards, as if a minister of the gospel needed them. But the guards did more than concern themselves with security. They kept the Bakkers' cars washed, the swimming pool clean, the cat litter swept up, and the refrigerator stocked with soda pop. They also replaced light bulbs, emptied the humidifiers, and daily set the appropriate temperature for the houseboat air. There were endless details that they had to take care of because the Bakkers had neither interest in nor time for such matters.

In addition, a full-time housekeeper received a salary of $45,000 annually. Tammy confessed that she never concerned herself with how much money she herself earned. "Honestly I do not know how much I made. I've never thought about it," she told Ted Koppel.[3]

As every parent knows, it is sometimes difficult to know what to buy a teenager for Christmas. At the age of sixteen, Tammy Sue found a full-length mink coat under her tree. Tammy Faye did not receive a mink that Christmas because, according to the furrier, Jim told him that his wife already had fourteen mink pieces. The Bakkers celebrated their twentieth wedding anniversary in April 1981 with ninety PTL employees, spouses, and guests at Cafe Eugene. Including the $1,000 tip, champagne, and lime sherbet, the anniversary party cost $96.44 per person, totaling $8,681.40.

Jim liked his executives to travel first-class with $800 briefcases, $70 address books, $74 Gucci toilet kits, and $120 Gucci pens. In a Hawaiian hotel Jim and Tammy stayed in the presidential suite at $350 a night.

Jim's aide, David Taggart, enjoyed the life of big bucks and expensive gifts too. David's older brother James worked as an interior designer and decorator for PTL. Despite the fact that their jobs were at PTL headquarters, they paid $660,000 for an unfurnished space in a New York City Fifth Avenue high-rise condo in March 1986, only five years after David became Bakker's aide. In the freewheeling PTL atmosphere, David had easy access to a company credit card. One set of charges totaling $9,132 covered six trips for himself, brother James, and friend Sandi Watson.

It might reasonably be assumed that as soon as Jim Bakker's March 19 resignation took effect, the excessive salaries, bonuses, and expense accounts would have ceased at once. Not so. Partly because of the confusion about who received what, Falwell and his knights-to-the-rescue were not on top of matters. On April 9, David Taggart signed a PTL check for $100,000 to his brother James for "consulting services." The documentation did not make explicit the nature of the services. As interior decorator, James had already been on payroll for $120,000 per year.

During the final eighteen months of Bakker's term at PTL, David Taggart and Jim Bakker together used $640,000 in cash advances on PTL credit cards. David took a $45,000 cash advance shortly before his 1986 European vacation. The finance director, Peter Bailey, said that Taggart informed him that he (Taggart) was in charge of keeping all credit card records to insure confidentiality.[4] Each month, PTL wrote out a check of between $40,000 and $50,000 to reduce the charge card expenses. Shortly before Bakker's resignation, the charge card expenses totaled $120,000. The limit of what could be charged on each of the two cards was $100,000.

The problem of sorting out the expenses of each individual executive and functionary at PTL is a bit like reconstructing a spilled bowl of soup. David Taggart, for example, charged $263,000 to one of PTL's charge cards in 1986. Of the charges, $216,000 remain undocumented. Some of the documented charges raise serious questions—$1,070 for eyeglasses and the $9,132 bill for air travel from Charlotte to New York City for David, James, and friend Sandi. Many other documents failed to show up, including construction purchase orders and invoices.

In March 1987 the elusive Taggart brothers purchased a two-story stucco house with double lot in southeast Charlotte for $315,000. For Christmas 1986, David and James gave each other black Jaguars, one a 1986 model, the other a 1987. The total cost was $87,765. Since moving to Charlotte in the late seventies, the brothers have owned three Mercedes, three Cadillacs, and one Corvette. With a penchant for expensive dining, the brothers picked up the tabs for $40-per-person meals and occasionally a $120 bottle of champagne. A few years after joining PTL, David bought Tammy a $25,000 pair of diamond earrings and his mother a $12,000 pearl-and-ruby necklace. Not surprisingly, the Taggart brothers wore designer clothes, and David was reported to be wearing a solitaire diamond ring worth $75,000 to $100,000.[5]

Available records indicate that when he was in his twenties David Taggart received about the same amount of money as Richard Dortch, who was not only twice David's age but the executive director of

PTL. The younger man was Bakker's personal aide and one of seventeen vice-presidents. David had been a piano player of no great distinction, whereas Dortch had worked his way up to key administrative positions in the Assemblies of God denomination. David's duties included arranging travel for Bakker, managing Bakker's office, buying his clothes and homes, notarizing documents, and greeting TV guests offstage. David refused to appear before the TV camera or the PTL audience.[6]

Bakker had also a highly paid secretary, Shirley Fulbright, who received $160,000 in 1986 and $50,000 for the first three months of 1987. Fulbright might have had a more powerful position than the board, however. One of her functions was to sign executive bonus sheets. At least one board member claims that the board voted the bonuses somewhat blindly: bonus authorization sheets detailing the amounts were not attached to board minutes or presented in the meetings. A separate accounting firm was hired to perform the executive payroll, keeping the executive salary and bonus information covert.[7]

Richard Dortch, silver-haired, erect, and self-confident, had been in denominational politics most of his adult life. Born only a couple of years after the Great Crash of 1929, Dortch had seen to it that his material needs would not go unmet. Before he was stripped of his official ordination in the late spring of 1987, Dortch had gained prominence more than once among the Assemblies of God. In 1983 he was appointed to the position of Bakker's chief deputy (executive director), having been a PTL board member for the previous four years.

Dortch's lifestyle was opulent. He and his wife Mildred bought a $170,000 home in Winter Haven of Polk County, Florida, in April 1983. Three years later they bought another Florida home, in New Port Richey of Pasco County, near the time they sold their Winter Haven home for $179,300. In May 1987 they sold their new home for $280,000. Their principal residence since 1983, however, has been their Lake Wylie parsonage in Pineville, North Carolina, just across the border from Heritage Village. PTL purchased this house, valued at $256,170. In the fall of 1987 the house was put up for sale, and PTL valued it at $789,000.[8]

Money trees seemed to thrive in the Heritage Village soil, and

Bakker had many friends who were willing to pick their fruit. Singer Vestal Goodman and her husband Howard received together a $500-per-month car allowance in addition to the use of a $178,000 Lake Wylie home. After being served with a June 12, 1987, eviction notice, the Goodmans chose to fight to keep their home. In an invoice-type memo delivered to the new PTL board, they stated that the house belonged to them because on April 2, 1986, the board had voted to gradually deed the Lake Wylie houses to the residents. The memo contended that PTL owed the Goodmans $319,000 for 1986. The figure included $178,000 for the Lake Wylie house, apparently in lieu of receipt of the deed. Vi Azvedo, another of the many PTL vice-presidents, took legal steps to acquire the deed to the Lake Wylie home he had been occupying.

In late May 1987, Richard Dortch, invoking the April 1986 board decision, instructed his attorney to write a letter to PTL requesting that the Lake Wylie parsonage he had lived in and its contents be transferred to him. Before leaving his position on the PTL show in April 1987, Dortch made the following announcement on the air: "I will continue to live in the parsonage of this ministry . . . but I will not accept any salary whatsoever, nor pension benefits or any other benefits for the next twelve months." He added: "God has spoken to my heart, and he will provide for my needs."[9]

Even after being dismissed from his position as PTL president in April 1987, Dortch was retained as consultant to PTL at a cost of $13,500 per month. Harry Hargrave of Dallas, serving as the new PTL chief operating officer, announced in late July that he had recently cut off Dortch's monthly salary. In partial justification, he explained that he happened to review the tape of the PTL show in which Dortch commented that he would not accept any salary or compensation for a year. Dortch complained that Hargrave's action made no sense, especially since Falwell and the PTL board had known of his comment well before he was terminated on April 28. The board must have had another motive for cutting him off so abruptly.

Dortch's legal representative speculated as to what the real motive was: Dortch possessed "a lot of information about how Mr. Falwell and company came into this position they are in. . . . I think it is fair to say there's another side. There are questions about whether the method by which Falwell came into power is a proper method." The lawyer went on to suggest that Falwell's position in the PTL controversy was legally on thin ice from the start.

On July 24, Falwell's board issued an audited report which claimed that in 1986 Dortch received $356,000, including $194,000 in bonuses. His compensation for the first four months of 1987 was $270,000, of which $203,000 had been classified as a bonus.[10]

Dortch fell into legal trouble in Florida when a Dade County prosecutor filed charges. Both Richard Dortch and his wife Mildred faced a maximum penalty of up to one year in jail and a $1,000 fine on each count. Dortch was charged with one count of homestead exemption fraud by falsely claiming to live full-time in his $280,000 Pasco County home in order to obtain a property tax break. Mildred was accused in a similar case in neighboring Polk County, where their home was valued at $179,000 in Winter Haven. She pleaded not guilty to three grand theft charges. In April, Dortch told the Associated Press that Mildred had handled the paperwork and that the exemption applications were merely an oversight.[11]

According to the affidavit and the *Tampa Tribune,* when applying for the Pasco County exemption, Mildred Dortch listed a license plate number of a rental Lincoln Town Car she had had for four days in February 1986 as proof of Florida residence, a requirement for the exemption. In October 1986 the Dortches sold their Winter Haven home near a golf course for $179,300. Their New Port Richey house in Pasco County sold for $280,000.[12]

Charlotte lawyer Eddie Knox asserts that Dortch was responsible for the exceedingly high salaries paid to top PTL officials in recent years. Large salaries began after Dortch started work as Bakker's chief deputy in late 1983, said Knox, who for years served as attorney for Jim Bakker. The *Charlotte Observer* in April reported that Dortch himself was among top PTL executives who received bonuses in 1986 more than double their regular salaries. They received additional bonuses in the early months of 1987 that approached the total amounts of their 1986 bonuses. Two other lawyers, Charles Chapel and Michael Wigton, left PTL in protest, sending a long letter to Bakker dated September 9, 1986. They charged that Dortch made all the decisions without consulting the board. They charged further that he presented himself as receiving input from Bakker and other responsible trustees. The lawyers remain skeptical of his claim to the input.[13]

Also on the PTL payroll until April 1987 were Richard Dortch's son Rich and daughter Deanna Collins, and the son of Dortch's friend, former Interior Secretary of State James Watt.[14]

The PTL structure has allowed executives to receive salaries and bonuses that would be the envy of many members of the upper ranks of several Fortune 500 companies. Excessive salaries in charitable organizations can lead the IRS to revoke their tax-exempt status. The accompanying table lists compensation made to top PTL executives and aides, including salaries and bonuses. The figures do not include, however, all the money that PTL paid for luxurious parsonages, utilities, maid service, security and other upkeep on Bakker's parsonage, and PTL-supplied cars. Neither do the figures include money spent on lucrative expense accounts that often went undocumented.

Recent PTL Compensation for Top Executives and Aides: Salaries, Bonuses and Other Compensation[15]		
(Figures Are Rounded)		
	1986	*January–March 1987*
Jim and Tammy Bakker (combined)	$1.9 million	$640,000
Richard Dortch, PTL executive director, Bakker's top deputy	$350,000	$270,000
David Taggart, PTL vice-president, top aide to Bakker	$360,000	$250,000
Shirley Fulbright, Bakker's secretary	$160,000	$50,000
Peter Bailey, finance director	$115,000	$70,000
Total	$2.885 million	$1.28 million
	$4.165 million	

It is noteworthy that during the first three months of 1987, all PTL executives except Jim's secretary, Shirley Fulbright, received bonuses in excess of fifty percent of their compensation for the entire twelve months of the previous year. Some, including Falwell, suspect there was a conscious effort to raid PTL coffers shortly before Jim's March 19, 1987, resignation. The accelerated compensation was accomplished via bonuses. Dortch and Taggart received bonuses during the first three months of 1987 that were approximately equal to all of their 1986 bonuses. The Bakkers "earned" $470,000 in bonuses during the first quarter of 1987, while they were both out of town and off the air for all but a few days. Jerry Nims, PTL's chief executive officer under Falwell, found that during a ten-day period in February 1987, $480,000 in checks went to Jim and Tammy. Those checks did not include cash withdrawals.[16]

According to a PTL audit released July 24, 1987, salary and expense accounts provided more than $4.7 million to the Bakkers and their top aides from January 1986 through April 1987. As shown in the accompanying table, compensation from January 1986 through March 1987 totaled $4.165 million. That amount grew by $535,000 by the end of April 1987. The difference can be explained by the fact that the Bakkers, Dortch, Taggart, Fulbright, and Bailey were still on the payroll in April and by the fact that documented expense accounts were included. By either design or incredible incompetence, the money trail became at times convoluted. The numbers continue to be revised and updated as auditors try to find a place for the previously missing pieces.

Jerry Nims said there exists no written agreement or other reasons to pay Jim Bakker past royalties for records, books, or tape recordings. Bakker claimed that he had not taken the $9 million in royalties that he thought rightfully his. Bakker had a point. If he had been content to keep an accurate account of his royalties and other PTL monies, he could have lived exceedingly well on them in the 1980s without taking a penny from PTL.

Ironically, the PTL headquarters building is in the shape of a pyramid. Wittingly or unwittingly, PTL played a game that in some ways resembles what bankers disdainfully call pyramidding, the illegal business practice of selling distributorships in lieu of goods or services. PTL's game resembled more closely, however, one of the Ponzi schemes, a phrase familiar to the U.S. Postal Service. According to Charlotte's postal inspector, R. M. Hazelwood, a Ponzi scheme emerges when there are debts to be paid off and "you create a fifth [project] to pay off the first project."[17] Hazelwood emphasized that *intent* is the key word: "If somebody intentionally made a broadcast for funds via either mail or air and requested funds for a particular project or donation or charity . . . and they never intended to use the money for that particular project, that would be in violation of mail fraud laws."[18]

The restless Jim Bakker seemed to grow dissatisfied with bringing in $15 a month from grassroots members. "You get what you ask for," he once told his chief of security Don Hardister. "If you ask for $15 a month, you'll get $15 a month. If you ask for $1,000, you get $1,000." Ignoring the small contributors, PTL under Bakker began to grow negligent about sending out promised gifts such as Bibles and receipts for contributions. Within two years a million and a half families had dropped off PTL's contribution list.[19]

Early in 1984 Bakker and Dortch convinced themselves that the idea of "PTL partnerships" was an idea whose time had come. By sending in $1,000, viewers could become PTL Lifetime Partners, which would entitle each to four days and three nights in the Heritage Grand Hotel every year for life. Dortch and Bakker made a big point of the $1,000 becoming a tax-free donation. According to the plan, Lifetime Partners could help PTL save money, since PTL would not have to pay interest money to banks.

In 1983 Jim's loyal friend Don Hardister was convinced that he had been privileged to witness the birth of the lifetime partnership idea through divine inspiration. Jim and he were traveling together in a car, when Jim suddenly asked Don to turn off and follow the dirt road. When they stopped at a clearing, which is now Heritage USA grounds, Jim jumped out of the car, snatched up a stick, and began sketching a design of the Grand Hotel in the dirt. According to *Time* magazine, Hardister heard Jim say ecstatically, "I feel like God gave me the plan to do it and pay for it. We're going to do it with cash."[20] When I asked Hardister if he had been quoted accurately by *Time*, he replied, "I can't vouch for their other quotes, but they quoted me accurately—the way I said it."

I heard what I thought was sadness in Don Hardister's voice. He acknowledged that the spring and summer months had been difficult for him. Referring to Bakker, he added, "You think you know somebody, but . . . well sometimes you just don't know." The evidence suggests that Hardister is the sort of man who does not take friendship and commitments lightly. He did not abandon the Bakkers easily, but in the end he had to walk away. The plan might have come from a more earthly source, building contractor Roe Messner perhaps. But there is no evidence to suggest that Jim knew Messner before early 1984.

Heritage Grand Hotel eventually turned from a dream to a sparkling material reality. On the surface, it was a honeymoon relationship between PTL and the Partners. How else could most of the Partners afford to join the ranks of the conspicuously affluent for four days each year for the rest of their lives? Those who were in the know, however, could see that the beautiful bubble might soon burst. For some, signs of mishandling of funds began to appear even before the December 1984 opening. Contrary to Bakker's spoken assurances, the $1,000 checks were not devoted exclusively to the Grand Hotel construction project. Checks from the Partners were commingled with other PTL funds from which general ministry expenses were paid. Ten million dollars had to be borrowed to complete construction.

Five months after the opening date, PTL raised fifty percent more revenue from Partners than the originally targeted $30 million. A disturbing reality burst the bubble. Bakker had hoped that guests who were not Partners would line up at the hotel's registration desk, since their money was desperately needed to offset obligation to the Lifetime Partners. Instead, Lifetime Partners lined up with receipts to prove they had already sent in their money—$1,000 each, to be exact. This meant that instead of pulling in money sufficient for self-operation, the hotel would generate still more debts. Even in the summer of 1987, Grand Hotel was losing $85,000 each month. PTL Lifetime Partners David and Sarah Combs filed a lawsuit against the Bakkers, charging fraud and racketeering. David and Sarah were refused reservations at the Grand Hotel several times on the grounds of no vacancies. When they phoned in for reservations by presenting themselves as new paying customers rather than Lifetime Partners, they were given reservations without delay.

To close down in order to reduce operating expenses, however, was to Bakker unthinkable. The risk-taker once again leaped headlong from the economic cliff by going on TV with new plans to increase the number of lifetime partnerships. With partnerships already oversold, Bakker and Dortch began selling more, thus increasing PTL's financial crisis. Not content with Heritage Grand Hotel, Bakker began selling partnerships for the projected high-rise Towers Hotel. Eventually he talked of bunkhouses, farmhouses, a thirty-room country mansion, and country club camping. New kinds of partnerships were concocted—silver, gold, diamond, victory warrior, and family fun partnerships.

At a rather heated creditor's meeting on July 22, 1987, at the Jefferson Square Theatre in downtown Columbia, South Carolina, Eleanor Eberhardt of Atlanta asked, "Why did construction never cease under Jim Bakker, but then as soon as Mr. Falwell came in, it was stopped and boarded up?"

"Because the source of the funds came from new projects, and we're not going to play that game," retorted Harry Hargrave, PTL's chief financial officer." It's wrong—and it may be illegal."

Robert Zanesky, attorney for the Association of PTL Partners, charged that Falwell made use of the PTL mailing list and took checks made out to PTL and deposited them in banks in Falwell's home town of Lynchburg, Virginia. Hargrave, who was pulling in $175,000 for his service to PTL, angrily denied the charge. When the Bakkers' attorney, Ryan Hovis, defiantly contradicted some of Hargrave's figures by citing detailed financial information, Hargrave fired back: "You not only have proprietary information that belongs to PTL, but someone has stolen that information and communicated it to you. . . . I'd like to know who it is and turn them over to the federal authorities."[21]

While he was head of the Heritage Village enterprise, a thick wall of insulation steadily accumulated around Bakker so that eventually he seemed cut off from the kind of ordinary useful criticisms that most people find essential for improving and correcting their ideas. Jim's sister Donna Puckett worked on PTL finances and was in charge of in-house audits, but there is no hard evidence that she generated warnings that penetrated Jim's wall of insulation.

At the hotel's registration desk and on the phones, things changed from bad to worse—justified complaints, shouting matches, and frustration without hope of resolution. After listening to one angry Partner for twenty-five minutes, reservations manager Joy Cole threw her

beeper against the wall out of frustration . Twenty of the twenty-
two people who had worked for her a year earlier had quit by July
of 1987.

Refunding money to some of the Lifetime Partners helped release
the pressure valve somewhat, but this served only to pull money away
from other areas where debts had accumulated. The summer of 1987
saw the Towers Hotel boarded up because the building contractor,
Roe Messner, had revived his suit against PTL, stating that he still
had a claim of $14 million in unpaid bills.

The key legal question is still the intent factor. If Bakker had
access to critical information on the partnership financial crisis and
if he acted persistently in direct conflict with the most elementary
steps to end it, then the question of intent is more precisely defined.
In the judgment of many, Bakker is clearly guilty of wire fraud and
mail fraud. PTL staff members insist that weekly reports went to
him regarding the number of partnerships sold. They scoff at
suggestions that Bakker was unaware of the ministry's financial
situation.[22]

At least three months before the Grand Hotel opened in December
1984, Bakker announced a plan to generate more revenues. PTL would
sell partnerships for Heritage Towers, with construction to begin late
in 1986. Over a year later, in mid-April 1987, Falwell ceased the
sale of partnerships. A total of $65.8 million had been raised through
the Grand Hotel partnership plan. More than $43 million had gone
into costs for the Grand Hotel, and Bakker originally estimated that
the Towers Hotel would cost $27 million. As of late summer 1987,
roughly $11 million, perhaps $12 million, had gone into constructing
the Towers despite the fact that Bakker and Dortch helped raise
nearly $70 million for its completion. PTL partners, creditors, and
government agencies have asked questions about the whereabouts
of the millions raised in excess of construction costs. As late as the
first week of April 1987, Richard Dortch sold price-reduced Towers
memberships at $900 each.

Routine commingling of funds at PTL could have helped create
the confusion that allowed men like Bakker and Dortch to say with
strangely twisted honesty that they did not understand the severity
of the PTL economic crisis. Taking refuge in a fog of mismanagement
is, however, not so much an excuse for mismanagement as an
explanation of how it came about. Confusion creates more confusion.

Many firms have learned that confusion is literally the practice of fusing together all the profit centers so that the trail of money easily becomes lost or obscured. To overcome this condition a corporation will sometimes divide itself into distinctive profit centers, each operating as a separate accountable small business under general directives from headquarters. Each profit center, therefore, maintains its own accounting and produces its own profit-and-loss statement. By contrast, even the offerings at Heritage Church were confiscated for use at PTL headquarters. When U.S. Bankruptcy Judge Rufus Reynolds visited Heritage Village USA incognito to try to gain insight into the case, he found the security guard more informative about the handling of money at PTL than all the financial records he had seen.[23]

Given PTL's antiquated bookkeeping system, the commingling of funds could have been the result of ignorance and negligence. Whether this system provides an excuse for the crimes committed or was developed with criminal intent is a question that the IRS and other government agencies were compelled to consider.

Apparently, Bakker had a long-range strategy. He would raise money for future building but use the money to pay off debts on *past* constructions and current operating expenses. This meant going into debt for each future building. The strategy called for continuing the process of increased construction until somehow the ones built in the past began to catch up economically and made money to help pay off new debts generated through later building projects. Bakker's dream included eventually constructing a $100-million replica of London's Crystal Palace, a nineteenth-century trading center erected in celebration of the emerging Industrial Revolution. For a long time a painting of the planned replica hung in the lobby of the 500-room Heritage Grand Hotel. (Dallas's Infomart, which Bakker might have seen on one of his visits there, is a replica of the Crystal Palace.)

Rumblings from the 160,000 to 190,000 PTL Lifetime Partners continued into late spring of 1988. The new PTL board insisted that if forced to refund money to all Lifetime Partners, PTL would fold. The South Carolina Tax Commission considered sending PTL a tax bill of about $10 million. And if the U.S. Postal Service rules that the partnership scheme is mail fraud, a penalty of up to five years faces Jim Bakker and Richard Dortch. The IRS is still not pleased with the baby-faced charmer of PTL fame. A particularly odd item that met with IRS disfavor was the $25,000 trip that Bakker and aide David Taggart took together to Palm Springs. The records call it a medical trip but fail to disclose the nature of the illness requiring a lavish trip to California. No medical insurance claim was filed. It would seem that a faith healer like Bakker could find a less expensive route to health care, especially as one who once boasted, after a televised preaching in Charlotte in 1974, "People were saved by the hundreds, cancers dropped off bodies, and tumors vanished."[24]

The *Washington Post* pointed out that Sun Myung Moon was sent to prison for criminal tax evasion and obstruction of justice—a case that hinged on a mere $25,000 in unpaid back taxes.[25] Bakker had more political clout than Moon had, but the charges against him were far more serious.

The federal special grand jury, hearing testimony in the criminal investigation of Jim Bakker and his former top aides, began on August 17, 1987. U.S. District Judge Robert Potter predicted that if the jury members met for one week every month, the investigation would continue into at least February or March of 1988. The topic of investigation was tax, wire, and mail fraud.

Throughout 1986 and 1987 the Reagan administration was charged with favoritism and foot-dragging on the Bakker case, because of Bakker's public support of the administration. Vice-president George Bush invited Bakker to a campaign party at his Washington home in the summer of 1986. After resigning from Bush's staff, Pete Teeley became PTL's Washington consultant, receiving $120,000 over an eighteen-month period. In 1986 Doug Weed, Bush's campaign link with evangelicals, was paid $75,000 by PTL to write a book about PTL's problems with the federal government. The book was never published. One member of the Justice Department who wanted to forget about all charges against Bakker insisted that an investigation was an intrusion of government into church matters. Other Justice Department members argued that being a member of the clergy should not exempt anyone from laws that all other citizens are required to obey. Former U.S. Attorney Charles Brewer of North Carolina said he was ousted from office because he defied firm instructions not to press for a criminal investigation of PTL. "That's the first time I've been told not to investigate something," he said.

Justice Department spokesman John Russell called Brewer's

charge "baloney." Brewer stood by his charge, however, and added that there was a deliberate attempt in Washington to slow down the investigation. Suspicion increased when Jesse Helms's former chief legislative assistant Tom Ashcraft was sworn in as interim chief federal prosecutor for North Carolina's western district before being nominated by Reagan or confirmed by the Senate. Helms is known to be a strong ally of TV evangelists.[26]

Under Falwell, PTL turned to the secular court to seek protection in bankruptcy laws. This move has created new complications in the church-state entanglement controversy. The consequences are probably far-reaching and, to a large extent, unpredictable.

8

A Personal Journey
Through Charismatic Mecca

Located on 2,300 acres in Fort Mill, South Carolina, Heritage USA had almost five million visitors in 1985. An increasingly popular attraction for tourists and Charismatic pilgrims, it employed in 1985 almost 2,500 workers. On January 26, 1986, the editor of the *Charlotte Observer* said that Heritage USA could soon be operating the biggest hotel between Washington and Atlanta. The new, squeaky-clean Heritage Grand Hotel is Victorian in design. The lobby features an ornately engraved piano and a swimming pool. A half dozen glassed-in elevators carry guests from the lobby to rooms on four floors. To the right of the fellowship lobby is a walkway leading to the enclosed promenade called Main Street, with a string of pleasant shops on either side.

I was not quite ready to leave the lobby and begin my stroll down Main Street because I wanted to hear what the articulate PTL lawyer from New York, Roy Grutman, had to say. He was still answering reporters' questions in the lobby.

The attorney's style seemed confidently ambivalent. He had entered the scene in a time of confusion, dancing to a tune played by Falwell and Bakker. At first lively and harmonious, the tune soon split into two, one played by Falwell and the other by Bakker. Lawyer Grutman had stumbled only slightly, and then quickly picked up Falwell's tune, forsaking Bakker's. One could only admire Grutman's footwork. But blowing in from Southern Louisiana was still another tune, played by evangelist Jimmy Swaggart. Grutman at first had interpreted it to be a hostile tune to which he most certainly would not dance. But Falwell had sent word that Swaggart was really playing in harmony despite appearances. Grutman reacted again in a confidently ambivalent manner.

When his interview with the reporters ended, Grutman left the hotel in a rush, stepping into a long black car. The magazine reporters left in another black car. I remained behind to make notes and take the walk down Main Street. I had already seen the home in which Billy Graham grew up. Bakker had had it moved in from Charlotte.

Before entering Main Street, I lingered at the entrance of the hotel restaurant. Too expensive. I set my face resolutely toward Morrison's Cafeteria at the far end of Main Street. I had been told that it was the largest Morrison's in the world.

Smoking, drinking, and using profanity are forbidden at Heritage. That did not concern me. What did concern me was the presence of three of my strongest sources of temptation—a bookstore, an ice cream parlor, and a fudge shop. I yielded and entered Ye Olde Bookstore, where Jim and Tammy's books were on sale. I saw a Tammy doll and books by scores of fundamentalist and Charismatic authors. On one shelf stood copies of a book by a famous liberal minister from Texas. I wondered who had been responsible for ordering those copies. There was a surprisingly large collection of books on divorce Christian-style. Twenty years ago a book on divorce in a Christian bookstore like this could not have been found. Because Jim and Tammy Bakker had experienced marital problems in the late seventies and early eighties, they decided to introduce into Heritage Village a ministry for troubled marriages. Until the public scandal of spring 1987, marriage and family workshops were scheduled regularly in the PTL Partner Center at Heritage Village Church. For Charismatics and fundamentalists, this move was nothing less than a revolution.

With a large plastic sack of books now in my possession, I left the bookstore and turned right. Continuing down Main Street, I saw on the left in the distance Susie's Ice Cream Parlor. Quickly I looked to the right, resolving not to indulge in the frozen cholesterol. To the right was a large jewelry shop. I stopped, looked at the merchandise, and wondered how often Tammy had stopped at a similar store to give her Pentecostal conscience permission not only to look but to partake. She had confessed that going shopping soothed her nerves. After checking the prices, I concluded that shopping therapy was not for me.

The stop at the jewelry store reminded me that years ago the wives of Pentecostal ministers risked a great deal if they ventured to wear jewelry. Today there are Pentecostal women ministers who seem far removed from aspects of their tradition. It brings about the old question—how many new threads can be stitched into a sock before it becomes another sock? How many changes in a religious tradition can be stitched into it before it ceases to be the same tradition? Perhaps the Pentecostal tradition is more like a growing tree putting forth new branches and new leaves while remaining in some sense the same tree.

Jim and Tammy Bakker have in effect declared that Pentecostalism maintains its continuity only if it changes. Heritage Village, with its sparkle and glamour, is a long way from the dusty, sweaty camp meetings that Pentecostals used to attend before air-conditioning came along and before they could afford something better than their sultry camp tents.

In my pilgrim's progress along Main Street, heading toward the cafeteria, I was assaulted by one of Satan's subtlest weapons. From the Celestial Fudge Shoppe came the aroma of chocolate more enticing than any I have ever known. I made the mistake of turning to stare at the chunks of fudge, huge chunks beckoning me. Powerless to resist, I entered the shop and was carried by the aroma of divinity and fudge from one display window to another.

Only a few moments earlier, inside Ye Olde Bookstore, I had seen a copy of Charles M. Sheldon's popular book *In His Steps: What Would Jesus Do?* At this precarious moment, I could not help wondering what Jesus would do if he had entered the Celestial Fudge Shoppe. Could he escape from this den of seduction without the telltale lingerings of fudge on his breath? Suddenly, I found myself turning around and leaving, glancing back over my shoulder like Lot's wife looking back longingly toward Sodom and Gomorrah. When I arrived back at the doorway, I did not pause. I had won the victory.

Various individuals—ministers, atheists, Jews, deacons, and secularists—have asked me a variety of questions about Heritage Village. The most persistent question is, "What does a twenty-three-acre theme park have to do with Christianity?" When Jimmy Swaggart was accused of plotting to take over Bakker's empire, he answered,

"What in the world would I want with a water slide?"

What indeed does a water park or a swanky hotel have to do with Jesus Christ? It is a fair question. But so is the question, "What does St. Patrick's Cathedral in Manhattan have to do with Jesus Christ?" Widows' checks helped build cathedrals in Washington and New York. The coins of peasants helped finance the construction and maintenance of Lincoln Cathedral in northern England. There is every reason to believe that monies that financed the magnificent buildings of worship on the Continent and in Russia were often forced out of the people.

In some ways Jim and Tammy Bakker are two twentieth-century bishops of their own church. Not unlike bishops in the Middle Ages, the Bakkers were dethroned by a rival churchman. For good or ill, Heritage USA is a return to the concept of the medieval village dedicated to the glory of God but often serving the glory of the ruling bishop. The word *cathedral* derives from *cathedra,* the Latin word for chair. In the Middle Ages the cathedral contained the official chair or throne of a bishop. Construction of the great Gothic cathedrals on the Continent of Europe began at the latter part of the twelfth century, when the bishops in the cities began to gain power.

When the Bakkers returned from California to Heritage Village in mid-June, 1987, they were adamant about reoccupying the parsonage they had left. Despite the eviction notice that Falwell and his board had instigated, the Bakkers refused at first to leave the parsonage. Why? I suggest that they had identified with the parsonage and Heritage Village in the way that medieval bishops identified with their villages and cathedrals. In short, the Bakkers appear to believe they have been divinely enthroned at Heritage Village and PTL. What we are witnessing, therefore, is the shaky beginning of a potential religious dynasty.

Many of the medieval cathedrals symbolized not only the power of the church but the pride and wealth of the town. It is not far-fetched to suggest that the wealth accumulated in Heritage USA symbolizes the pride and power of a new social class that includes Charismatics—a class of immigrants moving in, not from Europe or Mexico, but from across the social tracks and into the middle class. In late June 1987, I listened to a noted Pentecostal preacher speak at length to his large congregation on the need to be filled with the Holy Ghost and to speak in tongues. Just before his sermon ended, somewhat abruptly, he made a statement that summarized the attitude toward Pentecostal upward mobility. He looked straight at his people and said, "Let's push in and get our share!"

In the spring of 1981 I went to Lincoln, England, for a conference of social scientists studying new religious movements. Staying in the home of the canon of Lincoln Cathedral, I had the good fortune of meeting the former archbishop of Canterbury. On the following day I was given an extended guided tour by the canon through this famous cathedral, the largest in England. Standing on the roof of the gigantic structure, I looked out toward the North Sea and realized that some of my wife's English ancestors might have contributed to the building of this majestic triumph of architecture. Admiring the cathedral's stained glass, the towers, and the incredible precision of architecture, I realized that the sense of awe I felt was not peculiar to Christianity or any one religion. It was a human feeling that an atheist, Muslim, Buddhist, or Hindu might have. Southeast of Lincoln and across the Mediterranean Sea stands today still another majestic work of beauty—Islam's Dome of the Rock.

It is fair to ask if Muhammad would have approved of the building of the Dome and other great mosques around the world. Would the early Christians have approved of the building of Lincoln Cathedral and all the other cathedrals that claim to be Christian places of worship? It is fair to ask if the early Christians would have approved of Heritage USA. On the other hand, can contemporary Christianity be defined by what first-century believers might or might not approve of if they were alive today?

To me, the cathedrals offer a certain awe, beauty, and wonder that Heritage USA does not. On the other hand, I am not sure that the people who find Heritage USA to be a Christian center would find cathedrals to be greatly inspiring or moving. In many ways, the Bakkers' achievement at Heritage Village is a *shared* achievement. Heritage USA is also the vision of their supporters, a dream come true. The achievement is utilitarian in the narrow sense of the term, whereas cathedrals are not. The latter were constructed as if they were to be either the dwelling place of God or a creation of beauty for beauty's sake. By contrast, Heritage USA is the dwelling place of people, a place where Charismatics and others can celebrate and admire their own achievements. It is a prophecy or hope that has materialized before their eyes; a very special miracle that they personally brought about.

Heritage Village is also a utopian venture. Each generation of Christians in America seems to produce a mutation with dreams of building a Christian utopia on earth. Heritage USA and the PTL satellite network are the partial realization of a modern utopian dream. The old Pentecostal campgrounds were for the believers a brief but intense Holy Ghost heaven descending to earth. The new affluent Pentecostals and Charismatics still long for the Holy Ghost utopia. And for many of these believers, Heritage Village has become a sacred place, just as Jerusalem has been sacred for many Jews, Muslims, and Christians over the centuries.

Jim Bakker sensed the emotional power of the Jerusalem connection among fundamentalists and Charismatics. He also knew of the millions reaped by the Israeli government from pilgrimages to the Holy Land. With audacity, he set out to transfer some of the Holy Land mystique to Fort Mill, South Carolina. Refusing to seek out the advice that the best biblical archeologists and scholars have to offer, Bakker planned to recreate the streets of Old Jerusalem on the grounds of Heritage USA. His scheme would offer "an unforgettable cultural and spiritual experience for every visitor who has yearned to explore the land of the Bible."[1] In short, instead of transporting believers across the Atlantic to Old Jerusalem, Bakker can transport the sacred city to the Bible Belt and save vacationing pilgrims considerable money. What is more, Heritage USA-Old Jerusalem USA will lie between the Smoky Mountain National Park and Florida, two of the South's favorite spots for renewal.

A number of religions generate sacred sites for themselves. Every year hordes of Southern Baptists (the largest Protestant denomination in the Western Hemisphere) assemble at a very special mountain resort called Ridgecrest. Located a hundred miles northwest of Heritage USA, Ridgecrest has become a holy place where Baptists congregate for a special outpouring of the Spirit. It is also a place of fun and recreation—swimming, tennis, and hiking. Jim Bakker's Heritage Village is a Ridgecrest resort for Charismatics and others. But it differs from Ridgecrest in that it is also a place where people can live year-round. Jim Bakker knew what he was doing when he had the vision of erecting a sacred place for tourist-pilgrims that could serve as a permanent utopia for some believers.

What does the name "Heritage USA" have to do with Christianity? The answer to this question could fill an entire book. Briefly, I will suggest that Jim Bakker represents those who have blended their version of Christianity and Judaism with a version of American civil religion. Heritage USA is designed to be a sacred place especially for the pilgrims of this hybrid religion. Billy Graham in the first two decades of his ministry embraced this hybrid, mingling evangelical Christianity with a nationalistic civil religion and coming up with a kind of "Christian Americanism."[2] In the early 1970s Graham came to agree with those of his fellow evangelicals who criticized his confusion of evangelical Christianity with nationalism. Jerry Falwell in the late 1970s continued Graham's earlier confusion and developed the myopic notion that the United States had two and only two reasons for its existence: (1) to become the home base for Christian missionary efforts for evangelizing the world and (2) to subsidize Israel.

Jim Bakker sees eye-to-eye with Falwell regarding this political and religious hybrid. In fact, he has declared the Fourth of July, Independence Day, as "the birth of our own Heritage Village Church." He sees this date as profoundly significant, commemorating both the birth of the nation and the birth of Heritage Village Church. "All-day worship services with parades and fireworks are part of our 'Passover,' a time each year when we remember how God has miraculously delivered us from our enemies."[3]

9

Frocked and Defrocked Superstars

Testifying before the Federal Communications Commission in 1980, former PTL mission director Bob Manzano stated that Jim Bakker felt he had to "have one of two things going all the time, either a crisis or a project." Bakker believed that these two "hallmarks" were needed to motivate TV viewers to contribute to his ministry. Manzano told the FCC that Bakker threatened that the PTL ministry was on the verge of going under unless his supporters rushed money to him.[1]

Like a number of other TV evangelists, Jim Bakker appeared to believe that big was beautiful. But the bigger the dream, the more likely a crisis would develop. And few things seemed to be sweeter to Bakker than a well-publicized crisis. In 1978 PTL was virtually hankering for insolvency. The money received in the mail one day determined what bills would be paid the next day. Instead of tightening the belt, however, Bakker began dreaming of a new way to spend millions more on a truly big new project.

The justification that TV evangelists usually gave for throwing themselves into cliff-hanging debt year after year was the Great Commission that Jesus is said to have given his disciples: "And he said unto them, Go ye into all the world and preach the gospel to every creature." Bakker is only one among several evangelists who would tell their viewers that the literal fulfillment of the Great Commission was never truly possible until this present generation. Thanks to the "miracle of radio and TV," the gospel could literally be carried to every nation. During his first year at North Central Bible College, young Bakker revealed to his classmates his vision of fulfilling the Great Commission "to win the world for Jesus."[2]

It was not the vision of the Great Commission, however, that almost hurled the PTL roller coaster off its rails, but the rejection of both self-restraint and business common sense. Bakker had promised to give money through PTL to help ministers in South Korea and Brazil establish new religious shows on television. Along with failing to keep the promise, PTL in September of 1978 fell behind in its employee retirement fund. According to FCC testimony, tens of thousands of dollars were wasted. For example, work had to be stopped on Heritage USA because the contractor had not been paid, prompting the workers to walk out in the summer of 1978. The testimony of PTL board member Jim Moss revealed that one building had deteriorated so much that an additional half million dollars was needed before construction could resume a year later.

Jim Moss and Bill Perkins, then vice-president of PTL, came to believe that Bakker's commitment to Heritage USA undermined his commitment to evangelism and world missions. The PTL staff became confused and fragmented. In an October 1978 memo to Bakker, Perkins expressed his concern that the Heritage USA project had brought "conflicts, confusion and total disintegration of executive unity."

A radical shift took place in Bakker's priorities sometime between late summer 1977 and early 1978. On August 4, 1977, Bakker told viewers: "I believe from now on, as we pay for the facilities that are absolutely necessary to broadcast the Gospel, . . . every penny that comes in, over and above the actual minimal costs to keep us on the air and the budget, needs to go to world evangelism."[3] Only months later, however, Bakker drastically rearranged his priorities. Bill Perkins confessed to finding it incredible that his boss would require the greater percentage of the incoming money to be funneled off to the Heritage USA project at the expense of world missions. Bakker's decision to speed up the opening of Heritage USA shook Perkins profoundly. As a result of this decision, against the advice of many associates, construction costs were escalated as much as $10 million, Perkins claimed.

In response, Bakker described Heritage USA as bait in the endeavor to be "fishers of men," that is, to evangelize the world. How the bait was to be used remains unclear. In any case, the bait cost more than the whole of the fishing equipment, including whatever

Bakker took to be analogous to the boat.

A partial list of the projected units of the Heritage USA complex that Bakker regarded as bait in service of world evangelism includes a 500-room hotel (with a twenty-one-story addition under construction), the Main Street shopping mall, Kevin's House, a conference center, a home for unmarried mothers, restaurants, a TV studio, a sanctuary, an amphitheater, an animal park, Billy Graham's childhood home, RV campgrounds, recreation facilities, private homes, a cinema theater, a parsonage, and offices for such PTL programs as a prison ministry, an adoption agency, and food-and-clothing centers for the needy. Finally, there is a $10-million water park.[4]

It is currently impossible to find out how much money television evangelists as a group receive annually to cover their various new projects, routine organizational constructions and expenses, personal incomes, and ministry-related personal expenses. The most conservative estimate is $1 billion, the most liberal is $2 billion. A major source of the evangelist's income is royalties, a by-product of simply being on television regularly. In a letter to the editor, George Wright of Portland, Oregon, was on target when he observed, "Give somebody a TV pulpit and they're automatically best-seller authors, no matter the calibre of what they say."[5]

In the race to build bigger empires, TV evangelists become in some sense captives of their own serious game. This requires them to remain highly competitive with one another in appealing to customers willing to support their enterprises. Unlike the National Council of Churches's older model of the business cartel, TV evangelists are classical capitalists, each striving to form a monopoly. One reason that Falwell and Swaggart are concerned about the Bakker scandal is that it is bad for the business of television evangelism in general. Even though they are competing with each other, they realize that none among them wins if the fatted calf becomes diseased or dies.

Superstardom is a part of TV evangelism. Fame and money are not mere trappings of the business; they are its life blood. Power is a by-product that always beckons the evangelists.

Billy Graham had offers to high political positions at the national level and would have received considerable support had he wished to declare himself as either a congressional or gubernatorial candidate in North Carolina. Despite the fact that he had been somewhat like an unofficial advisor to several U.S. presidents (he had urged Richard

Nixon to seek the number-one job in the White House), Graham
has never seriously sought political office. He has always regarded
his calling to be second to none, including that of the U.S. presidency.
During the presidential terms of Eisenhower, Nixon, and Johnson,
Graham appeared to view himself more as a Daniel than as a King
David. (Evangelical Christians believe that Daniel was a real prophet
who had enormous influence on the King of Babylon.) Graham almost
always used the word "spiritual" to characterize the counsel he gave
to presidents. He thought of himself as belonging to the tradition
of the Old Testament prophets, whose spiritual advice was often highly
political.

In the early 1970s, however, Graham came to agree with his
wife that he was compromising his ministry by consorting with high-
ranking politicians. The complexities of the Vietnam war forced
Graham to see that he could not function as an Old Testament prophet
delivering a clear and uncertain message on national policy. "I'm a
New Testament evangelist, not an Old Testament prophet," Graham
began saying around 1973. By then, he had had his fill of politics.

By contrast, Pat Robertson has given no sign of being even slightly
ambivalent about his bid for power. In 1985 Robertson said he was
consulting God about whether to run for the Republican presidential
nomination in 1988. The former executive producer of the "700 Club,"
Gerard Straub, claims that as early as 1979 Robertson was consulting
him about his desire to become president. "Pat shared with me his
presidential fantasy and his firm belief that he was the one person
uniquely qualified to lead this nation."[6] Psychologist Edmund D.
Cohen, a convert from evangelicalism to humanism, says bluntly that
Robertson's lust for power is so consuming that if he were president
he would willingly override constitutional restraints in order to carry
out messages received telepathically from the deity.[7]

Jim Bakker's interest in gaining political power appears slight
when compared with Pat Robertson's and Jerry Falwell's. Problems
of fame and especially money, rather than political power, have been
the Bakkers' albatross.

Los Angeles Times syndicated columnist Cal Thomas, a former
vice-president of the Moral Majority, commented wryly about the
current battle among TV evangelists: "Instead of turning the other
cheek, we have turned to the other lawyer."[8] Thomas went on to

say that the unchurched are "hating God" because of the battle of the televangelists. Perhaps a more charitable look at the reaction of Americans to the Bakker scandal would reveal that most Americans are quite capable of distinguishing TV evangelists from the concept of God. Having a less-than-exalted opinion of TV evangelists and declining to send money is scarcely to be classified with God-hatred. The problem is not so much with the eternal deity as with the lifestyles of mortal evangelists.

When Falwell was forced to admit at long last that he and most of his fellow TV evangelists have not been as open and accountable as they should have been, Richard Cizik told Falwell to follow his own advice and join a national group for financial accountability. Cizik is research director for the National Association of Evangelicals. Arthur Borden, president of the Washington-based Evangelical Council for Financial Accountability, added that evangelistic organizations like Falwell's and the Bakkers' should give not only full disclosure, but "audited financial statements to anyone upon written request." PTL joined the Evangelical Council for Financial Accountability but withdrew after declining on release auditors' notes on its 1986 financial statements. Falwell was a member of this evangelical accountability group initially, but quickly pulled out. Billy Graham was the only major TV evangelist to join early and to remain a member in good standing.

The elevation to superstardom makes it easy for evangelists to lose touch with the financial realities of middle-class life in America. From January 1984 through March 19, 1987, PTL paid the Bakkers a combined $4.8 million in salaries, bonuses, and other payments, not including fringe benefits. In 1984 Jim and Tammy bought a $449,000 house in Palm Desert, California. In the same year they paid a total of $100,000 for a 1953 Rolls-Royce and a 1984 Mercedes-Benz. Less than two years later, they agreed to pay $90,000 for improvements on a mountainside home they had just purchased for $148,500 in Gatlinburg, Tennessee, one of the most scenic resort areas of the South.[9] Later, they sold their Palm Desert home and bought a house in nearby Palm Springs, where they moved after leaving the parsonage in Tega Cay, South Carolina. In June of 1987 the Palm Springs house was put up for sale at $700,000. This occurred only a week after Tammy had wept on TV because, she claimed, she and Jim had been reduced to their last $37,000.

That was not the first time the Bakkers had portrayed themselves as financially against the wall when they were in fact living high on the hog. During the summer of 1978, when PTL was skating on thin ice financially, Jim told supporters: "Tammy and I are giving every penny of our life savings to PTL." He went on to say that without a miracle of giving their ministry could collapse. That was a few days before Bakker made the $6,000 down payment on a houseboat.[10]

Richard Dortch, born during the Great Depression, was one of Bakker's close associates to receive handsome incomes. As PTL executive director immediately under Bakker, he earned $350,000, including bonuses of roughly $220,000 and a retirement account contribution exceeding $80,000. During the first three months of 1987, Dortch received about $270,000, most of it as a $200,000 bonus. One wonders how Dortch, who had been considered for the highest office in the Assemblies of God denomination, became Bakker's accomplice. Why did his influence at PTL and his closeness to Bakker fail to check the Bakkers' accelerating journey toward the land of excess? Did Dortch simply become blindly entangled in Bakker's web? Or did he help Bakker spin it more elaborately?

It is ironic that in 1983 Jim Bakker wrote the following advice:

> An old farmer once summed up the basics of poor economics by saying, "If your outgo is more than your income, your upkeep will be your downfall!" And that's exactly true. Most of the people who go bankrupt don't go under because they have little income . . . they just don't manage it well. They overextend themselves by spending too much too fast . . . by committing themselves to more "easy payments" than they can cover.
>
> Failure to use money wisely can cause more heartache and trouble than you can imagine.[11]

When Bakker resigned from PTL in March 1987, he owed $14.7 million to his building contractor; $4.5 million was still owed toward finishing the Towers near the Grand Hotel. By May 1987, the financial records of PTL were declared to be a nightmare of confusion and a labyrinth of mismanagement. As early as March, Jerry Falwell had already hinted of possible criminal charges against Bakker.[12] Later, there was serious talk of wire fraud and mail fraud.

Prior to 1983, Jim Bakker seemed to be aware that something was very seriously wrong with his organization. "I found myself spending much of my time trying to bail PTL out of financial crisis. Each emergency seemed worse than the one before."[13] Unfortunately, his diagnosis of the problem was only partly accurate. He correctly noted that his organization's phenomenally rapid growth in outreach and scope created financial crises. He inaccurately stated, however, that his financial problems "were not the result of waste or the bad use of funds."[14] He did try to set up a new budgeting system, but new resolutions and organizational innovations could not effectively offset Jim Bakker's gambling compulsion.

It may be that Bakker will never overcome his life-long compulsion to place his fate in the hands of a mythical Lady Luck. Unfortunately, his theology reinforces this by bestowing upon his compulsion the name "faith." For Bakker to demonstrate his great faith, a string of future crises will be required. In order to overcome this high-risk gambler's compulsion, Bakker would have to go against his past history and in some sense renounce what he has come to believe are miracles due to his faith.

10

The New Folk Theology

I once thought fundamentalist preachers were just guys who had found a way to make a lot of money. But now I think some of them really believe what they preach. It is still easy for me to question their sincerity." Those frank words, spoken by an engineer who shared a cab with me in Washington, D.C., call attention to one of the thorniest problems to emerge from the serious investigation of religion.

A sharp distinction must be made between (1) hard-core insincerity and (2) surface insincerity. The former compromises the heart of one's character and betrays one's deepest convictions. For good or ill, surface insincerity often serves one's convictions or belief-system. The danger comes when someone of influence like Jim Bakker seems unable at times to distinguish the difference.

An example of surface insincerity can be seen in the life of the famous folk singer and songwriter Bob Dylan. Driven by enormous ambition and a lust for fame, Dylan snubbed his old friends and knowingly manufactured his public image. He created a mythical background of himself as an orphan from New Mexico who lived on the road for several years. In fact, Bob Dylan was Robert Alan Zimmerman from a middle-class Jewish family in Hibbing, Minnesota.[1] Even though they are aware that Dylan (or Zimmerman) sometimes invents stories about himself, music critics ignore his questionable motives because they believe he is true to his music. It has an integrity and distinctive reality of its own. Just as a dam can be examined for the integrity of its structure, so a musician's work can be examined for the integrity of its structure. Similarly, belief-systems can be critically evaluated on their own right to determine the integrity of their structure. Like a dam or a musical composition, a belief-system stands on its own and must not be judged by the weaknesses of its human bearers and creators.

In his astoundingly revealing book *The Faith Healers,*[2] James Randi exposed the tendency of some faith healers to lie about their pasts. The renowned Methodist scholar Albert Outler once commented that in retelling their own conversion stories, individuals tend to exalt not only God but themselves. A distinction may nevertheless be drawn between the believers' motives and the history and content of their theology.

A new folk theology has emerged in the 1970s and 1980s in much the same way that a new folk music emerged in the 1960s. Just as Bob Dylan's music had roots in Woody Guthrie's music, so the modern folk theology of the Bakkers, Oral Roberts, and Pat Robertson had roots in the faith healers of especially the 1950s and early 1960s.

When Tammy Bakker was a child, she sang in the tent meeting of one of the most famous of the old-line faith healers and exorcists, A. A. Allen. "I was so small," Tammy recalled, "Mr. Allen would pick me up and put me on a chair in front of the microphone."[3] Even though he was in many ways a spontaneous, old-line Pentecostal evangelist, Allen proved to be an innovator by adding gospel rock music, combining it with old-time gospel music. Ten years ahead of his time in many ways, he was accompanied by a team of entertainers.

Allen maintained a running battle with newspapers. In 1963 the IRS sued him for $300,000 in back taxes, but he won the right for the A. A. Allen Evangelistic Association to enjoy tax-exempt status.[4] Like Bakker after him, Allen was a sensational and effective fund-raiser and was perhaps the first to formally advance the folk theology that has recently come to be known as the Prosperity Gospel. Allen made the stunning announcement in 1962 that God had bestowed on him a "new annointing and a new power to lay hands on the believers who gave $100 toward the support of our missionary outreach and bestow on each of them POWER TO GET WEALTH."

Knowing he had broken new ground in the revivalism business, Allen cast in highly dramatic form the new revelation of "the blessing of prosperity." In his mind, he was the absolute first in the history of Christianity to receive this revelation. In March 1963 in a Houston, Texas, crusade he told how it happened to him—"like a flash from heaven, a bolt out of the blue. . . . It was just as if a light had been turned on in my mind." In a booklet published in 1963, Allen printed what he purported to be a verbatim report of the divine revelation to him:

> I am a wealthy God! Yea, I am not poor. . . . But I say unto thee, claim my wealth in thy hand, yea, in thy purse and in thy substance. For behold I plan to do *a new thing in the earth!* . . . Yea, yea, yea, obey ye the servant of the Lord, for I have placed him in this place. Indeed I did call him forth from his mother's womb. And I have kept my hand upon my servant.[5]

Not only did Allen claim to be the first to receive this new commission, he was not a little jealous of fellow preachers who tried to horn in on his act. "God told me that he had given me power to bestow power to get wealth. He did not say it was given to every Tom, Dick and Harry, or to just anyone who says 'Lord, Lord.' "[6]

There are several interesting parallels between Allen's ministry and Jim Bakker's. Allen, for example, was accused of drinking, and someone inside his organization believed that Allen was being blackmailed. After Allen's demise, a well-publicized holy war erupted. In the Arizona courts his successor, Don Stewart, and his associates were charged with embezzling. In fact, only a shakeup of Stewart's board of directors finally restored to him firm control of the ministry that Allen had passed on to him. The Prosperity Gospel continued with Stewart and was also picked up by Oral Roberts. Jim Bakker, his fund-raising talent quickly acknowledged by his Pentecostal peers, became one of the leading formulators of the new folk theology of prosperity.

Folk theology has always played a major role in religious movements because it is communicated directly to the laypeople in their own language. One of the most successful folk theologies was developed by John Wesley, founder of the eighteenth-century Methodist movement. In the sixteenth century a leading voice of the Protestant Reformation, Martin Luther, preached and penned a folk theology that has survived five centuries. It was Luther who, by translating the Bible into German, helped create Modern German. Folk theology distinguishes itself by responding to practical crises in the faith of a great portion of the populace. It is neither systematic nor intended to be scholarly theology. It is deliberately devotional, motivational, and inspirational. It may also function to communicate a moral challenge or to make sense of a social and moral crisis that many laypeople have been thrown into because of historical circumstances.

There is little question that Jim Bakker, Pat Robertson, and Oral Roberts have contributed to the emergence of a new folk theology. It goes under several names: the Gospel of Health and Wealth, Prosperity Theology, Deliverance Theology, or the Gospel of Success. Ist principal twentieth-century roots trace back to the swashbuckling faith healers of the big tent and to popular God-wants-you-to-get-to-the-top sermons that reflect the theme of Norman Vincent Peale's best seller, *The Power of Positive Thinking*.

There is one key difference between the major modern proponents of the Gospel of Health and Wealth, on the one hand, and Martin Luther and John Wesley, on the other hand. Whereas Wesley and Luther had training in historical theology, Bakker and Roberts had none. Pat Robertson attended a seminary, but there is little indication that he has a great knowledge of the world of biblical scholarship. Whereas Wesley and Luther could engage the theologians and biblical scholars of their time in meaningful exchange, the big-time television Charismatics appear to have avoided testing out their new theology in scholarly give-and-take exchanges.

One of the marks of the modern Gospel of Health and Wealth is the slickness of its presentation. John Ankerberg is the only major television evangelist to come close to an intellectually respectable exchange of opinion in which each side gets a fair hearing. Jimmy Swaggart has his own panel of hand-picked experts who exchange views with him. But they sit while he stands, showing who is clearly the boss. For the most part, the panel is composed of his wife and a few admirers who already embrace Swaggart's folk theology.

The Prosperity Gospel of Bakker, Robertson, and Roberts is based on the following chain of arguments or premises from the faith-healing tradition: First, God has supreme power over everything, including Satan, who plays a major role in the thinking of Pentecostals. Second, God does not want anyone to be sick. In only rare cases, God may cause someone to be ill, but only for the purpose of demonstrating his healing power. Third, Satan and his underworld sycophants are the prime cause of disease and illness. Fourth, God can overcome the power of the demons *if* the diseased and afflicted develop a proper relationship with God. Fifth, the gift of healing that Roberts, Robertson, and Bakker claim to have is double-barreled. It allows them (a) to make war on Satan and demons (even exorcising them when they have possessed someone) and (b) to inspire and instruct the infirm and diseased so that they may establish a "right relationship" with God and thereby open up the channels of healing.

As simple as it may seem, at least on the surface, Prosperity Theology takes the points above and inserts the phrase *economic hardship* or its equivalent in the place of *disease and illness*. In the place of *wholeness* or *health,* it substitutes *economic prosperity* and even *wealth.* In short, God can heal both the body and the bank account.

According to this gospel, Jesus' death on the cross gained at least three victories for true believers: deliverance of the soul from sin and hell, deliverance of the body from Satan and disease, and deliverance from poverty and economic hardship in this life.

The modern advocates of this new Prosperity Theology turn to scripture for supportive proof texts. In John 10:10, Jesus is quoted as saying, "I am come that they might have life, and that they might have it more abundantly" (KJV). In his books and on TV, Pat Robertson relates stories of how believers set failing businesses back on the mountaintop of abundance and success by exercising great faith in Jesus and by contributing to Robertson's ministry. Oral and Richard Roberts are also fond of such testimonials. For Jim Bakker, Pat Robertson, and Oral and Richard Roberts, God has infallibly laid out steps that, if taken by Christian believers, will lead them to certain financial prosperity. A favorite scriptural text of the Bakkers is Philippians 4:19: "But my God shall supply all your need according to his riches in glory by Jesus Christ" (KJV). One of the most successful TV prophets of profit in Texas is the hard-selling Bob Tilton, who prays into the camera and loves to quote Deuteronomy 8:18: "But thou shalt remember the Lord thy God: for it is He that giveth thee power to get wealth" (KJV). For people like Tilton, God intends wealth to go directly to Christian believers, not to sinners and unbelievers. And to reinforce this belief, he quotes again a biblical text: "A good man leaves an inheritance to his children's children, but the sinner's wealth is laid up for the righteous" (Proverbs 13:22 RSV).

These jet-set materialists insist that the Bible is a book of promises, and that each biblical promise has the Creator of the Universe to back it up. As the new apostles of the "Name It, Claim It" religion, they name the blessing they want from God and then claim it as their rightful inheritance. Jim Bakker tells his people that when they pray for a new car, they should tell God what color they want the car to be. Flashing his movie-star smile on TV while hawking his packaged Biblical Success Course on cassette tapes for only a hundred bucks, Bob Tilton proclaims, "Jesus wants to bring you into your inheritance." Living in one of Dallas's posh enclaves, Tilton has already received his inheritance many times over and is anticipating more.

Can it be that these TV preachers were profoundly converted to the Gospel of the Golden Fleece by simply reading a few texts in the Bible? Can it be that they have erected their Prosperity Theology on a mere smattering of proof texts?

There are, after all, many biblical passages warning of riches and wealth. The English evangelical preacher John Wesley once said that if after his death it was discovered that he possessed more than twenty-five pounds (the equivalent to roughly $3,000 today), he should be counted as a knave and a dishonest man. Through the hands of the incredible Wesley passed a large fortune, which he spent on the poor and the deprived of London, Bristol, and Newcastle. Unlike the modern apostles of Prosperity Theology, Wesley did not believe he had the right to rake off great sums for his personal use. In 1776, when Adam Smith published his book *The Wealth of Nations,* Wesley issued a blistering sermon against the accumulation of wealth.

If the contemporary Prosperity Gospel is not really rooted in biblical proof texts, then in what is it rooted? Some have concluded that the obvious answer is unmitigated greed. The TV evangelists reply, however, by asking two poignant questions: Does the Heavenly Father *want* his children to suffer in sickness? Does he *desire* them to undergo prolonged economic hardship? For the forgers of the Gospel of Health and Wealth, the answer to each question is also obvious, and their theology is rooted in the answers to these two questions.

The fact is, nevertheless, that even among Christian believers there remains a staggering amount of mental and physical suffering and a great number of people who are struggling economically. Television evangelists seem to believe that people suffer or are financially strapped because they lack a proper relationship with God. Jimmy Swaggart once showed pictures of European Jews suffering agony and death in Nazi concentration camps. His point was simple. When people, like the Jews, are clearly not in a right relationship with God (after all, Jews are not Christians), then they cannot expect God to save them from earthly terrors such as the Holocaust. In fact, Swaggart and almost all evangelists hold that if the Jews do not convert to Christianity, they will be sent to the Eternal Concentration Camp.

It is frustrating when the "healers" have faith (as they define it) and the candidate for healing apparently has faith, yet there is no healing. The Pentecostal preacher Jack Coe in an Alabama meeting picked people up out of their wheelchairs and stood them up. If they fell, he pronounced them lacking in faith.[7]

After praying before the TV cameras year after year and pro-nouncing people across America cured of cancer, even though he had no idea who they were, Pat Robertson received a painful dose of reality. His wife could not be cured of breast cancer by the simple prayers and faith of Pat and others. On the day after the August 1986 Michigan Republican primary, Mrs. Robertson underwent a mastectomy.

There is a kind of Catch-22 in the definition of faith that Jim Bakker and other Gospel-of-Health-and-Wealth preachers urge on their audiences. The evangelists insist that if health and wealth do not follow as promised, then something was wrong with the faith process, not with the promise. This raises the question, "How can people know that they truly do have faith?"

Both Jim Bakker and Oral Roberts, as well as son Richard, include in the faith process something that Oral Roberts calls seed-faith. What it means in economic terms is that having faith and receiving the rewards of faith is like farming. Bakker explains:

You say, "I'm ready for the flood [of blessing]! I'm ready for God to pour me out a blessing."

Have you done what He told you to do? You have a part in this, too. God made me a commitment that He would bless you, but first you've got to do something—you've got to give to God. And then He'll come back to you.

It's like a farmer planting a field. He can go out to that field and say, "Okay, field. I'm ready. Give me some grain." But if he hasn't planted any seed, he's not going to get any grain. First he has to plant his seed, and then he can expect a harvest.[8]

Obviously, the ministry is the field. The money of the TV viewers is the seed-faith to be planted in the field. If they plant their tithes and offerings in the hands of Bakker or Roberts and trust them, it is the same as entrusting their money to the hands of God. It is an act of faith in God. Bakker writes, "Now people are confused about who they're supposed to give their tithes and offerings to. Let me tell you—*give them to God.* They're His."[9]

But who collects money on God's behalf? Knowing that he is not being specific, Bakker works his way toward an answer in a masterpiece of competitive fund-raising:

> If you want to know how much money to give to each church or ministry, ask God about it. He'll tell you what He wants you to do with His money.
>
> Just because something sounds wonderful doesn't mean that's what God wants for you. It might seem wonderful for you to help build a new sanctuary for your local church, but maybe that isn't what God wants right now. It would be wonderful for you to help build a home for troubled children in your community, but maybe it's not God's will for you to do that. Maybe He has some other jobs for you to do.
>
> You need to find out what God wants you to do and do it. Support those ministries that bless you and help you. If you attend a local church—and I hope you do—support it with your tithes. If you feel PTL ministers to you and you believe in what we're doing, then support us and help us stay on the air.
>
> Whatever you give to God, He will give back to you many times over. That's the secret of financial success—you can't outgive God.[10]

If Bakker's readers and TV viewers are disposed to spend money on their own projects without funneling any of it through churches or TV evangelists, Bakker takes off the velvet gloves and severely warns against such a practice. "When you rob God, it's going to come out of your hide! . . . Withholding from the Lord will place you under a curse of misfortune." Bakker goes on to specify troubles, bills, and emergencies that will befall those who fail to plant their money in the proper ministry.[11]

No proponent of the Prosperity Gospel has even begun to deal with the thriving economy of Japan, one of the most thoroughly non-Christian nations in the world. Today, Japanese workers individually have more money in their banks than do Christians in America. Japan is on its way toward becoming the world's richest country, and its prosperity cannot be regarded as having any substantive link with the bizarre economic theories of TV evangelists. The postwar Christian missionaries to Japan quickly learned that few, if any, free countries offered less promise of conversion than Japan. According to Richard L. Rubenstein, "After more than a century of strenuous efforts, with one of the world's largest concentrations of foreign missionaries, almost 5,200 in number, Japan remains more resistant to Christianity than any other developed country. Less than one percent of the population is Christian, and the numbers are declining."[12]

The Prosperity Theology of Jim Bakker and similar TV evangelists has been denounced as a message of vulgar materialism in the name of God. But it is more than that. Prosperity Theology represents the yearnings and ambitions of an upwardly mobile stratum of people who see themselves as having been too long at the nation's fringe. Like the grown children and grandchildren of immigrants, they have resolved to claim their birthright.

In the United States, two ways in particular are believed, rightly or wrongly, to be avenues leading to a place on the "inside." One is the avenue of money; the other is the avenue of higher education. Either avenue, according to the popular belief, will in time turn an outsider into an insider. There is little question that Pentecostals more than most Americans have seen themselves as outsiders. This is especially true of the older generation. Jim Bakker was one on the outside, and he admits that it sparked an intense sense of upward mobility in him and in Tammy.

In September 1965, when Jim was twenty-five, he decided that if he and Tammy were going to "work for the Lord in the community" of Portsmouth, Virginia, they should live "somewhere nice." Instead of going to a neighborhood where they could find an apartment suitable to their income, Jim and Tammy drove up to Number One Crawford Parkway, an expensive high-rise near Elizabeth River. Expecting to find in 1965 nothing but suites renting for $600–700 a month, Jim nevertheless approached the high-rise entrance. As it turned out, there was one efficiency apartment for $150 a month. It had a sweeping view of the river but lacked a bedroom. Years later, Jim commented:

> We never told anyone the apartment didn't have a bedroom. With so many doors opening off the huge living room, everybody probably thought the door leading to the furnace was our bedroom. We purchased a comfortable hide-a-bed and that worked out fine until the Lord could perform another miracle with accommodations.[13]

Giving the impression of being affluent was inordinately important to the Bakkers in their mid-twenties. Tammy took the high-rise elevator one day when "a society matron asked with her nose pointed high in the air" what floor she lived on. Tammy answered, "The seventh." The woman replied, "We live on the eighteenth," which was the most expensive floor in the high-rise. Within a year the Bakkers' financial situation had changed so that they were able to move to the eighteenth floor. Jim's later comment on this is profoundly revealing: "Then when the society matron would ask Tammy, 'And what floor do you live on?' she could say, 'Praise God, we've gone to the eighteenth.' "[14]

The fact is that the new Pentecostals are moving up economically in the world. As a consequence, they have with ambivalence become the selective partakers of this world's material goods. The function of Prosperity Theology is to justify their new social and material success. In order for this justification to carry weight, however, it must be done in the language of their own belief-system. In times past, Pentecostals were poor people. Since being poor has little advantage in and of itself, the Pentecostals of the Great Depression transformed it into a spiritual virtue. "Blessed be ye poor: for yours is the kingdom of God" (Luke 6:20 KJV). The simple life of self-denial uncluttered with worldly goods was made an ingredient of holiness and sanctification.

When Jim and Tammy were adolescents, sermons both praising the simple life and warning of the pleasures of worldliness shot like tongues of flame across Pentecostal pulpits. Blessings were ritualistically proclaimed as the reward for living a holy life of self-denial, good works, and manifest faith. "Manifest faith" was translated to mean deeds such as participating in church activities, Bible reading, witnessing to unbelievers, getting worked up at revival meetings, and offering prayers for healing and the baptism of the Spirit.

More than any other combination of factors, television and a new buying power among Pentecostals in the late 1950s and the 1960s called self-denial into question. Or, stated more accurately, not everything that the previous generation of Pentecostals classified as essential to the holy life was accepted by the new generation. As late as the 1950s a number of Pentecostal women did not cut their hair and had never been to a beauty salon to have their hair styled. They either could not afford such a luxury or looked upon it as a worldly extravagance. In time, the plain and colorless look became identified as old-fashioned rather than a mark of sanctification.

Ironically, it was male evangelists and ministers who unwittingly led the way in this reform. Pentecostal ministers began sporting colorful ties, artful tie clasps, and trendy suits and shoes. Some of them drove shiny cars and wore fashionable overcoats. It did not take some of the women long to realize that the preachers seemed increasingly concerned with their own outward appearance even as they delivered sanctimonious sermons to women about inward beauty. It was not uncommon to see a Pentecostal husband decked out in stylish clothes while his wife looked as if she were wearing a flour sack.

Late in the 1950s and early 1960s, Pentecostals began buying television sets. It is difficult to communicate to an outsider the feelings of guilt and anxiety that many Pentecostals had to deal with in order to give themselves permission to make this simple purchase. For some, TV dramas were the first theatrical productions they had seen apart from school plays. Hollywood films, even in the 1940s and 1950s, were denounced from the pulpits as the works of Satan. Pentecostal churches, however, did offer their people an alternate form of drama denied most Americans. The average Pentecostal church member could participate personally in powerfully emotional dramaturgies inside their own churches. During emotional revivals, the entire tent or church auditorium could suddenly transform into a stage, with the audience no longer spectators but players in the intense drama. Pentecostals have been criticized for the emotionalism of their religion. But in many ways, their religion provided the only truly acceptable way they had for enjoying a collective emotional experience.

Television made it possible for Pentecostals to grow comfortable with certain aspects of worldly entertainment that previously they had abhorred. Eventually, when Hollywood movies were shown on television, Pentecostals could pull down the shades and watch movies that they could not have watched at theaters. The eyes of other Pentecostals might have seen them enter the local theaters, but at home television could be viewed without fear of external censorship, although private censorship continued. (At the Heritage Village movie house, films are selected by a committee that determines their suitability to the Christian conscience.)

TV viewers have sent a staggering amount of money to Jim and Tammy Bakker over the years. In exchange, the upwardly mobile Pentecostal people, and many others formerly on the fringe but who now partially identify with Pentecostals, received from Jim and Tammy two absolutely essential gifts. First, the Bakkers mediated to them divine approval of their new ambition and success in the world. Second, the Bakkers took the belief-system that the Pentecostals grew up on and modified it in such a way as to give convincing *plausibility* to the rightness of the Pentecostals' new success in the world. The Bakkers did this while still quoting scripture and maintaining the religious terminology of Pentecostal orthodoxy. Like any reformulation, Prosperity Theology keeps much of the old and skillfully weaves into it the required new.

In gratitude, the people have freely sent their money to support not only the Bakkers' ministry but also the revised belief-system with which they identify. Both figuratively and literally, the supporters have bought into the new Prosperity Theology of the Bakkers, Oral Roberts, and Pat Robertson.

The following quote from Jim Bakker's chapter in *You Can Make It* entitled "How To Guarantee Success" offers a crystal-clear encapsulation of Prosperity Theology.

As a child of God, you ought to live in victory. Christianity is a winning way of life. God intends for you to be successful in every part of living.

Unfortunately, many Christians do not realize this. They

somehow have been conditioned to accept—indeed to expect—failure. Surrounded by an atmosphere of negativism and self-pity, they resign themselves to being second- or third-class citizens, inferior, end of the line. This attitude is not Scriptural. This lifestyle is not Christian.

Why, then, should His children, the citizens of His kingdom, live in defeat, failure, and want?

God's will is for your good. He has declared it in His Word, *Beloved, I wish above all things that thou mayest prosper and be in health, even as thy soul prospereth* (3 John 2). He expects you to be successful. He has cancelled the claim of sin and death in your life and placed all the power and resources of heaven at your disposal.

So it's not God's fault if you're not successful.

Don't blame God for your failure—He's given you all you need to be a winner. Through His love, His blessings, His Word in every conceivable way—He constantly assures you that you can make it.[15]

The element of gratitude and the sense of participation in the new folk theology is a major reason for the Bakkers' success in pulling in millions of dollars over the years. There is also the element of fear. A folk theology cannot get off the ground unless the supporters buy into it. The television viewers to whom the reformulated belief-system is meaningful know that it could all crumble. Playing on this fear, Jim looks into the cameras and talks the language of crisis. If the money does not come in, he tells them, the ministry that together they launched into uncharted waters could sink. The new Pentecostal and Charismatic venture is a kind of Titanic, making its way on the high seas in high winds. The band is playing in the ship's ballroom, and all the activities offer both excitement and structure to the lives of those aboard. But now and then the ship's captain, Jim Bakker, reminds the passengers that it is quite possible that they could all sink. Before long, the money pours in to save the ship.

PTL's emotionalism and willingness to provide entertainment have caused some outside observers to overlook the intellectual aspect of PTL. The intellectual factor comes in story form. Every religion offers a story or narrative to "explain" what is going on in the lives of the participants and in their world. It is not imperative that their belief-system be true; in fact, it could be largely fictional. What is imperative, however, is that those aboard the ship *believe* that it is true in some profound and significant way. Until this intellectual or cognitive aspect is understood to be absolutely essential to any religious movement, the fierce loyalty of its adherents will appear to outsiders to be scarcely more than groundless, pointless fanaticism.

Thus the Bakkers moved from the Garden of Success to the Garden of Excess. Their Prosperity Gospel actually encouraged social climbing and climbing to the top economically. What it failed to provide was an indication of the limits of wealth for the successful Christian. Indeed, the logic of the Gospel of Health and Wealth left the door wide open. If the Heavenly Father had infinite resources, then his children had access to infinite resources. What some Prosperity Theology proponents clearly failed to realize was that the children of the rich Heavenly Daddy might become spoiled children.

11

Accountability in High Places

When the PTL financial scandal was breaking in June of 1987, one of the most articulate and forthright of American priests, Andrew Greeley, made the following candid comment about financial scandal in his own Roman Catholic Church:

> I don't think the Catholics ought to throw too many stones, because what Jim and Tammy Bakker did was small potatoes indeed compared to the $2 billion Vatican banking scandal.

The Vatican City village is a country unto itself with its own diplomats and government. Archbishop Paul Marcinkus, a Chicago-born priest who became president of the Vatican Bank, is suspected of having murdered Pope John Paul I in September 1978. It would not be the first time that a pope had been liquidated. The quiet, new pope had begun to dig into the corruption of the Vatican Bank, which included the laundering of Mafia money through the bank.

John Cardinal Cody of Chicago was another man with a strong motive for exterminating the new reform-minded pope. John Paul I had decided to replace him with an honest priest. Cody's handling of the money of hard-working Catholics of his archdiocese was nothing less than arrogant and scandalous. During his despotic thirteen-year reign in Chicago, Cody did not know the meaning of fiscal accountability. He ruled over two and a half million Catholics, nearly 3,000 priests, and 450 parishes. He refused categorically to reveal exactly how much money passed through his control, but it exceeded $250 million a year. Serving as an example of the corrupting influence of unchecked power, Cody was abhorred by nuns, layworkers, and priests alike because of his fiscal secrecy and capricious methods.

Petitions for his dismissal would not be acted upon by the Vatican so long as passive Paul VI occupied the papal chair. But there was a priest named Albino Luciani who had been listening, probing, and watching. On August 26, 1978, Luciani became Pope John Paul I. His election made Cardinal Cody and several other priests with ties to Paul VI quake in their cassocks. Cody was to be replaced, and Marcinkus was to be compelled to give account of his handling of Vatican money and his dealings with underworld characters.

The new pope spent thirty-three days in office and died. John Cardinal Cody and Bishop Marcinkus could rest a little easier.[1] David A. Yallop, a tough-minded investigative reporter, has done much to uncover the circumstances of the pope's death. Yallop eventually concluded that the Vatican perpetrated the cover-up of a murder. "The Vatican began with a lie," he charged, "and then developed a tissue of lies. It lied about little things. It lied about big things. All of the lies had but one purpose: to suppress the fact that Albino Luciani, Pope John Paul I, was murdered sometime between 9:30 P.M. on September 28 and 4:30 A.M. on September 29, 1978."[2] Yallop has made a plausible case. No official death certificate has ever been issued. There was no thorough autopsy report despite (or because of) questions raised. The cause of John Paul I's death remains unknown. The Vatican spoke evasively of the death as "possibly related to myocardial infarction." A vow of silence was imposed on the papal household, and crucial evidence disappeared.

Andrew Greeley had supper with Robert Tucci, director of Vatican radio, on the night the pope died. Tucci phoned Greeley early the following morning to give him the shocking news. Greeley wrote later that he felt the way he had felt upon hearing that Kennedy was shot or that Pearl Harbor was bombed. The pope lay dead and the hope of his reform lay dead with him. Between Tucci's phone call and noon, the Vatican lied five times, Greeley later charged: "It did not tell the truth about (1) who found the Pope's body, (2) what time the body was found, (3) what the Pope was doing when he died, (4) what time he died, and (5) what was the apparent cause of death."[3]

The circumstances surrounding Pope John Paul I's death provide another example of what Greeley calls the pervasive abuse of power at many levels of the Vatican. The financial scandals of the last several years at the Vatican are a direct result of a system and policy of unaccountability.

Some American TV evangelists have finally confessed that their recent troubles were in part brought about because of their own lack of openness and accountability to the public. Falwell now claims to understand that the flow of money into his organization is a public trust. Greeley's arguments for openness and honesty at the Vatican are roughly the same arguments given by those concerned to bring real fiscal credibility to televangelism. Father Greeley predicts that unless a more democratic and open system is developed at the Vatican, Catholics "are going to continue to have disasters like the two-billion dollar Banco Ambrosiano scandal and a declining credibility of the Papacy in almost every area. . . ."[4] It remains to be seen just how much scandal American televangelism can generate and still attract supporters.

Not surprisingly, a significant drop in Catholic collections has come about. Contributions to Catholic churches have fallen fifty percent in the past twenty-five years. This means that Catholics give only half as much as Protestants to their churches, even though the average income of Catholics is slightly higher than that of Protestants. Greeley, who is also a sociologist, contends that Catholics in America vote with their money, which is the only significant way they have of voting.[5]

Contributions to television evangelists dropped immediately after the Bakkers' spring 1987 humiliation and the subsequent artillery of words among leading TV evangelists. Even the opposing lawyers in the so-called holy war took a few verbal swipes at each other. When Bakker's attorney Melvin Belli called Roy Grutman dishonorable, Grutman turned the other cheek and replied, "[I'm] trying not to become personal—I'm not talking about Melvin Belli and his multiple stewardess wives or about the arrogance of naming one's son Caesar. . . . Every step that Belli makes is one step lower down." Belli had charged that Grutman had been paid a half million dollars from PTL funds for his services. To this, Grutman replied that it was only $440,000, so far. After all, Grutman had put twenty lawyers to work on the bankruptcy case.

A 1987 Gallup poll showed that the credibility of TV evangelists has plummeted since a similar poll taken in 1980. Jim Bakker suffered a seventy-seven percent negative rating. The only big-time TV preacher to earn a high rating was, as expected, Billy Graham.[6] Polls are tricky and have to be interpreted in a sophisticated context, but one should not anticipate the demise of televangelism in this century. There are powerful needs in one stratum of the American population that televangelism meets. And there is also the fact that TV viewers easily forget and forgive. The Bakkers are counting on that.

If Jim Bakker goes to jail, he will not go for the reasons that the Apostle Paul or Martin Luther King went. But criminal behavior need not ruin an evangelist permanently, even if he is convicted and goes to prison, as in the case of Leroy Jenkins.

From 1979 to 1982 Jenkins served time in a South Carolina prison on conviction of not only conspiring to burn the homes of a former business associate and a state trooper who arrested his daughter for speeding, but plotting to assault an Anderson *Independent* newspaper reporter who wrote a series of stories about him. In May 1987 Jenkins offered Jim Bakker $100,000 a year and Tammy $75,000 to perform on a show similar to their PTL show. Jenkins claimed to have plans to transmit programs via satellite to cable television systems that reach about two million subscribers, but he neglected to identify the cable system. Whether or not he actually had anything beyond a plan is unclear.[7] Jenkins obviously realized that if he could persuade the Bakkers to sign a contract with him, he could then get a cable system.

Before taking up residency in prison, Jenkins lived in a style worthy of Tammy herself. His mansion was filled with glitter and ornate objects, many of them gifts. To justify his opulence, he stated:

> I like that. . . . I like real loud and nice things 'cause I never had them. . . . Most people in my crusades have made commitments . . . chandeliers, Cadillacs.[8]

When Billy Graham first came under fire regarding the handling of collections at his evangelistic crusades, he was deeply hurt by what the *Atlanta Constitution* wrote in criticism. Licking his wounds and swallowing his pride, he went to the National Council of Churches for advice. This act reveals something about Graham's character. First, he went to the National Council for help, even though he was not a part of the organization. In fact, he stood in considerable disagreement with the council's somewhat liberal theological perspective. Second, even in the 1950s, when he was farther to the right than he is today, Graham did not presume that evangelicals had a monopoly on moral integrity—a lesson that Jerry Falwell has begun to learn the hard way.

Graham took the National Council's advice to place himself on a salary paid by the Billy Graham Evangelistic Association. This meant that Graham cut himself off from every commission or "love offering." Billy Graham currently receives $78,800 annually, one-fourth of which is a housing allowance. In addition, he receives royalties on three of his fifteen books. He accepts no speaking fees.

Oral Roberts does not disclose his salary. It is known that he receives salaries from Oral Roberts University, City of Faith, and the Oral Roberts Evangelistic Association. The Tulsa home that he occupies is worth half a million dollars. His Rancho Mirage, California, home was once assessed at $553,602.

Local pastors have often suspected that after traveling revivalists of the big tent finished their brief stay in the community, they drove off with their pockets lined with the color green. Like other adventurers in private enterprise, however, most would-be traveling evangelists have ended up in debt or making an insignificant income.

Show number 1567 of ABC News "Nightline" gave the series the highest rating it has ever had. It was Ted Koppel's May 27, 1987, interview with Jim and Tammy Faye Bakker. After introducing his topic and his guests, Koppel asked the Bakkers not to wrap themselves in the Bible when they replied to his questions. Less than a minute later, a long excerpt from Jerry Falwell's devastating attack against Jim Bakker was shown. After a commercial break, Koppel worked up to a question he knew he had to ask before the evening slipped away:

KOPPEL: . . . Jerry Falwell today claims that now that the accountants are beginning to sort their way through all the paperwork, that they have found that over the past year, for example, you paid yourselves, or the board paid you, in salary and in dividends and in bonuses, a total of $1.9 million. Now, that's a far cry from nothing, isn't it?

JIM BAKKER: Uh huh. Yes, and I'm not sure of those figures, but I think we've made a lot of mistakes, and I'm sorry about it, and the—the board of directors, with me out of the room, always voted our salary. We—Tammy and I—had nothing to do with our salary. And that doesn't excuse it, because we are the president, or were the president of the ministry, and we should have said no. And we did say no many times, but our board cared about us, and they would tell us that "Jim and Tammy, you earn every penny that we give you." In one week, I raised $30 million, at least one time last year, and Tammy's records and our books have brought in literally millions of dollars, and instead of royalties, we took a salary controlled by the board of directors, and I feel that we—we should have said, "No, . . . we will not receive this." And the board did it out of love, they cared about us, they really did.

KOPPEL: Well, let's just talk numbers.

TAMMY BAKKER: And they told us they thought we were worth it.

KOPPEL: I'm sorry?

TAMMY BAKKER: They told us they thought we were worth it, because I would go every time and tell them, you know, we don't deserve it, and they will all tell you I have said that to them.

Later in the interview, Jim Bakker claimed that he was so busy working for the Lord that he had no time to handle his own checkbook or his own finances.

Over a month before the now famous "Nightline" interview, however, the most experienced investigator into the PTL structure, Charles Shepard, called on some of the men who had served on the PTL board of directors. The three who agreed to be interviewed said they did not remember authorizing $1.1 million in bonuses to Bakker during his last fifteen months as the TV ministry's president and chairman. Jim Bakker was himself a member of the eight-man board, as was Richard Dortch, PTL's executive director who received over $350,000 in salary and bonuses.

The three board members—a retired Charlotte businessman, a Texas hotel executive, and a Texas pastor—professed in separate interviews to be surprised at the amount of money that the Bakkers and Richard Dortch had received. "Whew!" said A. T. Lawing of Charlotte. "Well, I just, I can't hardly believe that." Lawing had served on the board from 1973 to 1987, when the scandal broke and he was asked to resign.

Ernie Franzone, a former vice-president of the Brock Hotel Corporation, confessed, "I completely trusted Jim Bakker. I completely trusted Reverend Dortch. If you want to call it blind trust, I guess you could say it was." The three board members each said they did not know Bakker's base salary. In fact, Lawing, the retired owner of a service station equipment firm, said, "The salaries were completely secret from the board." The third man, J. Don George, the pastor of an Assemblies of God church of 4,500 members in Irving, Texas, said he just assumed that Bakker's annual salary was somewhere between $50,000 and $75,000. The Reverend George claims he was favorably disposed toward voting for a handsome Christmas bonus because he sincerely believed that Jim Bakker's salary was under $75,000.

Figures obtained by the *Charlotte Observer* showed that Bakker received $800,000 in bonuses in 1986. "Wow, that surprises me," Franzone exclaimed when Charles Shepard quoted the figure.

Something similar to a pea-and-shell game was going on at the board meetings. The game was run primarily by Jim Bakker and Richard Dortch. Lawing, Franzone, and George admitted they could not document specifically the amount of bonuses they had approved. They could not remember because they were not allowed to keep minutes and other PTL papers drawn up at board meetings.

When Charles Shepard asked about the bonuses for Dortch, who was himself a board director, George answered that one of the other board members—Charles Cookman or Almee Cortese—would suggest that "We must do something for brother Dortch." Acknowledging that he would certainly be more inquisitive if he had it all to do over, George explained, "We were never privy to the type of information that would have allowed us to know the financial impact [of our decisions]."

"We played follow the leader," Franzone openly admitted. All three board members said that in recent years they had been called on to approve bonuses, but not salaries for Bakker and Dortch. George claims that he had the impression that the Bakkers were living from paycheck to paycheck, "a kind of hand-to-mouth existence." This impression came, said George, from certain other members of the board and especially from Richard Dortch.[9]

George, Lawing, and Franzone further denied that the board had approved bonuses and salary increases in 1987. Figures obtained by the *Charlotte Observer* in April of 1987, however, show that the Bakkers and Dortch were paid $670,000 in the first three months of 1987. There is no unequivocal record that this money was approved. The problem lies in part in the 1983 PTL bylaws, which fail to specify who sets executive compensation.[10]

I asked one *Charlotte Observer* reporter how an organization like PTL could be run so shoddily. He replied that Jim Bakker had created his own kind of organization to suit his own purposes and to give himself wide discretionary powers of manipulation. PTL under Bakker was not run like a local church whose members elect the treasurer and receive regular financial reports. Nor was it run like a corporation.

Former PTL executive Bill Perkins said of Jim Bakker, "I came to the conclusion that . . . he wanted to be a wealthy man, but he didn't want to appear to be."[11] But it is obvious that this is simply not true. For a devotee of the Prosperity Gospel, it is important to appear wealthy because wealth is viewed as an external manifestation of internal grace.

People who have associated with Bakker in a variety of ways have been struck by what they call his simple childlike faith in the promises of the Bible. A large number of Christians could doubtless easily recognize passages in ancient literature that cater to childish self-indulgence. They could also recognize similar passages in their own scripture. Such passages are often ignored, however, or pushed into the background like an embarrassing relative. Jim Bakker has embarrassed fundamentalists and main-line Christians alike by not only recognizing these passages but treating them openly as divine principles and promises.

Millions of contemporary Christian belivers cannot take at face value certain biblical promises. As adults who have faced the realities of life, they recognize the promises to be grandiose and childish. Some examples follow.

I tell you this: whatever you forbid on earth shall be forbidden in heaven, and whatever you allow on earth shall be allowed in heaven (Matthew 18:18 NEB). Church fathers fought over this obscure passage for centuries, bitterly contesting as to who had fallen heir to its putative power. When the Protestant Reformation emerged, haggling over the passage resumed.

Again I say unto you, if two of you agree on earth about anything they ask, it will be done for them by my Father in heaven (Matthew 18:19 RSV). A perfect Catch-22.

For every one who asks receives, and he who seeks finds, and to him who knocks it will be open (Luke 11:10 RSV). Instead of recognizing this to be an inspirational pep talk conspicuous for its useful vagueness, some Bible teachers have taken it so seriously as to build elaborate fences around it in order to prevent believers from using it to satisfy personal desires. The proper context for interpreting this choice text of salesmanship is as elusive as the text is vague.

Is any among you sick? Let him call for the elders of the church, and let them pray over him, anointing him with oil in the name of the Lord; and the prayer of faith will save the sick man, and the Lord will raise him up. . . . (James 5:14-15 RSV). Few Christians are childish enough to take this at face value. It is a promise with a long list of disclaimers and disappointing qualifiers.

Blessed are the meek: for they shall inherit the earth (Matthew 5:5 KJV). This may be delivered as an after-dinner joke at a convention of real estate brokers. Oral Roberts claims with a straight face that he is going to inherit a large piece of real estate when saints like him return from heaven to rule the planet with a rod of iron.

Be careful about what you pray for; you might get what you asked for. This proverb cannot be found in the Bible, but Christians occasionally quote it to one another as a sound piece of advice.

John Wesley spent a good deal of time worrying about what would happen to the Methodist people when they began increasing their incomes. Methodists encouraged frugality and industry, and discouraged wasting their lives in gambling and drinking. As a consequence, Methodists in England began to accumulate riches. Wesley faced this fact squarely and worried that pride, worldliness, and contempt for the poor would emerge along with the riches. He encouraged philanthropy as an antidote and practiced it. In the nineteenth century, however, Methodists rose to middle-class respectability and forgot about the poor, except for token efforts.

> The lower middle class and middle class believed on both theological and economic grounds in individualism, in every man's being free to do what he likes with no obligation to any other man beyond that of not harming him. . . . For by this time [i.e., the nineteenth century] Nonconformist England had but two main concerns, making money and achieving personal salvation.[12]

Two of Jim Bakker's close friends from earlier years, Sam Orender and Roger Flessing, believe they saw a drastic change take place in him. When the Bakkers left South Carolina after turning the keys of PTL over to Falwell, Orender drove from Los Angeles to Palm Springs to see the Bakkers, hoping he might be a friend to them in their hour of darkness. Unable to reach them by phone, he drove to the Bakkers' California home, which he discovered to be surrounded by people. Even though Orender had served as vice-president of PTL only a few years before, the bodyguards turned him away. He had met Jessica Hahn in 1980, had been at the Clearwater, Florida, hotel, and knew about Jim's desperate affair with her. As a friend, he had kept the secret. Almost seven years later, he was turned away. "Jim's changed," Orender reflected. "Money will change people. I'm sure it would have changed me more than it did Jim. But he isn't the same."[13]

Despite all their stories about supernatural miracles taking place in their lives and about soaring up to the third or seventh heaven in the Spirit, evangelists remain flesh-and-blood earthlings. If they lack training in the Aristotelian principle of moderation, they cannot be expected to cope with a drastically altered lifestyle.

What can be said about a religion that literally teaches its people to spawn tales of miracles, gain insight by clairvoyance in the name of Jesus, pursue an education by divine telepathy, and attain wisdom by treating the Bible as a Sears catalogue of limitless promises? If this is what a religion teaches its people, then why should a Jim and Tammy Bakker be a surprise to those who taught it to them?

The real surprise is that the hard-won common sense of the Pentecostal people still maintains a firm hold on reality despite perpetual indoctrination in the faith of the twilight zone. Jim and Tammy represent the inhuman stress and strain that the propaganda hype had created, so that they eventually lost their grip on reality. When an evangelist arrives at a point where he can no longer recognize great chunks of reality near at hand, then the religion that helped put him in that precarious shape owes him the means for pulling him back closer to reality. Those who want to restore the Bakkers to a new position of leadership will, probably out of compassion and kindness, set him up so that he may drift even farther into the twilight zone.

12

The Baptism of Pleasure

Jim Bakker's Gospel of Health and Wealth contains a highly significant truth that deserves to be cut loose from the arrogance and excesses that have ensnared it. In its own way, it is a poorly conceived but daring attempt to free religion from its ancient attachment to masochism. For centuries, religions of various sorts have glorified suffering. Deliverance Theology represents an attempt to break the habit of regarding earthly life as either a vale of tears or merely a test to determine who is worthy of gaining happiness in the next life. In short, Prosperity Theology is a confused but persistent attempt to restore *pleasure* to earthly existence and to give a theological justification for doing so.

Over the centuries a number of priests and preachers seemed to receive their greatest pleasure from calling down thunder and lightning against earthly pleasure itself. They have vetoed pleasure on earth only to promote heavenly hedonism. Despite the fact that people differ profoundly in what they find to be sources of pleasure, the unshakable fact remains that human beings everywhere are incurable hedonists—seekers of sources of pleasure. If they were not, the appeal of heaven and the abhorrence of hell among fundamentalists and Charismatics would end overnight. There is not a preacher alive who in all earnestness will tell his flock that when they arrive in heaven they can have anything their sanctified hearts desire except pleasure and enjoyment. The appeal of heaven itself is built on the rock foundation of hedonism. If hell were thought to offer pleasure and enjoyment, it would no longer be regarded as unenticing.

We cannot cease being practicing hedonists so long as we live. We have choice only in turning from what we take to be one source of pleasure to another. In our rational moments, we sacrifice one avenue of pleasure because we see that in the long run it corrupts and destroys other avenues and sources of pleasure. This is not to say that individuals and groups are always wise and sufficiently informed as to the sources of pleasure they choose or the style of life they elect for the sake of promised pleasure. It is to say that to be human is to be concerned both to gain pleasure and to avoid pointless pain.

When people are cut off from sources of pleasure and joy on earth, they may find pleasure in contemplating the pleasures of the next life or at least in contemplating relief from displeasure. Jim Bakker saw early in his ministry, however, that religion in America today will attract few followers if its promise is pleasure in the next life only. What the new Pentecostals and Charismatics are about is the cultivation of new sources of pleasure in the here and now. They may believe that they are bringing a little of heaven to earth, but behind the belief are hedonistic believers craving pleasure and joy. While either mild or furious battles continue over what "truly" gives pleasure, the fact remains that every religious movement is borne by people driven by the hedonistic principle. People are, of course, more than pleasure-seekers, but they never cease being hedonists so long as they live.

In one of his earlier books, *Love Against Hate*, the noted psychiatrist Karl Menninger quotes a challenging passage from Rebecca West regarding the principle of pleasure or hedonism:

> If we do not live for pleasure we shall soon find ourselves living for pain. If we do not regard as sacred our own joys and the joys of others, we open the doors and let into life the ugliest attribute of the human race, which is cruelty. . . .[1]

As an ethic to live by, hedonism considers no act to be evil in itself but judges each act according to whether it increases the net pain and suffering of oneself and others. Until the rise of the new Pentecostals and Charismatics is seen as an assertive but stumbling effort to develop a Christian hedonism, the movement will never be profoundly understood.

Religious masochism itself carries, however feebly, the flame of hedonism. It is an attempt to adopt one burden of suffering in order

Murray/SIPA

In the 1970s and early 1980s, Jim and Tammy Bakker were to all appearances on top of the world, with a growing television ministry and plans for a huge complex in Fort Mill, S.C. But few knew that behind the scenes lurked marital and financial problems and Tammy's growing addiction to prescription drugs.

The theatrical televangelist Jimmy Swaggart presented damaging evidence against Jim Bakker to Assemblies of God officials in the summer of 1986. Less than two years later, in the spring of 1988, the tables were turned when Swaggart was forced to confess his own sexual misadventures.

In March 1987, Jim Bakker, who had publicly condemned "the sin of fornication," confessed to a single sexual encounter with Jessica Hahn and turned the attention of a nation to televangelism's seamier side. While Bakker charged that Hahn was an experienced professional who had helped to trick him into the liaison, Jessica maintained that she was just "an innocent church secretary."

It came as a surprise to many Pentecostal PTL supporters when Jerry Falwell, a fundamentalist Baptist, was handed the reins of the deposed Bakker's ministry just a few days after Bakker confessed to his encounter with Jessica Hahn. Bakker later charged that Falwell had tried to "steal Heritage USA."

Though Heritage USA, a 2,300-acre "Christian Disneyland," is the third most popular theme park in the United States, it has been a huge financial burden to PTL ministries almost since construction began in 1978.

In April 1987, evangelist John Ankerberg of Chattanooga, Tenn., stunned the press with charges that Bakker had had multiple sexual encounters and that the widely publicized experience with Jessica Hahn was only the "tip of the iceberg."

Controversy also surrounded faith-healer Oral Roberts in 1987. News-making items included his proclamation that God would "call him home" unless he raised $8 million for missionary work; his claim that a 900-foot-tall Jesus had told him to continue building his City of Faith; and his mention of the time he had raised an infant from the dead.

Though Tammy Bakker became the butt of many jokes, a relentless barrage of reporters gave her plenty to weep about by acquainting the fascinated public with the most intimate—and shocking—details of her personal life.

to offset what the believer takes to be an even worse burden of suffering. When Martin Luther and other reformers of the sixteenth century focused on "justification by faith and not by works," they were in effect casting off the yoke of religious masochism. They were saying that the individual cannot earn divine approval and acceptance by self-inflicted punishment disguised as penance. Justification comes by faith, that is, trust in the goodness of the deity. Every child should be so fortunate as to be made to feel that he is loved for no better reason than that he exists.

Whatever may be said to condemn the deceptions practiced by faith healers, there lies behind the folk theology of the Gospel of Health a conviction that disease and sickness are not inflicted by God on individuals to punish or test them. A surprisingly large number of people need permission to accept health and happiness. For various reasons, some people were made to feel in childhood that they had no claim to happiness and health unless they "proved" themselves. The Gospel of Health and Wealth preachers serve to challenge the self-hatred frame of mind. When Jim Bakker and other evangelists proclaim "God intends for you to be successful in every part of your living," they are proclaiming nothing less than a revolutionary "good news" for individuals who have long been enslaved by the dehumanizing mindset of masochism.

Unfortunately, the Gospel of Health and Wealth has failed absolutely to provide a sensible explanation of why or how sickness and defeats come about. It has no doctrine of tragedy to call upon. Too often the gains over masochism made by the Gospel of Health and Wealth are lost by the cruel and heartless way in which some preachers give the impression that any sickness or failure is at the bottom line a *moral* failure on the part of the sufferers. They are made to feel that if they had generated more faith (and not failed to mail in seed-faith checks), the demons that produce disease and defeat would have gained no foothold in their lives. Therefore, so the tale goes, the victims have only themselves to blame. Bakker makes this point in his own glib way: "So if God doesn't keep us from success, and the devil can't—why aren't more Christians successful?"

He concludes, "The answer is obvious—*they defeat themselves.*"[2]

Having pulled their followers out of one lake of masochism, Bakker and the faith healers toss them back into another lake. Oral Roberts sometimes worries about his inability to deal with the stubborn fact that faith does not seem to solve all severe problems of suffering and defeat. Because he has a debt-generating business to take care of, however, he has to give more thought to ways of pulling in money than to ways of deepening his understanding of tragedy. Despite the philosophical and theological poverty of the Gospel of Success, the seed of a tough-minded Christian hedonism remains in it and deserves to be cultivated and developed.

Materialism is an obsession with the accumulation of material objects for their own sake. While material goods are essential to the maintenance of pleasure, materialism has little to do constructively with hedonism. Jim and Tammy Bakker foolishly allowed their earlier glimmerings of Christian hedonism to succumb to corruptive materialism.

While visiting the Bakkers at their lakeside home in South Carolina, Roger Flessing observed the delivery of a new houseboat to the Bakkers. Jim looked upon the boat as a gift from God. Before it had even been docked, he began to describe the next one he had in mind to buy: far bigger and much better equipped.[3] The Bakkers appeared not to have disciplined their growing desire for exceedingly expensive objects.

Money began to pour into the PTL coffers during the late 1970s and the 1980s, but Jim allowed this success to grow quickly out of perspective. The discipline required for spending money wisely was lacking. Jim Bakker simply had not be *trained* to manage millions of dollars, just as he and Oral Roberts received no discipline or training in forging a theology. Their theology became one of excess, their spending increasingly extravagant. Oral succumbed to his City of Faith obsession, causing his theology to grow increasingly bizarre, while Jim fattened his obsession for more and more expensive toys.

Big money, superstardom, and the fast-paced life did not appear to generate greater net pleasure for the Bakkers. To the contrary, the pleasure of their marriage relationship waned significantly. Before the TV cameras they maintained a good front, but behind the scenes their marriage began falling apart. Even that wonderful source of pleasure called sex became a source of displeasure for Tammy. She tried to deal with her pain through prescription drugs. Meantime, instead of cultivating and relishing the pleasure of old friendships, Jim and Tammy began losing valuable friends.

The new Pentecostals and Charismatics have found a way of making the Prosperity Gospel fit with the Armageddon mentality that many of them inherited from fundamentalists like Falwell. Bakker and the other Pentecostal evangelists embrace a view of the Second Coming of Jesus called premillennialism. Christ will come again to earth to rule on earth for a thousand years (the millennium) and will appoint Christians to positions of government and power. Oral Roberts is only one among many who expect to receive such an appointment. Before the Second Coming, the Rapture will take place. According to one version of premillennialism, the Rapture will occur seven years before Christ returns to set up his thousand-year kingdom. During those seven years, all true Christians will partake of the Marriage Feast of the Lamb, after having been taken up to heaven in the Rapture. On earth, however, all non-Christians (including the Jews) will suffer great agony during the seven-year stretch. This ordeal is called the Great Tribulation (or Jacob's Trouble).

After the seven years of absolute pleasure for Christians in heaven and misery for non-Christians on earth, Christ will descend from heaven to make holy war on Satan and his subordinates. This anticipated bloody confrontation will take place in Israel and is called the Battle of Armageddon.

All the troubles currently in the Middle East are interpreted by premillennialists to be the fulfillment of prophecies found in the books of Daniel, Ezekiel, and Revelation. A sinister figure called the Antichrist will emerge at the outset of the Great Tribulation. He will deceive almost all non-Christians into thinking he is a great reformer, whereas in fact he will be the greatest deceiver of all time, the incarnation of evil.

Before becoming a presidential contender, Pat Robertson would issue gleeful prophecies of doom and global ruin, of Europe plunging into economic disaster, of the U.S.S.R. and other eastern nations declaring war on Israel, of unprecedented human suffering, of farm foreclosures and political chaos, of famine and earthquakes followed by hurricanes, followed by droughts accompanied by unparalleled volcanic eruptions. During the Great Tribulation, people will rush up to mountains and cry for the rocks to roll down on them. At the Rapture, Christian pilots will be sucked from their jets, leaving the jets and their non-Christian passengers to plunge to the ground. According to some premillennial preachers, half-human beasts from hell will appear on earth and roam the streets, raping and plundering without restraint.

In short, the grisly premillennial vision is a fit of cosmic rage against the greater portion of the human race, a rage conceived in resentment, nurtured in revenge, and cloaked in robes of righteousness. It is the lust for an unholy vendetta gone berserk. It is revenge in the name of the Lamb of God.

The rage grew in part out of the delusion of "winning the world to Christ," a delusion that has turned sour because down deep its advocates are compelled to face up to the global reality of the increase in the number of Muslims, secularists, and other non-Christians in the world. The myth of the worldwide revival has gone flat.

Of all the major TV evangelists who embrace the premillennial vision, Jim Bakker has been the least intense about its bombastic, violent details. As Bakker approached his fortieth birthday, the goal of his grandfather and of his own youth to win the world to Christ began to seem increasingly remote if not far-fetched. Apparently, Jim Bakker began to suspect the existence of a serious crack at the heart of his belief-system. He did not have, however, the theological and intellectual training to equip him to deal with this crisis. Instead of devoting time and hard intellectual effort to wrestle with profound theological issues, Jim Bakker took another route. He continued to feed himself with the intellectual pabulum of his youth, threw himself deeper and almost blindly into his work, and substituted the vision of Heritage USA for the vision of winning the world to Christ. Virtually all of this drastic change in his life seems to have taken place with scant theological or philosophical appraisal at the conscious level.

If his irresponsible bookkeeping methods could be momentarily set aside, much of Bakker's Heritage USA project might well qualify as a sensible, down-to-earth goal. Jerry Falwell admitted that as a vacation resort for Christians (by which Jerry usually means adherents to various types of evangelicalism and fundamentalism), Heritage USA was a sound idea. Jimmy Swaggart rejected it as too hedonistic. To someone who dreams of winning the whole world to his religion, the development of a water park and resort hotel seems by comparison insignificant. For those Christians who look upon the Swaggarts of the world as barkers for the grand delusion, however, a family amusement park can be refreshingly real.

World evangelism has had a long track record of failure, according to noted Anglican missions researcher David Barrett. His research indicates that about 300 plans to Christianize the world have been formulated since Jesus' era, and 250 of them "collapsed or fizzled out within five, ten or fifteen years." The reasons for the failures, as cited by Barrett, are "administrative fiascos, personality clashes, irrelevant doctrinal disagreements, prayerlessness, apathy, shortages of funds, embezzlements, absence of workers, rise of other agendas, diversion to other interests."[4]

At least half of these reasons are the product of one deeper reality: On the whole, believers over the centuries have come to sense that the vision of worldwide evangelization was doomed from the start. Apathy was not the cause but the consequence of the disillusionment. Before the close of the first Christian century, bitter disillusionment had already set in with a vengeance. The Book of Revelation reveals the raging of a mad believer who sensed that the grandiose dream would never come true.

The idea that Christians can have fun in harmless ways in a water park is something that Pentecostals have long needed. Ordinary Pentecostals cannot be expected to find all their pleasure in speaking in tongues, preaching, and trembling in the baptism of the Spirit. There is nothing grandiose or earthshaking about a water slide, which is perhaps one reason some preachers dislike it. Swaggart seems to find pleasure in thinking of himself as an earthshaker and dreaming of turning the whole nation back to his version of God. By contrast, Bakker grasped the simple notion that harmless play and recreation can be a part of the Christian life.

In his preachings, Jimmy Swaggart represents the Pentecostals who have been more cautious in their rush to gain new sources of pleasure. Most of the excess and extravagance of Swaggart's version of religion is channeled into his ministry of traditional preaching and spreading the Pentecostal style of worship. Knowing that outsiders regard Pentecostals as arm-waving, noisy, and exuberant in their worship, Swaggart appears to gain pleasure in flaunting the Pentecostal style. While he would be the first to reject having the word "hedonism" as applied to his religion, the fact remains that to Pentecostals their style of bouncy, fast-beat, muscle-moving music is a powerful source of intense pleasure. After listening to this kind of soul-stirring music in one of his crusades, Swaggart stood up at the microphone and, with a beaming grin, exclaimed, "Hallelujah. . . . That's old-fashioned, heart-felt, Holy Ghost, heaven-sent, devil-chasing, sin-killing, true-blue, red-hot, blood-bought, God-given singing of the gospel!"

In short, the music was not only intensely pleasurable but had on it Swaggart's personal stamp of approval and sanctification. He in effect told his people that it was okay to enjoy the thrill of their kind of music as opposed to rock music. Later in the year, in an interview, Swaggart said that even rock music in itself was not wicked. Rather, the wickedness came through the evil spirit behind it and the association with drugs, sexual promiscuity, and perverse lyrics.

By defining Heritage USA as a Christian environment, Bakker succeeded in communicating to many that playing for no purpose beyond the pleasure it brings is perfectly acceptable in the eyes of their God, a lesson that old-line Pentecostals in particular have needed. Coming out of this religion, Jerry Lee Lewis sometimes seems unable to grasp that some pleasures come free and can be enjoyed without destroying oneself as if to pay a happiness tax.

Bakker's colossal mistake was not the building of Heritage USA but the failure to inform his supporters and his staff about the radical change he was making in his theology. Unfortunately, he could not inform them, if my thesis is correct, because he was not altogether aware of what was going on in his own thinking. The reevaluation of the very meaning of Christianity that began to take place in his mind was not something of which he was profoundly conscious.

Because television evangelists present themselves as authoritative spokesmen of heaven, their followers often fail to detect changes that take place in their theology. Like Bakker, Oral Roberts has recently made a profoundly significant shift in his thinking. He has moved far away from Swaggart's hell-fire and damnation theology, even though both men were ordained as Pentecostal ministers. Swaggart remains convinced that all Jews who do not become Christians will go to hell. By contrast, Oral Roberts said plainly, "I'm not going to tell you that they're going to hell." He further assured Larry King that the Lord would do right by all the Jews who believe "according to the light that they have. . . . I don't understand all the theology, but I know I serve a God who is going to do right."

Despite the chicanery and guile endemic to the faith-healing business and the hollow boasting about his own healing powers, Oral Roberts does seem to have heartfelt compassion for the sick. Ironically, the infamous pitch for money that besmirched his reputation the most was probably dictated by his best motives. When he made the appeal for $8 million, he believed there were only 400 medical missionaries throughout the world. He said on "Larry King Live" that he had visited forty-six nations in which he met not even one medical missionary. He then added, "I've seen those thousands of wretched people in those little villages—filth, sickness, squalor. Missionaries preach about God but [with] little or no concern about people's bodies."

One branch of Roberts's Pentecostal background could not have tolerated sending physicians to another country because it regarded physicians as instruments of Satan. In light of that fact, Roberts's late 1970s obsession to build a medical center in Tulsa is at first confounding and then revealing. Roberts called upon all his considerable economic and political clout in Oklahoma to gain approval of the medical center— City of Faith, as he called it. He did this despite the fact that Tulsa already had 1,000 hospital beds not being economically utilized. Roberts's new hospital with 777 beds was erected not because Tulsa needed it but because Roberts needed it. Without it, he would eventually die as just another faith healer who, while raising more money than the others and making a bigger sensation on television, made no important contribution to the advance of human health.

It became apparent that without the hospital Oral Roberts's healing crusades would make no lasting mark on the pages of American religious history, to say nothing of medical history. In North America, Australia, New Zealand, and Europe, the middle class largely holds medicine in high regard but faith healers in low regard. Oral Roberts's crusade in Australia proved to be a deep and bitter disappointment to him. Whereas Roberts was treated as a charlatan, Billy Graham had been politely received there. Roberts desperately needed to find a way to link his putative faith healing to the institution of medicine, thus gaining for it respectability by association. Without this link, his ministry would remain a sideshow. Already he had linked the faith-healing business to the television entertainment business. But to be regarded as the star and producer of one of America's most successful entertainment shows in the 1960s was not enough for Oral Roberts.

His desire to link faith healing with the respectable, legitimate medical profession became, therefore, more than a desire. It became nothing less than an obsession. Against incredible opposition and sound advice from friends and informed people in medicine, Roberts risked a great deal to build and maintain a hospital whose beds could be filled only by flying patients in from outside Tulsa.

His obsession to build the medical center at Tulsa was also inspired by embarrassment and guilt, for his continued compassion for the sick collided with the growing realization that too much of his faith-healing ministry was mere talk. He confessed to Larry King that no man alive has failed more than he in efforts to heal the sick. There is every reason to think that Oral Roberts did make a profound and very personal connection between the success of his medical center and the meaning of his own life, so that if the original purpose of the new medical center failed, his ministry on earth would seem empty. He would therefore die, or in his own words, "be taken home."

On the surface, Roberts appears exceedingly confident about having been given the power of healing. A careful study of the man, however, reveals considerable shifting and ambivalence. His preoccupation with holistic medicine and holistic healing is a move into an area of useful ambiguity that allows for exploration and experimentation in the healing process. It also provides room for equivocation and playing with words like "spiritual" and "psychological" in hopes of finding a way to give them status and a role in medicine. The successes of medical research in the second half of the twentieth century have been astounding. Pentecostals and others with a faith-healing background have not been oblivious to these successes. As they climbed up the socioeconomic ladder, their antipathy to the medical profession decreased significantly while their suspicion of the extravagant claims of faith healers increased. This change was not lost on Oral Roberts.

PART IV:

Marriage and Adultery

"When you help the shepherd, you are helping the sheep."

13

Televangelism and the
Money-Sex Revelations

In the twentieth century, the clergy are still going hard at one
another. Jimmy Swaggart and a half dozen associate pastors felt
it necessary to make a plane trip to Lakeland, Florida, in the
late spring of 1987 to set Brother Karl Strader back on the straight
and narrow. Pastor Strader has been straying from old-line Pentecostalism and snuggling up to the new Charismatics, who are too
loose for Swaggart and the hard-core Pentecostals. Rumors began
spreading that Pastor Strader, whose "Carpenter's Home Church"
seats 8,000, had become too accepting of Catholic and Episcopalian
Charismatics.

Swaggart had raised questions about whether Mother Teresa of
India was really saved. According to the tall preacher from Baton
Rouge, the good Catholic woman's works of charity would not save
her from the flaming pit of damnation. As for Brother Strader—
well, he had begun to live dangerously, upsetting the God of heaven
by playing Christian "rock" music on the Florida church's station
WCIE.

On Phil Donahue's talk show in the early 1980s, two members
of the clergy squared off on a topic that has to be a first in church
history. Evangelical Charlie Shedd defended oral sex within marriage,
while archfundamentalist Tim LaHaye searched through the scripture,
trying desperately to come up with proof texts against it. Down in
Southern Louisiana, Swaggart came out swinging against oral sex.
In Oklahoma, Oral Roberts has yet to make a public comment, pre-
ferring to stay out of family politics on this topic.

In his ninety-minute TV news show, Jerry Falwell accused Bakker of homosexuality and said it dated to the 1950s, when Bakker was a teenager. Whether it was a naive exploration period that some adolescents pass through quickly was not made clear by the accuser. Whereas Falwell did reveal what he took to be the details of the Bakker-Hahn misadventure, he remained vague about the details of Bakker's alleged homosexuality.

Billy Graham once compared sex to dynamite, which is not the best analogy but one that communicates the dangers of sex in a generation when books on its joys have become best sellers and Dr. Ruth hands out sex tips on TV. America has been going through a sexual revolution since the sixties, and PTL has felt the impact of the revolution. Wherever two or three Charismatics gather to speak in tongues in the name of Christ or for any other purpose, there in their midst will always be the potential for sexual misadventure.

A former PTL executive recalls the shocking summer of 1977. "We were at an outdoor Jesus rally in Pennsylvania. Bakker knocked at the door and said, 'I think [two vice-presidents] are wifeswapping.' At first [one VP] denied it, but then he admitted it."

Bakker reportedly demoted the two executives but did not fire them. It was in this same year that Bakker allegedly visited a prostitute three times for a purpose other than saving her soul. Charlotte's WSOC-TV broke the story. Bakker insists that they concocted it from their vain imaginations.[1] John Ankerberg still claims that Bakker had affairs with both prostitutes and homosexuals around the world. In reply on TV, Bakker more than once challenged Ankerberg, Falwell, and others who had made the charge to bring the alleged witnesses out of their closets. "Where are they?" Bakker asked.

Ankerberg, prematurely white-haired, enjoys a good scrap. His TV shows are theological boxing matches. He obviously takes great pleasure in inviting on his program representative Catholics, Jews, Masons, Jehovah's Witnesses, secular humanists, and others whom Ankerberg regards as advocates of "false religion." The format of his TV program is simple. The guest is cross-examined about his or her religion. Ankerberg tries to show at what point his guest's religion missed the boat and became a false religion. He then argues that his brand of evangelical Christianity is the only true religion. Sometimes, he selects video excerpts of guests to present at a later time, which gives him another opportunity to demonstrate to his audience the falsehood in all religions except his own.

It cannot be said that Ankerberg's format is always evenhanded. TV evangelists, however, have seldom come close to giving under any conditions a fair and objective account of the views of their philosophical opponents. John Ankerberg's approach is a full cut above them all as a venture in religious education. The worst, hands down, is Jimmy Swaggart, who does not so much deliberately distort the views of his philosophical rivals as keep himself unbelievably uninformed of their arguments.

Swaggart has become a fierce opponent of the public schools and abhors what he believes educators would do to children in sex education courses. Tim LaHaye, comparing current public education in America to the Jonesville tragedy, wildly charges that there is a "demonic humanism" set loose in the schools, so that children are taught that marijuana is harmless and are encouraged to take drugs. Like Falwell, Swaggart appears to share LaHaye's hostility toward sex education in the public school because he thinks the teachers would cause their students to become obsessed with sex.

The sexual revolution has nevertheless arrived, spilling over into the very citadels of fundamentalism. Like most social revolutions, it has generated both constructive and destructive consequences. Tim LaHaye and his wife have traveled about the country offering Family Life Seminars in response to the new sexual consciousness.

After Tammy Bakker turned frigid toward her husband but began to thaw toward music star Gary Paxton, Jim made a trip to Clearwater, Florida. Fellow evangelist John Wesley Fletcher imported a young woman from New York, Jessica Hahn, to meet Jim Bakker there, for she admired Bakker as much as she admired Elvis Presley. Later, Jim would explain that he had been "wickedly manipulated" in his vulnerability at the Clearwater hotel. Stephen Winzenberg was in Clearwater at the time, having arrived to do a taped radio interview with Jim's close friend, Efrem Zimbalist, Jr. When Winzenberg saw Jim Bakker, he assumed that he had flown down from Charlotte to help the TV station in its fund raising. The Florida station was already supplying the PTL satellite network with several new Christian programs, including a singles program with Arthelene Rippey (who later cohosted PTL with Richard Dortch after Bakker's resignation).

Jim Bakker loved Florida. Tammy and he had been guest

preachers for the Christian TV station's first annual golf tournament. A couple of times a year the Bakkers would broadcast their PTL show from a Christian retreat in Brandenton, Florida. They would air it outside before a large audience, with Tammy providing one song a day.

A few insiders knew that Jim and Tammy's marriage was sailing through choppy waters at the time. Their marriage counseling sessions in California helped them through the storm. It was from these sessions that they obtained the idea of offering counseling and marriage enrichment sessions for Christians who came to Heritage USA for general spiritual enrichment. Though the Bakkers had lived through the sexual revolution without its having a positive impact on their marriage, the California sessions provided new insights and introduced them to some of the constructive aspects of the sexual revolution for married couples. They resolved to introduce some of those insights and positive contributions into the family seminars at Heritage USA.

The flow of mindless movies and TV soaps about extramarital and premarital affairs seems endless, but the profound sexual revolution *within marriage* appears to be a mystery to the TV networks. Perhaps this is for the good. What has happened for married couples in America is a little amazing when viewed from a distance. Only three or four decades ago, some Protestant ministers and numerous Catholic priests could be heard heatedly condemning married adults for using contraceptives. Several changes, mostly positive, have come about since those awkward and guilt-riddled days.

First, the ancient link between sexual enjoyment and the production of children has become a matter of choice rather than a requirement or a game of roulette. For centuries, members of the clergy looked upon sex as primarily a procreative function. Sexual intercourse solely for the sake of the pleasure it gave to the married couple was labeled as selfish. Until the year of his death in 1939 Pope Pious XI was telling the poor that if they could not afford to have more children, they should give up sexual intercourse and thereby "preserve in wedlock their chastity unspotted."[2]

If Pope John Paul I had lived a year or two beyond his thirty-three days in office, the Catholic church's current official view on birth control might have been buried. In 1967 the indecisive Pope Paul VI had asked for additional reports on artificial birth control.

He had listened to Cardinal Ottaviani's endless warnings against making artificial birth control devices acceptable for good Catholics. When Paul VI asked for opinions from other regions in Italy, the patriarch of Venice, Cardinal Urbani, called a meeting of all his bishops within the region.

The question of artificial birth control was aired and debated. One man was selected to draw up the report—Albino Luciani. No one knew that this quiet, inquisitive man would soon be the new pope. He had been selected to write up the report because birth control was a topic he had been researching for several years. He had consulted sociologists, doctors, and theologians, and had written articles and given talks on the topic. A pastor at heart, he had done what Ottaviani had not done—talked with married couples and solicited their opinions and insights. Luciani had grown up surrounded by poverty, and it was clear to him that his friends and loved ones, including his brother Edoardo, had more children than financial means to care for them.

By April 1968, Luciani's report had been written, debated, and rewritten. Cardinal Urbani read it, approved of its content and conclusions, and sent it to the pope. When Paul VI told Urbani that he highly valued the report, Urbani passed the praise on to Luciani. It will doubtless come as a surprise to many to learn that the main thrust of the report was the recommendation that the pope approve of the anovulant pill developed by Professor Pincus and that it become the Catholic birth-control pill.

Less than a year later, Paul VI reaffirmed that only abstinence and the rhythm method were acceptable. Luciani was dismayed. Meantime, the Vatican Bank invested in the Istituto Farmacologico Sereno, which was making money on one of its top-selling products, an oral contraceptive called Luteolas.[3]

An additional change that has taken place within marriage in America is the overcoming of a great deal of ignorance about some simple techniques of love-making, sexual play, and intercourse. Still another is the removal of the stigma that some of the church fathers attached to sex per se.

Several influential priests have looked upon women as swamps, traps, or graveyards. One medieval monk referred to women as "vomit and odure. . . . How then can we ever want to embrace what is merely a sack of rottenness?" St. Jerome called woman the door of the devil; St. Maximus called her the shipwreck of men; and St. Athanasius, the guardian of orthodoxy, called her the clothed serpent.[4] The Latin Church father Tertullian regarded sex even within marriage to be degrading.

Some priests and nuns have found sexual desire to be merely a distraction from a vocation for which they believe themselves chosen. Onigen, a third-century Christian theologian, discovered that declaring himself a priest did not eliminate his sexual desire. To rid himself of this nagging interference, he voluntarily castrated himself. One of the most famous priests of medieval Christendom, Abelard, was castrated involuntarily for having fallen in love with a woman named Heloise and getting her pregnant.

Reacting to those who have proclaimed themselves morally superior because of their celibacy, some Protestants have gone to the opposite extreme by proclaiming celibacy to be not only unnatural but perverse. This reaction both confuses the unnatural with the perverse and fails to understand that monogamous marriage is itself partly unnatural. It is nevertheless a remarkable and beautiful achievement, although some church fathers thought it an indication of human weakness.

The new sexual consciousness among Pentecostals today has eliminated considerable guilt about their sexuality. The clergy had for centuries a strong, vested interest in infecting the people with a sense of being wicked for having sexual desires. Salvation was conveniently distributed through the clergy as a necessary antidote to the guilt attached to human sexuality. Since sexual passion was not extinguished by either water baptism or the baptism of the Spirit, the clergy as the brokers of salvation easily gained tenure in their vocation. The Protestant Reformation, far from attacking the notion of original sin and its accompanying guilt over sexual desire, jockeyed for the dealership rights of the salvation presumed necessary to cover the guilt of original sin and sexual passion.

On August 2, 1987, two Christians, Clifford and Joyce Penner, appeared on "Straight Talk" (an offshoot of the "700 Club") to talk about Christians and sexuality. Since Pat Robertson's TV partner, Ben Kinchlow, was on vacation, Scott Ross was left alone to moderate the show. In a frank, tasteful, and informative session the Penners answered questions ranging from premature ejaculation to masturbation. It was one of the most sensible and balanced discussions of sexuality I have heard on TV. Had they been a part of the audience, most sensitive humanists, Jews, and American Catholics would doubtless have praised the Penners for their constructive and forthright answers. Word Books of Waco, Texas, published the Penners' book *The Gift of Sex* in 1981. Both the book and the TV session stand as clear testimony to the sexual revolution's influence on one of the most conservative branches of Christianity and to the hope that a new sensitivity to the collective wisdom of various traditions, including the conservative traditions, lies on the horizon. Dr. David Clark, former vice-president of marketing at CBN, saw the new CBN radio talk show "On Line" as a new venture in evangelical forthrightness.

The playful side of the sexual relationship between wife and husband has for centuries been dampened by the serious threat of the wife's becoming pregnant. It is not difficult to understand, therefore, that many women became frigid, especially in times when death in childbirth was far more than just a remote possibility. But better birth control technology has reduced frigidity in modern women, including Pentecostals. If there is any sexual problem with the new freedom, it is that of learning how to deal with the proliferation of options and the rising performance expectation among those who insist on turning sex into a test.

Another revolutionary sexual change that has occurred with a number of Americans is the acknowledgment that sexual intercourse is for the woman's pleasure too. The idea that the man was the lord of the household and that his wife was by marital contract bound to submit herself to be used for his sexual pleasure meant that after he had gained *his* pleasure in bed, she subsequently gained *her* pleasure in recalling that she had stoically performed her duty to him alone. Thanks to a number of changing circumstances, including larger homes providing more privacy, *mutual* sexual pleasure has become something of an application of the Golden Rule in marriage.

The current pope, despite his largely ignored attitude on birth control, has come to understand the imperative of respecting the wife's feelings both in and out of the marriage bed. The press completely misinterpreted a statement made by the pontiff on this subject. He did *not* state that marriage is adultery, as if he were a throwback to a woman-hater like Tertullian. John Paul II's point was that Catholic men must give up the demeaning practice of treating their wives as objects. To turn one's spouse into a thing is a form of unfaithfulness because it fails to consider his or her feelings and wishes. Unwittingly, perhaps, the pope is opening the door to Christian hedonism—as long as mutual pleasure prevails rather than the narrow egoism that is popularly confused with hedonism.

In 1983, after his December 1980 encounter with Jessica Hahn, Jim Bakker wrote the following words under the heading "Don't let Satan deceive you":

> And in the heat of lust, who thinks of the awful price being paid for a moment of passion? No one expects to feel so guilty, so ashamed . . . so dirty. No one intends for those he really loves to be hurt. No one expects to end up *diseased*—permanently marked with an insidious infection like herpes for which medical science can find no cure![5]

The threat of AIDS was not widely known in 1983. By the spring of 1987, Richard Dortch had to inform the Assemblies of God governing board in North Carolina that Bakker did not have AIDS.

Jerry Falwell suggested that Bakker was involved somehow in the raping of Jessica Hahn. Not only did Bakker deny Falwell's charge, but he wrote the following a little over two years after meeting Hahn:

> Let me be completely blunt about the sin of fornication and adultery. The vulgar slang expression often used for the sex act or partner is "piece." In a sense, it is an apt term because each time a person is involved in an illicit sexual act, he or she is literally breaking off a piece of himself, a piece of his mind, a piece of his body, a piece of his soul—and destroying it forever.[6]

On a TV interview Bakker denied John Ankerberg and Jerry Falwell's charge of homosexuality, but he looked into the camera and said he wanted homosexuals to know that God loved them. In words that were at least as hard-hitting as Falwell's, Bakker had stated in 1983 that by exchanging wedding rings, homosexuals "flaunt their perversion and make a mockery of marriage."[7]

Of course, there are two distinct possibilities about Bakker's answer to the homosexuality charges: he told the truth or he lied. It could be that Bakker became involved in some form of man-to-man interaction which Falwell and Ankerberg would label as homosexual but which Bakker would not. Or Bakker may have regarded homosexuality as wrong for most people but not for himself because he enjoyed a special relationship with God. A friend suggested this possibility to me and told the following story. Several years ago a young ministerial student in the Midwest was in love with a young woman who, like himself, held to the fundamentalist faith. They did not attend dances at school or in the community because they and their church regarded dancing as sinful. Despite this, they frequently slept together even though they were not married. The young ministerial student's reasoning was that since both were divinely called, he to be a minister and she to be a minister's wife, they were not bound to a law that was given to restrain the unspiritual.

Another charge against Bakker that is equally as sinful as his alleged bisexuality, in the minds of his followers, is that of adultery. Christianity has never found a truly satisfactory way of dealing with clergy who have broken the seventh commandment. Castration was the punishment for medieval priest Abelard. In later centuries, public confession and humiliation were sometimes required as punishment, serving as a form of social castration. Nathaniel Hawthorne's *The Scarlet Letter* was a poignant protest against this practice. More recently, a noted evangelical author and lecturer resigned the presidency of the conservative InterVarsity Christian Fellowship after confessing that he had had an affair. He had hoped that his resignation would not be necessary after he had fulfilled "all the biblically defined steps of confession, repentance and restoration." Rumors and unfounded stories continued to spread, however, and eventually prompted him to submit his resignation.[8]

Throughout America, stories abound about local pastors or priests who have had sexual affairs. The stories are truly ecumenical, transcending all denominational barriers. A Church of Christ elder in Texas had an affair with a strikingly beautiful woman not of his faith. According to the elder, the young woman was destined for hell, not because of her affair, but because she held to the wrong faith. Throughout the affair, while engaging her body, he earnestly sought to save her soul from damnation, the bed becoming at one moment a lover's nest and at the next moment a pulpit. The woman eventually ended the affair, the relationship having left her both unfulfilled and unsaved.

Fundamentalist and old-line Pentecostal preachers seem at times to believe that crime and brutality in pluralistic America are largely the result of the sexual revolution. They blame the Supreme Court. Jimmy Swaggart once pointed his finger at the TV camera as it zoomed in, and with volcanic wrath in his voice, he rebuked a Supreme Court justice. Swaggart said that someday the U.S. judge would stand before the Heavenly Judge to give account of his moral failures.

"The Supreme Court kicked the Bible out of the public schools," another preacher charged, "and they brought in *Playboy* to take its place."

The fundamentalists and old-line Pentecostals abhor what they call the new morality of do-it-if-it-feels-good. They charge that the sexual revolution has carried in on its wave the curse of moral relativism. In denouncing evangelical Christian writers for not taking a stand against oral sex, Jerry Falwell lashed out with the warning that the hottest place in hell was reserved for such writers.[9]

Both Falwell and Swaggart's favorite scapegoat—the humanists— had been falsely accused of generating all manner of moral corruption in America. Then suddenly Pandora's box broke open, and out popped one moral flaw after another—all allegedly committed by a TV evangelist named Jim Bakker.

Bad blood had continued to develop behind the scenes between Jim Bakker and Jimmy Swaggart over the case of Marvin Gorman, a Pentecostal preacher who was forced out of his key position as pastor of First Assemblies of God in New Orleans. By his own admission, the Reverend Gorman committed what he called an immoral act with a woman in 1979. He was not dismissed from his church, however, until the summer of 1986, Jimmy Swaggart having had a hand in the dismissal, Gorman charged. Bakker took Gorman's side. Gorman has filed charges against Swaggart and fourteen other individuals and churches. Charging them with being a part of a conspiracy to defame him, he asks for $90 million in damages.

In an impassioned plea before his Heritage Village Church on July 20, 1986, Jim Bakker called for forgiveness of his fellow minister:

One of the great ministers of this country . . . has just been destroyed. . . . I want to tell you who destroyed him. You say, "Himself?" No.
The church. The church. The church. I don't know how

much longer I can go on. I'm watching my brethren be destroyed one at a time and the church isn't doing anything about it. All you do is gossip about them. . . .

My brother is hurting. Where's Jesus? Are you all so perfect that we can go stone him today?

If I was his congregation—and I hope someone tells them—I would not receive his resignation. I would say no, no, no more. . . .

We leave the unsaved in the pulpit, we kick out the good men who made mistakes instead of rebuilding them, instead of restoring them. My heart is broken. Woe unto you that cast the first stone. . . .[10]

Before his ejection from the New Orleans church, Marvin Gorman had been a major influence in the Assemblies of God denomination. In 1985 he placed second in the race for the position of general superintendent of the denomination. He had served also on the powerful executive presbytery of the Assemblies of God. Unfortunately, he became the second member of that prestigious presbytery to be removed in recent years for sexual misconduct.[11] Critics believe that because Jimmy Swaggart had inordinate ambition to become the major influence in the growing denomination, he exerted his influence by seeking to purge from it those who did not embrace his old-line version of Pentecostalism. Swaggart's defenders insist that his real concern was to purge the denomination of immorality and false doctrine. Jim Bakker's insinuation that Swaggart was attempting a "hostile takeover" of Heritage USA and the PTL satellite grew out of this longstanding infighting within the Assemblies of God denomination.

The legal structure of PTL and Heritage USA prevents either from being taken over in the way a hostile takeover develops in the corporate world. Bakker probably did not intend to use the phrase in this technical way. His fear was primarily that Swaggart would exert pressure on the Assemblies of God presbyters to purge Bakker from the denomination. Reading the handwriting on the wall, however, he volunteered to resign from the denomination rather than face what he perceived as a hostile governing board. This partly accounts for his going to a Baptist like Falwell rather than to the Assemblies of God presbyters.

In another denomination Jim Bakker might have been treated

differently. The Assemblies of God denomination is growing rapidly
and its leaders appear deeply concerned with gaining the respectability
that they believe was denied them over the years. In most denominations, conduct that violates sexual standards is normally handled off
the front page. Even in Bakker's case, Baptists John Ankerberg and
Jerry Falwell wanted to go to Bakker privately about his adultery.
Ankerberg decided to draw up a letter to send to Bakker personally
after obtaining the signatures of Swaggart and Falwell.

After being asked to sign the letter, Swaggart had second thoughts
about the whole idea. As a consequence, on March 12, 1987, he
wrote a letter (which he said he did not mail) to John Ankerberg
to explain why he did not want to send even a private letter to Bakker.
The *Charlotte Observer* published a copy of the letter. The Bible
text to which Swaggart refers is Matthew 18:15 (KJV): "Moreover
if thy brother shall trespass against thee, go and tell him his fault
between him and thee alone: if he shall hear thee, thou hast gained
thy brother."

Dear John:
I tried to call but could not wait. I had to leave for Dallas.
Frances and I have discussed this letter with my name attached
at great length and are not comfortable with it and I will
explain.

John, I know how the mind of Bakker and Dortch work.
They will take the letter and show it over television, deleting
the part they do not want to read. They shall say, "We had
to take these two men [Swaggart and Ankerberg] off television, and then they went on a 'witch hunt' to hurt us." [Bak-
ker had removed Swaggart from the PTL network because
of his public criticism of certain Catholic beliefs. Bakker represented the new Pentecostals who wished to establish connections with people of every denomination, especially with those
having Charismatic leanings. Ankerberg has been highly critical of Catholic beliefs, but unlike Swaggart, he found a way
to give representatives of Catholicism and other rival theologies
the opportunity to speak on his program.]

Furthermore, I have already approached Dortch, gave
him the evidence and he lied to me about the situation. I

even told him I would like to meet with Bakker, but all to no avail.

As far as I am concerned, Matthew 18 has been satisfied with these people.

Last of all, if any of this should ever go to trial, they would use the letter in any way they could.

The *Charlotte Observer* will do its part. The Assemblies of God has finally started to move on this, and they will do their part.

Please believe me there is absolutely no chance of Bakker and Dortch stepping down for any type of rehabilitation. First, they will try to lie their way out of it, but the documentation should be irrefutable. Then they will pull out of the Assemblies of God.

Their last step will be to institute a barrage, which has already begun, to elicit sympathy from the general public. That will be their modus operandi.

If there are severe difficulties and problems I will bear the brunt of it, not anyone else.

I realize that your course of action is correct. However, you do not know these people as I know them and I do not want my name attached to a letter sent to them. I know what you are thinking, but it really will not work, and I will be surprised if Falwell will allow his name to be used for obvious reasons.

If you have any other suggestions, I will be back tonight and we can talk then.[12]

The pattern is clear. Religious people inside and outside the churches have problems and sometimes become problems to others. This is to be expected—they are only human. But something else has also become clear. The attempt of TV evangelists to establish themselves and their religion as the foundation of society and ethics simply will not wash. In many ways, TV evangelists, far from providing society with a moral foundation, become society's parasites by offering pseudo-healings and salvation, which for the most part simply add to the troubles of fellow mortals who already have enough earthly troubles.

John Wesley Fletcher had a problem that became a problem

for some of his fellow evangelists and pastors. Whereas some of the preachers were intoxicated with heady dreams of power, Fletcher was sometimes intoxicated with the wrong spirits, the kind that emerge from a bottle. After being dismissed from the Assemblies of God in 1981, the traveling evangelist's business dwindled. The man who handled Fletcher's dismissal was none other than Richard Dortch, who at that time was the Illinois district superintendent of the Assemblies of God, a member of PTL's board, and a member of the Assemblies of God's executive presbytery.

Before becoming an outcast from his denomination, evangelist Fletcher had been a popular guest on the "PTL Club" in 1980. Jim Bakker and he would sometimes "tag-team preach" on the show, working the large audience to a peak of excitement. After losing his credentials in 1981, however, Fletcher was no longer welcome on PTL.

Fletcher's motive for bringing Jessica Hahn and Jim Bakker together at the Florida hotel on December 6, 1980, remains in dispute. It was Fletcher who in 1983 dialed the *Charlotte Observer,* and, without identifying himself, told a reporter to remember the name Jessica Hahn.

On the surface, it appeared to be an act of revenge for the severe punishment he had received for his drinking problem. Later, reflecting on his deed, he explained that he did it because he had been "so upset and angry over the lack of compassion and understanding for people who had fallen from God."

Fletcher was understandably disturbed by Richard Dortch's use of a double standard. On the one hand, Dortch went far out of his way to cover up Jim Bakker's encounter with Hahn. On the other hand, he caused Fletcher to lose his credentials.

In 1981, only months after bringing Jessica to Florida to meet Jim at the hotel,'John Wesley Fletcher was on trial before the Assemblies of God's highest governing board in Illinois. It was then, in a private meeting with superintendent Dortch, that Fletcher told of Jim Bakker's hotel encounter with Jessica Hahn.[13] By reminding him that even the highly successful and esteemed Jim Bakker also had feet of clay, Fletcher apparently hoped to become the recipient of Dortch's compassion.

For a minister to be defrocked is much more serious a matter than a layperson's being fired from a particular job. It is close to being stripped of a part of one's identity and of one's means of self-support. Fletcher, fearing this loss of identity, told on Bakker in an effort to appeal to Richard Dortch's understanding and mercy. He did not find either. Years later, Fletcher said he blamed neither Jim Bakker nor Jessica Hahn for what happened at the Florida hotel. "I blame myself," he said.

In 1985 Fletcher again reminded Dortch of Bakker's illicit encounter with Hahn. Dortch was not sufficiently moved, however, to intercede effectively on Fletcher's behalf.

Since the very beginning of Christianity, the churches have been plagued with the question of what to do with leaders who fall significantly below the standards by which they are required to abide. Different denominations have somewhat varying standards. Local churches within the same denomination can often have considerable diversity of expectations.

Many first-century Christians took a chillingly hard line against those among their ranks who yielded during times of persecution. If anyone denied Christ after having once become a Christian, the penalty was nothing short of losing both salvation and the possibility of being restored after the persecution had passed. In short, Christians who lapsed or denied being Christians succeeded in irrevocably sealing their eternal doom with no chance of being saved a second time.[14]

Other early Christians were more lenient. To support the practice of accepting back into the fold anyone who under threatening circumstances had denied Christ, they turned to the example of Peter. According to the Gospel of Matthew, Peter denied Christ after having boasted that even if the other disciples fell away, he would die rather than follow their example. Peter denied even knowing Jesus and invoked a curse on himself to emphasize his denial. All the disciples were restored except Judas, who had committed suicide. Furthermore, the same disciples who had fallen away were now given the highest commission to make more disciples, to baptize, and to teach.[15] The lesson is clear. Fallen men with feet of clay can be not only restored, but given positions of leadership.

Generations since have been divided on how to deal with the imperfections of the clergy. There is no reason to think that one universal solution will be found by the present generation. The Assemblies of God would have had no choice but to remove Jim

Bakker from the ranks of their ordained servants had they put him on trial. Even if there had been no sexual misconduct charge against him, Assemblies of God elected leaders could have called in Bakker years ago for a thorough investigation of his mishandling of funds. If they are going to continue to fight the attempt of governmental agencies to police the flow of money inside religious institutions, the denominations are going to have to police themselves. Fiscal accountability will have to become the eleventh commandment.

Today, there exists a degree of moral relativism among television ministers that has precipitated, in some cases, a weakening of ethics. In order to advance pleasure and to reduce meaningless pain, rational ethical regulations have proved to be necessary for the human species. Like traffic regulations, sensible ethics serves ideally to make the life of pleasure and enjoyment more secure by protecting it from both recklessness and stagnation. The Bakkers drove at breakneck speed through too many of life's stop signs and ignored too many warning signs. Finally, they collided with reality. And now, as Tammy said, "We're hurting." Jim could end up hurting in prison.

14

Love and Marriage for Woebegone Saints

According to evangelist John Wesley Fletcher, Jim Bakker, during his marital troubles of 1980–81, spoke to him of suicide. At the age of forty, Jim felt rejected by his wife, who had found a new interest in a man unlike Jim in many ways.

Gary S. Paxton, a product of the radical 1960s, wore funny hats and sported a gigantic beard that made him look like a cross between Moses and a character from the movie *Deliverance*. For one of her album covers and a PTL appearance, Tammy dressed up in a Paxton-like beard and hat. Paxton, with a hippie attitude and an outlandish appearance, stood in perfect contrast to the clean-cut, small-shouldered Jim Bakker. They got along surprisingly well, though, partly because Jim always admired people successful in the secular entertainment world. Tammy and Jim treated him as if he were a king, and he in turn seemed genuinely to enjoy their company.

Despite his style, Paxton was serious about at least two things—music and his career. His friendship meant a great deal to both Jim and Tammy, especially to Tammy. She came to appreciate what he had done for her. He had taken her twangy, country, hound-dog voice and worked with it until it was no longer a joke. At the 1985 Angel Awards in Los Angeles, Tammy was awarded Best Female Vocalist for the album *The Upper Room*.

Gary Paxton's wife, Karen, was reported to have said that Jim fussed at Tammy "about her makeup, her wig, her hair," sometimes leaving Tammy in tears. Tammy slept in her makeup, and Karen Paxton had a theory: "Tammy always felt she was not beautiful,

149

and she wanted to be beautiful. . . . Apparently [Jim] made her feel ugly." According to Jessica Hahn, Jim said in 1980 that he was not sexually satisfied with Tammy and that she was not satisfied with him.[1]

As early as 1970, after the Bakkers' daughter was born, Tammy was so immersed in depression that a wall built up between the couple. She didn't want a physical relationship. "That's bound to offend any man," Jim complained.[2] During her pregnancy, Tammy had never been happier. She made friends with Linda Wilson, whose husband Roger worked at Pat Robertson's CBN. "For the first time in my life I had a true friend," Tammy later recalled.[3] Then, without warning, Tammy was buried in an emotional avalanche. In the very first hospital experience of her life she found herself going through labor for two days. In the hospital the sheltered Holiness woman felt exposed and was literally left naked for all the doctors and nurses to see, since the doors were left open. She was turned into an object and felt that her undressed body was on display. To compound her terror, the doctors feared they might lose both mother and child.

When the baby finally arrived, Tammy did not realize what had happened. It was necessary to assign nurses to her through the first night. Never had the nurses seen anyone react to drugs so drastically. Tammy hallucinated, trying to kill mice and spiders.

A week later she was back at work. But when the new euphoria wore off, she broke out in hives, looking like someone with measles. Unable to sleep, she felt her life coming unraveled. She could not laugh, cry, or pray. Each time Jim tried to touch her, she broke out in a cold sweat.

A few more weeks of this behavior drove Jim to despair. "Tammy, if you don't love me, don't let the baby stand in the way of a divorce!"

Returning to the hospital, she begged the doctor for help. Tammy claimed that the man shrugged and said, "Well, you have to pay a price for anything that's good."

Tammy said the nurses later informed her that she had been given an almost fatal overdose of medication.

To complicate matters, she felt she had lost her salvation during all those unnerving months. At times she thought she was going to die.[4] Jim had virtually no insight into what was happening. When he mentioned divorce, Tammy was shocked and confused.[5]

Unlike most Baptists, Assemblies of God believers are convinced that Christians can lose their salvation. Tammy was worried sick about falling from grace and going to hell. Even before becoming pregnant she had the haunting feeling that she was on the verge of committing the unpardonable sin of blaspheming the Holy Ghost, an act which would spell absolute and irrevocable doom with no forgiveness in this life or the next.

Anthropologists studying the beliefs and practices of other cultures have sometimes observed the powerful physiological effects that certain beliefs have on the individual, especially if others in the culture accept the validity of those beliefs. In the case of the believer who accepts being cast into the role of "the dying person," a neurological and endocrinological process is set off, leading to organic dysfunction and sometimes death. In his book *Primitive Behavior,* W. I. Thomas points out that while a belief itself may refer to nothing in the objective world, its effect on the individual is real and can be objectively studied by others.

In the summer of 1976 in Franconian, Switzerland, twenty-two-year-old Anneliese Michel came to believe that she was possessed. Her symptoms included hallucinations, spasms, writhing, and speaking in "devilish tongues." Her deeply pious Catholic family believed in possession and accepted her strange behaviors as satanic in origin. Bishop Josef Stange of Wurzburg entrusted two priests to administer what they regarded as an exorcism, using the seventeenth-century *Rituale Romanus.* A desperate battle between the exorcists and the presumed Satan followed, lasting for many months. Anneliese had been a robust young woman, five feet eight inches tall. The priests used fasting as a weapon against Satan, and apparently it did not occur to them that they were starving her body. She weighed only seventy pounds at the time of her death. In 1978 the priests were convicted of negligent homicide.[6]

During many of the Renaissance Inquisition trials, people often confessed to crimes that were entirely illusory. Perhaps the greatest of all theological and pathological con jobs is the doctrine of original sin by which everyone is labeled guilty of the crime of being born a finite human mortal deserving to be tortured day and night forever. Psychiatrist Karl Menninger's chilling *Man Against Himself*[7] provides case after case of individuals who came to believe that it was required of them to be tormented or partially destroyed, even if they had to inflict the torment on themselves. The famous Russian novelist Nikolai Gogol allowed an ignorant Eastern Orthodox priest, Matthew Konstantinovsky, to set him on a path of self-torment. Gogol conjured up images of hell fire and eternal torment and fell into the role of a miserable sinner irrevocably doomed, beginning with torturous thoughts that he could not dispel. While under the influence of the fanatical priest, he destroyed the second volume of his greatest novel and renounced Pushkin, who is to Russian literature what Shakespeare is to English literature. Possessed by the fixed idea of damnation, Gogol increased his self-inflicted torments until he died at the age of forty-three. His death was in effect a suicide.

Tammy Bakker's torment, whether self-inflicted or not, became unmanageable. Fearing that she either had spoken or was about to speak out against the Holy Ghost and therefore achieve damnation forever, Tammy cried out, "Oh Jesus, I want to go to heaven more than anything in the world. Please don't let me have sinned against the Holy Spirit, because I love You so much."

According to her testimony, a voice taunted her: "Say something against the Holy Spirit." The voice would not leave her alone. "Day in and day out," Tammy later explained, "my mind was so tormented that I would rather have died than go through the torment of that year."[8]

In 1970 Tammy began the first of her seventeen years of dependency on prescription drugs. In her book *Run to the Roar,* she says it was God who gave her the courage to face the fear of flying. She regularly supplemented her prayers, however, with Valium.

In 1987 PTL disclosed that on January 13 Tammy had been hospitalized at Eisenhower Medical Center in Rancho Mirage, California. Located on the grounds is the Betty Ford Center, a chemical-dependency recovery hospital. Tammy was treated there for thirteen days.

The Bakkers described on videotape their trip to their Gatlinburg, Tennessee, home to let Tammy recover from the flu. They explained that she took aspirin, Aspergum, and a variety of over-the-counter medications and antibiotics prescribed by the doctor. Earlier, on a flight to California, Tammy began hallucinating, seeing demons, insects crawling on the floor, a cat, and people on the private plane's wings. She even put on her coat in an attempt to leave the plane in midair. Doctors recommended that Tammy take a year's leave of absence from TV, but the Bakkers decided it would be too difficult to comply with that recommendation.

In 1984 hospital tests had revealed a fast heartbeat in Tammy. On the verge of a nervous breakdown, she was told she was consuming too much sugar and caffeine. Jim revealed in 1987 that Tammy had suffered attacks of hives and hyperventilation for seventeen years. Unfortunately, the allergy medication and nasal sprays kept her hyper, leading the doctors to prescribe tranquilizers. Along with weeks of the detoxification program, Tammy received outpatient treatment and counseling.[9]

In 1975 a new excitement came into the lives of the Bakkers, an excitement that promised a better future than Tammy's constant love-hate relationship with drugs. Country singer Gary Paxton and his wife Karen began making appearances on the "Jim and Tammy Show." Karen and Tammy spent most of their time together eating and shopping. Like most recent converts, Gary appeared extremely religious in those days. At McDonald's he would bow his head and say grace over a Big Mac and fries, making even Jim feel fidgety.

Tammy grew increasingly enamored of Gary, who had once been the lead singer for an eccentric rock group called Hollywood Argyles, known for their hit "Alley-Oop." Ambitious to become a major gospel singer, Tammy found in Gary the understanding tutor she had dreamed of finding. Instead of criticizing her voice and her new style of dressing that offended Jim, Gary focused on the better qualities of her voice and helped her develop them. Tammy grew in confidence under the tutelage of a professional who cared.

The summer of 1980 proved turbulent for Jim Bakker. Clouds of jealousy formed. A special bond between Gary Paxton and Tammy grew until it became obvious to their friends. Tammy denied that the relationship was sexual, and Karen Paxton still insists that the relationship was not consummated. Normally cheerful and upbeat, Roger Flessing urged the Bakkers to consult a marriage counselor. With the counselor's help, the marriage survived the stormy summer.

Emotionally, Karen Paxton was deeply wounded. Feeling betrayed by both Tammy and Gary, she eventually ended the marriage. Jim Bakker grew increasingly morose. On a Monday morning Gary was scheduled to appear on the "Jim and Tammy Show." He did not appear. From that day forward, his name was not mentioned on the show. No explanation was offered, and the regular members of the show did not have to make inquiries. They knew that the boss, having had his fill of Gary Paxton, had sent him packing.

After leaving PTL, Gary Paxton became involved in a shooting incident when he caught burglars helping themselves to the belongings in his van. He had at one time raced cars and had driven at the Daytona speedway. In 1978–79 he produced a number of acclaimed Christian records; but sometime after getting shot by one of the burglars, he began to move away from Christianity.

Unfortunately, the breach between Tammy and Jim did not heal after Paxton's abrupt departure. Although not a man to argue or voice his anger loudly, Jim seethed with inner rage, which he expressed with what seemed to be deliberate cruelty: He had his wedding ring melted and turned into a twenty-year service pin. In the season to be merry, he bitterly presented the pin to Tammy as a Christmas present. Only weeks earlier he had slept with Jessica Hahn in order to make Tammy jealous (he claimed) or to get revenge (some counselors might suggest). In any case, the Florida hotel encounter did not drive Tammy back into Jim's arms.[10]

A few weeks after the hotel incident was seemingly over, Jim appeared in the office of Fred Gross, a clinical psychologist who founded the Christian therapy program at Palmdale, California. At Bakker's specific request, Gross appeared as a guest on PTL's weekly show on March 24, 1987. Gross told the following to the audience: When he and Bakker went to a private study for the counseling session, Jim was in absolute agony. Finally mustering the courage to speak, Jim told Gross that he had committed an indiscretion in his life. "A onetime incident," said Gross, "something that happened real quickly, in a time of real need in his life." Sobbing and shaking violently, Bakker had to be held, according to the counselor. "He was so totally distraught and out of control that he was racked with pain and guilt from the head to his toes."

After about ten minutes on their knees together, Gross continued, he and Bakker found themselves prone on the floor, Jim's face buried in the carpet. "He was kicking the floor. He was writhing. He was retching." Gross added that he wanted everyone to know that during that ordeal of three and a half hours, "Jim Bakker asked God to forgive him. He confessed his sin in detail. He apologized to God."[11]

Bakker's counselor proved to be a good audience to the evangelist's

sobbing, writhing, and retching. Assuming that it was genuine—Bakker
has always been able to produce instant tears—some burning questions
remain. Were his tears an expression of sorrow over having done
something that might ruin his career? Or were they tears of grief
over what he had done to Jessica Hahn? Bakker said he wanted
a heart that was clean before God. The counselor said of his client,
"He apologized to God." Jessica Hahn claimed that she never received a truly decent apology. Bakker claimed he did apologize, but
Hahn said it sounded to her more like a warning. "He told me I
would be accountable to God if I caused trouble."[12]

According to the California counselor, Bakker walked the straight
and narrow during the six years after his encounter with Hahn. It
would be more accurate to say that this is what Bakker told the
counselor. Only Jim knows how he spent all his time during those
years.

According to Jerry Falwell, Bakker told him that he had been
with a whore. Bakker also vaguely insinuated that Jessica had a
repertory of love-making that indicated a professional range of experience. But according to what John Wesley Fletcher told Charles
Shepard of the *Charlotte Observer,* Jessica was "just an innocent
church secretary" eager to meet a noted TV evangelist she admired.[13]
She had been sending his ministry $15 a month.

Why would a Christian minister like Fletcher bring an innocent
church secretary and Jim Bakker together in compromising circumstances when he knew that Bakker was vulnerable? Fletcher, Hahn,
and Bakker agree that Bakker felt rejected by his wife at the time.
Sam Orender, who later became disillusioned with Bakker, was in
Clearwater when the incident occurred. He heard Fletcher's own
account, and what he heard led him to believe that Jessica had been
brought to Florida to have sex with Jim.[14] Did Jessica, however,
know what the purpose was? What exactly were Bakker and Fletcher
expecting?

The hotel incident can be summarized from various accounts
provided by Jessica Hahn. Jerry Falwell says the November 1987
Playboy account coheres substantially with what Jessica had earlier
told him.

It began with a phone call on Thursday, December 5, 1980. She
was looking forward to a weekend in her home on Long Island when

evangelist John Wesley Fletcher phoned to say he had a surprise for her. He told her that his friend Jim Bakker and he were doing a telethon in Clearwater Beach, Florida, and that she was invited to take a plane to Florida to become a part of the audience.

It was not a call entirely out of the blue. Fletcher had been in Jessica's hometown earlier that year. "Furthermore, I baby-sat for his son the summer of 1974 while John [Fletcher] was in a revival meeting in New York. I knew the family—the son, daughter and Shirley [his wife]—very well," Jessica later explained in her affidavit. "I was just his fourteen-year-old baby sitter—a kid." At the age of fourteen she also left the Catholic Church to become a Pentecostal after her close friend died of a brain tumor.

On the phone, Fletcher added that his family would be in Florida. Jessica grew excited. It would be great to see the Fletcher children and Shirley again. She liked the family. She would gladly exchange the cold December weather in New York for sunny Florida for a weekend. And she was thrilled to learn she could watch the filming at the studio and meet the people involved in it.

Fletcher seemed pleased with her enthusiastic response and promised to phone again soon. He kept his promise and on the following day, Friday, he informed her that a prepaid one-way ticket on Eastern Airlines was waiting for her. "Dress up because we'll be going to lunch with a lot of people," he told her. "Then we'll go to the studio."

Jessica Hahn went to New York's La Guardia Airport on Saturday, December 6, and took the jet. She says she left a virgin but returned the victim of two men who, she later charged, took advantage of her. Had she known what was going to happen before the end of that miserable day, she says, she would have remained in Massapequa, New York, where she was church secretary at the Full Gospel Tabernacle.

John Wesley Fletcher was wearing a light blue sweater when he met her at the Florida airport. According to Jessica's testimony given later, Fletcher helped with her luggage and they walked to a rent-a-car counter. "Don't I look great?" he asked her, proud of his blue sweater. "Jim [Bakker] is glad you decided to come, Jessica."

She was elated about meeting the Reverend Bakker, whom she had seen on TV and admired. She admired Tammy also. Jessica was glad she had been invited, but says she became confused when, en route to the hotel, Fletcher informed her that Jim was having a hard time with his wife. More disturbing was the news that the Bakkers were going through a separation, Tammy having left for California. Jessica apparently would not get to meet Tammy.

Jessica listened to Fletcher reveal details about the Bakkers that made her uncomfortable, details that she felt she had no right to know. Today, Jessica insists that she thought John just wanted to impress her with how close he and Jim Bakker were and that she had not even a whisper of suspicion about her trip to Florida until she learned from Fletcher that Tammy was not with Jim.

Since her early teenage years, Jessica had apparently been too trusting of ministers. It should be noted that she grew up in the Roman Catholic Church and in a Catholic family that looked with awe upon priests. She claims that even after arriving in Florida, no alarm went off in her head as she listened to evangelist Fletcher give her a somewhat modified version of the story he had given her on the phone Thursday.

When at last they arrived at the parking lot of the Sheraton, they stepped out of the car and went immediately to the fifth floor. Stopping at the door of room 538, Fletcher fished the key from his pocket and unlocked the door. As soon as they entered the hotel room, Jessica went to the closet. "I was fussing with the closet. I was trying to get the closet open." She testified later that she noticed two double beds in the room.

"Here, forget that," Fletcher said to her and handed her a glass of wine. "Take this."

"I guess he thought I needed it to relax. I took the wine and I just drank it."

Traditionally, Pentecostals have been sternly opposed to alcohol. Jessica had no way of knowing that John Wesley Fletcher had gone on drinking binges following some of his most outstanding preaching experiences.

Jessica says she remembers Fletcher telling her something about how "down" and "run ragged" Jim Bakker was, and that Bakker had no sex life with his wife whatsoever. Jessica recalls that Fletcher told her something about Tammy's affair with singer Gary Paxton. "Jim no longer feels like a man," Fletcher said.

To understand the incident it is helpful to know the background of John Wesley Fletcher. In 1970, at the age of thirty, Fletcher left his Durham, North Carolina, job as ambulance driver and mortician's helper to become an evangelist. He had been convicted five times of writing worthless checks, and he left behind four unsettled suits over more than $3,800 in unpaid bills. Johnny Chase, a minister in Wanchese, North Carolina, who has known Fletcher since the 1960s, had the following comment to make about Fletcher: "He's one of those people who has built up a track record over a period of years that would make you cautious."[15]

Graduating from tent revivals, Fletcher entered big-time evangelism when he appeared on PTL with Jim Bakker. Complaints about Fletcher's drinking, however, led to his release. The term of his ordination within the Assemblies of God lasted only four years, from 1977 to 1981. He was dismissed in 1981 for excessive drinking. Today he works the faith-healing circuit, traveling across America. He married early in 1971—while a Durham County, North Carolina, deputy sheriff searched for him in the hope of collecting a lawsuit judgment.[16]

Fletcher did not graduate from high school until he was twenty-one because he spent two years in the ninth grade and also two in the tenth. Pastor Louie Schultz of Durham and two church associates recalled Fletcher's driving a Cadillac and wearing expensive clothes while he occasionally assisted at the Assembly of God Revival Center in Durham. They heard rumors that he was involved in a nightclub. Years later, while preaching in New York, Fletcher admitted he had run a topless restaurant before becoming an evangelist.[17]

A Durham citizen who has known Fletcher for twenty-five years but wishes to remain anonymous recalled seeing Fletcher in a bar in Durham's Voyager Inn in the mid-1970s. "He sat down with me and told me he was making a lot of money as an evangelist. He used these words: "Some were called [to preach], some were sent, others just packed up and went.' " The funeral home owner who once employed Fletcher recalled Fletcher's visiting his hometown in the late 1970s. He talked to him about "having his own jet plane, about having a Cadillac, that he was just rolling in money."[18]

In September 1987 Fletcher was called before the federal grand jury investigating Jim Bakker's alleged violations. At that time, Fletcher still faced a $765,000 lawsuit in Oklahoma City. According to Jerry McLain, Fletcher took him to Atlanta, Georgia, in March 1986 for the purpose of discussing business. McClain accused Fletcher of having taken "physical liberties unbecoming a normal person, never mind a man of the cloth" in the hotel room.

"Come here. . . . I want you to see something," Fletcher reportedly said to twenty-one-year-old Jessica in the Florida hotel room. They walked onto the terrace and looked out over the pool below. Fletcher pointed. "There's Jim Bakker."

She saw him at the poolside, which had a refreshment stand, bar, and band nearby. She heard the beat of Caribbean music. She says she felt comfortable because she saw in the distance one of her heroes of the faith in person, Jim Bakker, who was with his daughter, Tammy Sue.

When eventually Fletcher went out of the room, leaving her alone, Jessica took a shower and dressed. Even though she was puzzled at the time about some of the pieces of information that Fletcher had given her regarding the Bakkers, Jessica today insists that what happened to her next came as a total surprise.

"No sooner was I dressed, than John came back with Jim," who wore only a white terrycloth swimsuit, Jessica recalled. "We met eye to eye. We must both be about five-foot-four."

"I didn't know women from New York were so beautiful," Jim said.

Jessica later reported that a feeling of nausea came over her. She had not eaten for several hours. This was a strange situation, one for which she was not prepared. She says she felt dazed but resolved not to embarrass herself. "I thought there was something wrong with me. I didn't want to come across as uneasy. I tried to believe that Jim and John were being normal." Later she wondered if John Wesley Fletcher had slipped something into her wine.

Jessica said six years later that Jim seemed to her to be hyper. "He was rubbing his thighs a lot, like, you know, let's get down to business." As John and Jim joked with each other, she said, Jim grew increasingly hyper until all at once he became "tranquil for a moment, like he does on TV when he cries." Jessica could scarcely believe her ears now. Jim Bakker was telling her he didn't know how he was going to make it.

"Tell her! Tell her!" Fletcher kept interrupting. Tell her what your problems are. Maybe she can help."

Jessica says she heard Fletcher's words and wanted to say to him, "I can't help, I don't even know this man."

Years later when the question arose as to why Jessica made no protest at this moment, she answered, "What was in my head wouldn't come out of my mouth." She reportedly felt she had no will of her own. "By then, if John had told me to stand out on the terrace and jump, I probably would have done it. That's how I felt."

Some women would have suspected something awry and tried to make a quick exit from the hotel room. But those who have never come under the control of clerical authority will perhaps not easily understand why Jessica Hahn did not walk out.

The incredible control that the notorious Siberian priest Gregory Rasputin exercised over the Russian czar, Nicholas Alexander, and his wife Alexandra is a well-established fact of history. "Bloody Nicholas," as he was often called, submitted to the priest in ways that are nothing less than astounding. If a Rasputin had tried to exert similar control over a leader like Thomas Jefferson, the priest would have been told to hit the road. But the Russian czar, despite his ruthlessness and autocratic rule over his people, lacked both the insight and the strength of will to dismiss the priest.

The truth is that individuals respond differently to the power of the clergy. The following is a quotation from the Mormon Church's Word Teaching Message, June 1945:

When our leaders speak, the thinking has been done. When they propose a plan—it is God's plan. When they point the way, there is no other which is safe. When they give directions, it should mark the end of controversy. God works in no other way. To think otherwise, without immediate repentance, may cost one his faith, may destroy his testimony, and leave him a stranger to the kingdom of God.[19]

Forty years later, apostle Dillin Oaks of the same Mormon Church gave the following warning on pages 24 and 25 of the "1985 CES Doctrine and Symposium":

Criticism is particularly objectionable when it is directed toward Church authorities, local or general. . . .Evil-speaking of the Lord's anointed is in a class by itself. It is one thing to depreciate a person who exercises corporate power or even government power. It is quite another to criticize or depreciate a person for the performance of an office to which he or she has been called of God. It does not matter that the criticism is true. . . . David recognized that we are never justified in any gesture or act against the Lord's anointed.[20]

Millions of intelligent, self-reliant Mormons today appear to accept this control their leaders have over them with little question. The threat of being cut off from the kingdom of salvation by crossing the clergy is nothing new. It should not be surprising, therefore, that a Charismatic young woman like Hahn should feel at the very least ambivalent and confused when one of the leaders of her church makes advances toward her.

A quantum leap in the meeting in the hotel room took place. "Tammy has made me feel belittled," Jim told her. "I don't know how I will come out of it. I don't feel like a man; I feel like I don't amount to anything."

As Jessica later told her account of the incident, she was in tears. "He said that sexually he wasn't satisfied with [Tammy], and she wasn't satisfied with him. He also told me Tammy was very big and that he couldn't be satisfied by her. Those were his words exactly. Those were Jim Bakker's words—Tammy is very big, and he cannot be satisfied."

In her sworn testimony, Jessica recalled how sick she felt and how confusion enveloped her when Fletcher suddenly interrupted Bakker and said, "I'm going to leave. I want to go to the beach."

Five minutes later he returned, knocking on the door. "Here's some Vaseline Intensive Care," he said. "Jim likes back rubs."

"No, I don't think so," Jessica replied.

As soon as Fletcher left again, Bakker made his move. Jessica claims that he began pulling her close to him.

"I really do need somebody. I've been going through hell," he said.

Still not wholly able to believe what her senses told her, Jessica replied that she had never been with a man: "I've never had intercourse with anyone."

Jessica says she remembers Jim pulling off the bedspread and saying, "I hate bedspreads." Sitting in the chair and watching in disbelief, Jessica felt him pull her over to him on the bed. "I really think you can help me," he said.

He then removed his bathing suit, untied her sash and removed her plum wrap-around dress, leaving her in her underclothes.

"Why don't you hire somebody?" she said, pushing away from him.

It is at this point that Jim Bakker's account of events differs most sharply from Jessica Hahn's. He claims that she was experienced and portrays himself as inexperienced and incompetent, if not temporarily impotent.

"You can't trust anybody," Jim is supposed to have replied to Jessica's question as to why he did not hire somebody.

"What makes you think you can trust me?" she asked.

"Because I know about you. I know where you've been for the past few years. I know what your life is about. You're not someone who is going to try and hurt me like the others. You're here to help me, and by helping me you're going to help a lot of people."

Jessica claims she told him she felt ill, but he seemed not to care for anyone's feelings other than his own. He unsnapped her bra and stripped her of all her clothes, she said in sworn testimony.

She said she felt helpless; that he was choking her.

"He started almost from the top of my head and didn't stop for what seemed like an hour and a half. He did just everything he could do to a woman . . . and he wouldn't stop. I told him I didn't want to be pregnant. He said, 'Oh, I've had an operation.' Once wasn't enough. He had to keep finding new things to do. I just couldn't stand him. I just wanted to pull out his hair." Her pain was indescribable, she later said, claiming that he forced her to perform oral sex with him.

"He finally stopped and said, 'I could go on, but my daughter is here.' He got up, brushed his hair with my hairbrush, and put back on his bathing suit. He then said, 'I'll see ya.' "

Jessica testified that she then stood up, draped a sheet around herself, and said, "I asked you not to, and you just kept on. Why?"

Jim is reported to have laughed faintly. "Don't worry about it; you'll appreciate it later." Then he left.

Dizzy and shaking with the chill, but relieved that the ordeal was over at last, Jessica made her way to the bathroom and threw up. She says she tried to turn the swirling confusion into a temporary oasis of order as she showered and brushed her teeth.

When John Wesley Fletcher returned, Jessica wanted to pound the evangelist with her fists. "Why didn't you tell me what you were planning? Why didn't you tell me what you were doing?"

"Just think how many people you're helping," Fletcher replied (according to Hahn). "Jim is a shepherd, and when you help the shepherd you help the sheep."

"Why are you here?" she demanded.

"Well, it wouldn't be fair, would it, being I made all the arrangements for Jim and then you left me out?"

"I can't function. I want you to leave. You've got to go."

"I'm not going. I made the arrangements and I feel that you have to do for me. . . ."

The above dialogue is strictly Jessica's version. Fletcher offered no sworn testimony until late September 1987. Jessica claims that Fletcher literally tore off her robe and said, "I'm going to keep on, Jessica, until you scream. You won't remember Jim; you'll remember me." He then put her on the floor.

Both men were twice her age, and both treated her roughly, she claimed, as if she were an object. Fletcher swore before the judge that he forced no one to do anything. He said he confessed all to God and his family shortly after the hotel incident.

Having satisfied himself, Fletcher got up and began dressing. Jessica recalls what he said: "I've got to get ready for the show. I've got to preach tonight."

Later that day, alone in her hotel room, Jessica turned on the "PTL Club"—partly out of habit and partly to assure herself that the two evangelists had really left the hotel. "I heard John say to Jim Bakker, 'You had a good rest today.' And Jim answered, 'Yeah, I need more rest like that.' John then added, 'The Lord really ministered to us today. We need more ministry like that.' I felt they were making fun of me right on television."

At 8:35 on Sunday morning, December 7, Jessica Hahn took the $129 in cash that Fletcher had given her for the plane ticket and boarded Eastern Airline's Flight 168 from Tampa.

A few days later Jessica received another phone call from an evangelist. It was Jim Bakker asking for forgiveness and for assurance that she would not talk. According to Jessica, he told her that he not only had much to lose, but carried a lot of responsibility on his shoulders. "He told me I would be accountable to God if I caused trouble. Jim said he would pray for me."

Other phone calls followed just to remind her to remain quiet about the hotel incident. To Jessica, the message was clear: "If I talked, I would be in big trouble."[21]

The question of Jessica's expectations has to be considered. At the Florida airport or at least on the way to the hotel, her initial expectation had to have changed somewhat because she now knew she was not going to meet all of Bakker's family. Did she expect to meet Jim Bakker alone? Is it possible that she still expected Bakker to be accompanied by other members of his staff? The information that Fletcher gave Jessica regarding the strained relationship between Jim and Tammy would have set off loud alarm bells in the heads of some women, although not all. Keeping in mind that she was only twenty-one, Jessica might very well have gone to the hotel out of trust. There is reason to believe that she was predisposed to trust ministers inordinately. Perhaps she found in them a father figure.

From the time that she graduated from Massapequa High School, Jessica worked full-time at Massapequa's Full Gospel Tabernacle with its minister, Gene Profeta. Religion had been exceedingly important to her since her early teens, when one of her close friends died. It was only natural that ministers became significant figures in her life. Even at the age of twenty-seven she placed inordinate faith in Falwell's promise to help her. She became disillusioned and angry when the help did not materialize.

The question of whether Jim Bakker raped Jessica Hahn also has to be raised. Two points need to be made in seeking an answer. First, there is no evidence to support the hypothesis that Bakker acted with premeditated intent in forcing Hahn to have intercourse. Rape can happen more or less spontaneously, that is, it can be unpremeditated. Second, if there is any truth in her claim, Jessica was either ambivalent about having sex with Jim or outspokenly against it. Fletcher seems to believe that Bakker had intercourse in mind when he went to the hotel room, and that he expected to find Jessica agreeable to having a sexual relationship with him.

If this is indeed what happened, then Jim Bakker appears to be guilty of unpremeditated rape. It is essential to realize, however, that the reconstruction of the actual scene is based in part on the purported memories of Jessica and Jim, as well as of John Wesley Fletcher. The memories are not fresh after several years. Furthermore, in times of high-voltage emotional conflict, putative memories can often be highly unreliable even when spoken sincerely.

There is another factor that might have been at work in the dynamics of the hotel incident. Is it possible that Jim had begun to fear that something existed deep down in him that prevented him from being attracted to Tammy? And was that "something" causing her to find him sexually unappealing? Could it be that he—Jim Bakker—considered himself homosexual? If he could have one chance with Jessica Hahn to prove himself, then perhaps he would know that he was a whole man.

John Ankerberg and Jerry Falwell seem absolutely convinced that Jim has had sexual relationships with men. It now seems likely that the alleged evidence will never be brought out for critical evaluation in a court of law. Therefore, the charges must remain temporarily conjectural as the allegations continue to come in from various sources.

John Wesley Fletcher continues to preach. He denies having forced himself on Jessica. Late in July 1987 he and Johnny Paycheck announced plans to record together *The Outlaw and the Preacher,* a gospel record. Fletcher is the preacher. Paycheck, best known for his 1978 hit "Take This Job and Shove It," is the outlaw. He was sentenced to nine and half years in prison for a barroom shooting in Ohio.

The October 5, 1987, *People Weekly* article on Jessica Hahn carries the sensationalized title "Bearing Body and Soul." The article is for the most part sensitively written. The author speaks of Jessica at twenty-one as "almost unimaginably naive." She is portrayed as a rather sheltered young woman whose life was devoted largely to her work. Jessica claimed that before Bakker and Fletcher took advantage of her, she had had only two dates. Some of the angry reactions to Hahn seem to stem from a belief that no woman has a right to be that naive at twenty-one.

The fact that Jessica posed for *Playboy* photographers caused Phil Donahue on his show on September 29, 1987, to question the credibility of her account of the hotel incident. However, it seems the Jessica Hahn of today cannot be wholly identified with the Jessica Hahn of December 1980.

One man in the Donahue audience seemed to imply that for taking money for her *Playboy* interview Jessica was a prostitute. He and others making this charge overlook the fact that she received no money for having sexual relations with anyone, which is what defines prostitution. She was paid for telling her own version of the story, partly to correct or supplement the news media versions. She received no additional money for the pictures in *Playboy*; in fact, the pictures were her idea originally and not the magazine's.

Of the $115,000 that PTL paid her in cash, $90,000 went to her legal representative, Paul Roper, who was not even a certified lawyer at the time. It might be said that Hahn was naive in more ways than one.

Jerry Falwell hopes to earn at least $1 million for his life story. If Jessica Hahn earns that much, too, then perhaps her readers can enjoy the fact that in her new life she has encountered good fortune. Perhaps some women would be willing to have intercourse with two evangelists in one day for a million dollars, but Jessica Hahn says she was not given the option of choice. She insists that she was cruelly forced to comply with the evangelists' wishes and that she was treated like an object rather than a person. Her feelings and wishes, she contends, were completely brushed aside because the men regarded her as a tool to serve them.

The November 1987 *Playboy* article is much more explicit and disturbing than the account revealed here. Equally disturbing is the charge by Rocco Riccobono that he had slept with Hahn two years before the Florida hotel incident. His friend Joanne Posner claimed to have been an unseen witness to the performance. However, Hahn's New York lawyer, Dominic Barbara, discovered that Riccobono was less than a sterling character, having been arrested for public lewdness (later reduced to disorderly conduct) and cocaine possession. He had once been caught literally with his pants down in the men's room of a Hicksville, New York, train station. A Vietnamese refugee claimed to have had a sexual relationship with Jessica four years after the Bakker incident. The relationship, he said, took place in a vibrating brass bed. Another man, Barry Hawkins, claiming also to be an ex-lover, said Jessica was the most expensive woman he had ever met: "Gold and diamonds and silk dresses." Hahn denied all the allegations and predicted that other men with shady motives would make similar claims.[22]

As if the plot were not already thick enough, a prostitute in Charlotte, North Carolina, claimed that she was surprised when Jim

Bakker called on her for sexual services. Bakker denied that he had gone to her.

Neither Jim Bakker nor John Wesley Fletcher has a corroborated history of being straight with the truth. If it could be shown, rather than alleged, that Hahn's history has as much deception in it as either Bakker's or Fletcher's, then her testimony would be not only damaged but demolished.

The nude pictures in *Playboy* are of Hahn at the age of twenty-seven, not twenty-one. She had kept quiet for over six years after the hotel incident. One male therapist I talked with suggested that her willingness to pose in the nude might be a delayed reaction to having lived virtually in the closet for six years with the thought that she had been rendered dirty and stained. By posing for *Playboy,* she wished to reveal that she was not dirty but beautiful and that she was no longer the victim but a woman in charge of her own life. North Carolina journalist Gail Mathabane, who was raped by a stranger when she was only thirteen, offered a similar explanation in a special article for the October 6, 1987, issue of the *Charlotte Observer.* She calls Hahn a brave and courageous woman.

It is very possible that Hahn does not clearly understand why she posed for *Playboy.* News columnist Ellen Goodman, who thinks the *Playboy* interview has the ring of truth about it, conjectured that Hahn believed she was still a victim and that in posing for the magazine she was in effect taking control of her own victimization. "Only I'm at the controls," Hahn said.[23]

My own conjecture is that penniless Jessica Hahn felt overwhelmed and guilty, not for taking money for her story, but for taking an inordinate amount of money. In short, feeling she might be exploiting the public, she offered to atone for her guilt by exploiting herself in public. In addition, she might have felt wicked for having been raped. Apparently, a number of rape victims judge themselves as immoral even though they were victims. If Hahn had already condemned herself, then posing for *Playboy* might have been a way of confirming her self-condemnation. I do not, however, take my own conjecture so seriously that I firmly believe it. Nor do I believe any other conjecture purporting to explain the *Playboy* exposé.

No explanation could have any great merit until the significant details of Jessica Hahn's life are uncovered. Those details are not likely to come forth soon, and indeed there remains the ethical question of how much right the public has to the details of Hahn's private life. The fact that she chose to pose nude is one thing; that she therefore has lost all rights to privacy is quite a different thing. Having gone public with the story, leveling the charge of rape against two TV evangelists, Hahn has guaranteed that her private life and past life will be under scrutiny for years to come. Except for the money in Hahn's case, there is still little to be gained in accusing a man of rape even if the woman is telling the truth.

Rape in the United States is apparently much more prevalent than many experts imagined only a few years ago. Psychoanalyst J. M. Masson was fired in 1981 from his position as projects director of the Sigmund Freud Archives because, he claimed, he discovered that Freud had suppressed his research on the rape and seduction of female children. Masson charged that Freud, giving in to the pressure of male medical doctors of his time, changed his story by saying that the women had not suffered real traumas of seduction and rape in their youth but had dreamed them up.[24] According to FBI reports, between 1977 and 1986 the incidence of rape increased by forty-two percent—making it the most rapidly growing crime in the nation. This upsurge might, however, reflect a new trend toward reporting "date rape," a crime which until recently had been largely ignored.

Surveys suggest that some men commit rape but define it not as rape but as their "right."[25] Men differ considerably regarding the question of when—at what point in male-female interaction—a woman gives up her right to say no to a man's sexual advances. Some men believe that if a man has taken a woman out to eat, paid for the meal, and has succeeded in getting her to visit his apartment (or getting himself an invitation to her apartment), then she has crossed the line of no return. She has lost her right to deny him his right to take her to bed.[26]

One colleague suggested to me that a number of men regard themselves as not responsible for controlling themselves once they have been strongly aroused. "It's like falling off a building. Once you start, it's too late to stop. The man just can't be expected to stop in midair, so to speak."

The Jessica Hahn case raises the important problem of clarifying what rape is. Rape is defined by law as sexual intercourse with a person against her (or his) will or without consent. Currently, the main victims range between the ages of fifteen and twenty-four. Some women appear so ignorant of the law that they believe forcible sexual intercourse is not rape if perpetrated by a friend or relative. Others feel that they are legally vulnerable if they did not put up a fight against sexual aggression, and some men seem to have grown up to sincerely believe that under certain conditions a woman's silence or even her protests are merely her way of consenting.[27]

What is puzzling about the Hahn case is the ease with which individuals develop intense biases about it despite the fact that they have only a sprinkling of the supposed information. My own strongest conjecture is that Hahn went to Florida with no conscious expectations of having sexual intercourse with either Bakker or Fletcher. If I read Fletcher accurately and fairly, he concurs with that conjecture. There is, however, no conjecture on which I would bet any amount of money.

PART V:

Power Plays, Envy, and Jealousy

In October 1987 PTL attorney Roy Grutman referred to Jim Bakker as "a defrocked minister who is uncontestably either a rapist or an adulterer, allegedly a pervert, and a financially devious and false steward who abused the trust of the credulous and who . . . may be a criminal as well."

15

Jerry and the Charismatics

Jim Bakker wanted Texas TV evangelist James Robison to succeed him as temporary host of the "PTL Club." Jerry Falwell knew of Bakker's preference in the spring of 1987, when he was still handing out a few complimentary statements about Bakker. On the surface, it seemed that the big, wavy-haired James Robison was a shoo-in for the position as "PTL Club" host. After all, in the summer of 1980 Falwell and Robison had worked together to convince their candidate Ronald Reagan to come to Dallas to speak at a big rally of the Religious Roundtable. Falwell had supported Robison's designation as up-front man and vice-president of the board of the Religious Roundtable in 1980. At the rally it was Robison who stole the show with his fiery speech. Reagan created a minor stir with his mild attack on the theory of evolution.

With Reagan sitting only a few feet from him on the Dallas platform, Robison exclaimed:

> If necessary, God would raise up a tyrant, a man who might not have the best ethics, to protect the freedom interests of the ethical and the godly. . . .

From the same platform he shouted before a cheering audience:

> I'm sick and tired of hearing about all the radicals and the perverts and the liberals and the leftists and the Communists coming out of their closets. It's time for God's people to come out of their closets, out of the churches, and change America! We must do it. . . . Our preachers are . . . to warn the people the enemy comes. . . . We're being attacked by satanic forces.

Between 1980 and 1987 something happened that cooled Falwell and Robison's admiration of each other, so that Robision was never offered the job of "PTL Club" host. In late-June 1987, Robison sent an open letter ten pages long to Falwell, stating that he intended to cancel his scheduled July 13 guest appearance on the PTL network unless Falwell answered certain questions publicly. Robison also called on Falwell to appoint more Charismatics to the PTL board. Two weeks later, Falwell announced that he would recommend to his board members that they open membership to Charismatics. Partly because of the resignations of Charismatics like evangelist Rex Humbard and James G. Watt, the board had become a fundamentalist-dominated enclave. On July 24, 1987, Falwell announced that Dr. Thomas Zimmerman had been invited to join the all-fundamentalist PTL board. Zimmerman is a Pentecostal who served as general superintendent of the Assemblies of God for many years. A Baptist from Jerry's home state of Virginia was also invited, which would scarcely give the Charismatics equal voice on the board. "We're not trying to mollify anyone," Jerry sternly insisted, vowing that he nevertheless would pursue a policy that was fair.[1]

Some Charismatics are convinced that Falwell set out to trick Bakker into turning the organization over to him. "Jerry Falwell called us long distance," Tammy Bakker charged, "and he told us that Jimmy Swaggart was going to do something terrible to our ministry. He said there would be a class-action suit, and he said a lot of things, told us a lot of things." Swaggart asked Falwell straight out if Tammy's charge was true. Falwell denied even having had such a thought. Both Jim and Tammy Bakker assured Swaggart that it was true. Caught in the middle, Swaggart said he would have to leave it with the Lord. The most charitable interpretation is that an overly confident Falwell, not fully aware of the problems he would face, quite naturally appointed his fundamentalist brethren to the board in a move of desperation. Charismatic Pentecostal Richard Dortch was kept on the board until it became known that he had served as middleman for funneling PTL hush money to Jessica Hahn's lawyer. His dismissal left the Charismatics with no strong voice on the board.

Even though James Robison had been a Baptist evangelist for years and was now a Charismatic like Jim Bakker, he was not forcefully recommended to the PTL board by his former friend Falwell. The reasons are still in dispute. Perhaps it was because Robison had become a Charismatic, and Falwell seemed consciously determined to repress the influence of Charismatics on the Board. If Robison's move toward the Charismatic faith did not cause a rift between Falwell and him, what did cause it?

In 1977 Robison was expelled from a Fort Worth TV station for verbally attacking homosexuals, which prompted an organization of gays to demand TV time to answer Robison. At the same time, Falwell was denouncing homosexuals, too, using language similar to that of his then-friend James Robison. By invitation from Robison, the noted Texas lawyer "Racehorse" Haynes joined the fight against the TV station. Like Falwell, Robison was a fighter, and he resolved to use Racehorse Haynes as legal counsel.

Haynes had successfully defended Fort Worth one-time multi-millionaire Cullen Davis against the charge that he had shot his twelve-year-old stepdaughter in cold blood. Desiring to save Cullen Davis's soul, Robison went straight to Davis and helped turn him into a born-again believer. Soon Cullen Davis was on the road as a lay evangelist who specialized in denouncing evolution and the public schools (which he calls "pagan schools"). It was the angry, flamboyant James Robison who helped Davis gather into one pile what they claimed were expensive pagan art objects that Davis had purchased over the years. With great fury and feelings of righteousness, they raised a hammer to the art objects and smashed them to pieces.

For Robison, this particular display of rage was progress. "When I was a kid," he once told his audience, I considered everything but murder. I was mean. I'm talking about sadistic! Cruel! I killed animals . . . deliberately. I killed a dog—just threw it on the floor until it died. I killed a cat. Put it in a fire. . . . God, I was bad. I was filthy."[2] Today, he still entertains a theology that predicts that someday his God will cast not cats or dogs, but Jews, Buddhists, humanists, and all other non-Christian human beings into a raging fire that will not be quenched. According to his own testimony, Robison as a youth secretly planned rapes, although he never carried out his plans.

By the mid-1980s, Robison had fallen out with many of his fundamentalist Baptist brethren. Moderates among Southern Baptists had never been taken with him. Some were repelled by his bombastic manner and regarded him as a man filled with hatred. Charismatic theology began to appeal to both Cullen Davis and James Robison. The latter began defending the practices of speaking in tongues and casting out demons, claiming on one occasion that he had been involved in raising someone from the dead. Such claims always make the majority of Baptists raise a skeptical eyebrow.

Jerry Falwell, an independent Baptist, had ridiculed the Charismatics' proclivity for faith healing and speaking in tongues. Bakker's hard-core followers charged that Falwell had earlier classified modern speaking in tongues and faith healing as works inspired by the devil.

When Robison sent word that he would refuse to appear as a guest on PTL until Falwell answered some questions, Robison was requesting his views on speaking in tongues, faith healing miracles, and exorcism. If Falwell held that these kinds of Charismatic works were Satan-inspired, why would he wish to place Charismatics on the PTL board? Robison's call for public answers to his questions placed Falwell in a dilemma. He would have to either repudiate his earlier negative comments about Charismatic views or show how he could work closely with Charismatics whose religious ecstasy he regarded as at best nonsense or at worst the wicked work of demons.

Christians have never been altogether comfortable with miracles. In medieval times, everybody wanted to get in on the act, every village had its yarns about miracles. Theologians have tortured language unmercifully with attempts to distinguish miracles from magic. Bitter quarrels have broken out among believers over the issue of miracles, some groups claiming to have miracles on their side, others denouncing alleged miracles as superstitions generated by hell itself. Today, a large number of Christians fear that the proliferation of phony miracles is steadily turning Christianity into a laughingstock. Another group, equally vehement, insists that without present-day miracles Christianity would be merely another humdrum religion. As if that were not confusing enough, some who believe in other religions are convinced that they have an inside track on miracle production. An African Muslim challenged Billy Graham to a miracle-healing contest several years ago. Billy quickly turned down the invitation. Oral Roberts did not volunteer to pick it up. I have often wondered why he did not. The prophet Elijah boldly challenged the prophets of Baal to a high-noon miracle contest on Mt. Carmel. According to the highly partisan writer of I Kings 18, Elijah won the contest and then executed his competition.

The outcome of the conflict between Falwell and some of the Charismatics is not easy to predict. James Robison has clearly cast his lot with the Charismatics. In the late 1970s, when he was still a Baptist without Charismatic frosting, there was serious talk of James Robison's becoming the new Billy Graham. Robison himself once exclaimed that God had a man in every generation to carry his torch. None of the current well-known evangelists, however, is likely to assume the role that Graham has played for over thirty years.

Though he didn't identify himself with Charismatics, Graham at least did not accuse them of being in league with the devil. In fact, he spoke at Oral Roberts University and maintains his friendship with Oral. He also appeared as a guest on Jim Bakker's PTL show, and over the years has proved to be a skilled politician among denominational leaders. Ultrafundamentalist Bob Jones, Jr., refused to pray for Billy's ministry because Graham was too willing to cooperate with Catholics and liberals. Graham gets along well with Charismatics because he does not try to work too closely with them. And no Charismatic suspects him of having designs on PTL or any other agency that has been even loosely identified with Pentecostals and Charismatics. Moreover, he has over the years mostly winked at the scandal of faith healing.

Falwell could not avoid dealing with the Charismatics as long as he remained the PTL helmsman. He has said more than once that if he had known what he was getting into, he would have declined Bakker's offer to take over PTL. In response to the question of why he did not resign much earlier than he did, Falwell gave two reasons: He said he had a Christian duty to see to it that those who invested their money in PTL and Heritage USA received what they were promised. Also, he believed he had to soothe the financial scandal created by Jim Bakker since it was a serious threat to all TV ministries. Falwell seemed to think that loss of faith in TV evangelists somehow signified a decline in religious faith. At the end of March 1987, in an appearance at Cocoa Beach, Florida, he said, "If Heritage Village were to go down the tubes, it would affect every Christian in America."

The fact is that someone else could have replaced Falwell at the helm and accomplished at least as much as he. Unless he believed he was serving as God's indispensable appointee, there was probably another reason for his staying on at PTL. He did not know how to walk away from a fight. (When he did resign in October 1987, it was because the fight was over and he had lost.) Still another reason was offered by some ministers, including one who knows Falwell quite well. They believe that Jerry, to put it bluntly, coveted Heritage USA. In short, he came to believe that the general idea of a Christian resort/retreat was a capital idea, one of Jim Bakker's greatest.

One thing is clear. Falwell was forced to come to terms with the Charismatics. James Robison's open letter and demand for an open reply served notice on Jerry that the truce he claimed to have worked out raised as many questions as answers.

As early as the first century A.D., some Christians were quarreling about the propriety of speaking in tongues in public. The apostle Paul told Christians in Corinth that speaking in tongues mainly benefited the individual and had minimal value to the community.

> Well, then if I do not understand the meaning of the sound the speaker makes, his words will be gibberish to me, and mine to him. You are, I know, eager for the gifts of the Spirit; then aspire above all to excel in those which build up the church. . . . Thank God, I am more gifted in ecstatic utterance [tongues] than any of you, but in the congregation I would rather speak five intelligible words, for the benefit of others as well as myself, than thousands of words in a language of ecstasy (I Corinthians 14:11–12, 18–19 NEB).

Paul had to deal with the problem of believers speaking in tongues at a public worship service in the city of Corinth. He asked, "Hence if at a gathering of the whole church everybody speaks with 'tongues,' and if outsiders or unbelievers come in, will they not declare you are insane?" (Moffatt translation). The word that Paul used for insane is the term for religious frenzy. When the citizens of ancient Sythia witnessed the raptures and ecstatic behavior of the worshipers of Bacchus, they scoffed at the idea of believers possessed by a god who drove them into insanity. Paul did not want the Corinthian Christians to be mistaken for a group of wild religious lunatics.

Near North Dallas sits a large Charismatic Church run by TV faith healer Bob Tilton. Besides specializing in preaching the Gospel of Wealth and Health, he hangs crutches on the walls of the auditorium. Like the sound of thousands of swarming hornets, a great noise sweeps across the large auditorium when the congregation begins speaking in tongues. Richard Roberts was the guest preacher on one Sunday evening. To the believers, the putative healing miracles and speaking in tongues became a spiritual rhapsody. Their faith had summoned God down from heaven. To them, the sound was sweet and heavenly.

To some observers, the display of "tongues" is a manifestation of lunacy; to others, it resembles the shouting and screaming of happy fans at a basketball game. Although faith-healing antics can be damaging, the tongues experience is harmless and seems quite meaningful to the participants. What infuriates a number of non-Charismatic Christians is not so much the practice of speaking in tongues as the strong claims made by Charismatic preachers. Instead of designating tongues as a human form of worship or as an expression of faith alongside other such expressions, Charismatics are prone to treat speaking in tongues as a supernatural miracle that accompanies the baptism of the Holy Spirit. Sparks of anger fly when Charismatics claim that those who speak in tongues possess a higher spiritual status than those who do not. Some Charismatics treat speaking in tongues as *the* manifestation of immersion in the Spirit.

Fundamentalists have sometimes charged that speaking in tongues is a self-serving practice in which individuals indulge to gain prestige without contributing anything to anyone but themselves. Speaking in tongues requires no talent, no training, little effort, and accomplishes nothing except to increase one's status within a particular circle. Many maintain that it produces little fruit of the Spirit, no charitable work, and little or no help to anyone except the individual who engages in it. The fur really flies when one group of fundamentalists goes so far as to brand modern speaking in tongues as the work of Satan.

Charismatics reply that speaking in tongues reveals to the whole assembly that the power of God is still at work, that the devil can be defeated, and that God is producing an abundance of miracles for those who live in the Spirit.

Some contemporary Christians plainly do not believe in supernatural miracles. According to Christians who embrace the doctrine of the Sufficiency of Universal Revelation, God works entirely without supernatural interruptions. If God resorted to miracles, he would be working against his previously established order in Creation. Nature as God's orderly self-disclosure contains an abundance of healing powers and blessings. Medical science is the attempt to appropriate aspects of God's orderly Creation for the purpose of improving human health.

Christians of this persuasion are actually thankful that the Creator does not suspend the laws and regularities of nature in order to work supernatural wonders. If even a tenth of the billions of prayers requesting miracles were answered in one year, the majestic cosmos that is the universe would collapse into chaos. Christians who think this way hold that an orderly creation free of disruptive miracles is the best gift that the Creator could offer his human creatures. They rejoice that Creation's patterns and regularities can be learned and appropriated by human beings universally. They compare the gift of nature to an automobile that parents give to their teenage children. In gratitude, the children should take the gift and learn how to use it intelligently and responsibly. Trying to run one's life by supernatural miracles is like trying to drive a car by miracles. Both approaches reflect a failure to develop responsibility for one's decisions. If nature's patterns and laws were interrupted by supernatural responses to pleas for miracles, then neither farmers, pilots, rodeo riders, truck drivers, carpenters, librarians, nor anyone else could rely on anything.

According to these strict Universal Revelation Christians, when farmers plant corn, they do not count on miracles. They depend on the regular order of nature to hold fast. If miracles popped into existence the way some people would like (or think they would like), everything would collapse in confusion. Life would be so unpredictable as to be a sea of misery. Working would go out of style because there would be no connection between individual effort and consequences. People would try to solve problems by praying rather than by working and thinking.

Charismatics think Jerry Falwell is arbitrary in his choice of what to accept as a modern miracle and what not to accept. He often seems to pick and choose the miracles that suit his private purposes. When he wanted to raise a few million for PTL in May 1987, he went on TV and prayed for a miracle. When the money came in, he chose to describe the victory as the "May Miracle." He believes that the power of demons and Satan is still felt in the world, but he wavers on the question of miraculous exorcism. He claims that the Holy Spirit miraculously heals the broken heart through the Word preached by pastors like himself, but he becomes wishy-washy when faced with the question of the Holy Spirit's miraculous healing of broken bodies through preachers of deliverance. He admits that God raised the dead in biblical times and that he will raise many at the Rapture, but he seems to lose faith in the power of God over death in the present. As for speaking in tongues, Falwell appears to think it was a wondrous and good spiritual manifestation in biblical times but is a sign of lunacy or possession in the present age. In short, the Charismatic and new Pentecostal critics of Jerry Falwell see him as lacking boldness in preaching the whole counsel of God.

The Charismatics do appear to have a point about the somewhat arbitrary way in which Falwell labels events miracles. One of of his latest fund-raising projects was "The Resurrection Committee," composed of those who made a one-time $1,000 contribution to PTL. According to Falwell's theology, Jesus was resurrected miraculously. The new 1987 Resurrection Committee presumably was designed to help bring about the financial resurrection of PTL. The choice as to whether to label achievement of this goal a miracle seemed entirely arbitrary.

The problems PTL had after the spring of 1987 were so severe that a compromise had to be struck between fundamentalists following Jerry Falwell and Charismatics associated with leaders like James Robison. First, the financial salvation of Heritage USA would have to come from a range of customers extending beyond the fundamentalists and Charismatics. Business was business, which meant that Heritage USA had to try to turn to the mainstream. Given Falwell's ability to use biblical texts and divine impulses to suit his purposes, there was every reason to suspect that he would find biblical and prayerful support in widening his circle of customers. On August 12, 1987, PTL's chief executive officer announced plans to explore the possibility of building parks similar to Heritage USA. He spoke of constructing a place just like it on the West Coast. "We've identified what we feel is a target market of 70 million people . . . : the evangelical community in this country."[3]

Second, it is important to realize that even if Heritage USA were run by Buddhists, it would still be a resort center for parents who want to take the kids to a pleasant village where they can feel safe and reasonably secure. If the bookstore and other sections of the complex can provide more options for mainstream customers, Heritage USA might eventually attract more customers with money to spend.

Jim Bakker had actually solved the problem of what to do with both faith-healing performances and speaking in tongues on his "PTL Club." He dispensed with them on the set (thus pleasing the non-Charismatics). At the same time, he said a few hundred words each week in favor of faith healing and speaking in tongues (thus satisfying the Charismatics). The real problem was not that of speaking in tongues. By reading the Bible in light of PTL's financial crisis, Jerry Falwell was able to find a way to tolerate Charismatics' speaking in tongues at some of the Heritage USA worship services. A church located in Dallas, Texas, has worked out a compromise that the new PTL board and the Heritage Village ministers might consider. Some of the members of the Dallas church speak in tongues and others do not. At the morning worship service, speaking in tongues seems to be unacceptable. At the Sunday evening service, it is quite acceptable. This gives the church members options without anyone greatly infringing on the convictions of others.

The problems of so-called faith healing are, by contrast, so enormous that there is little room for compromise. Some of the new Pentecostals and Charismatics will simply have to understand that a large number of Christians and non-Christians look upon faith healers not only as misguided, but as con artists and tricksters who prey on the afflicted. It is not simply a question of disagreement over the interpretation of scriptural texts, but the more critical question of elementary decency and morality.

In the 1960s things got out of hand and Pentecostals themselves had to take a fresh look at faith healing. Outlandish claims, to say nothing of outright lies and tricks handed out by certain faith-healing evangelists, caused a large number of Pentecostals to call for discipline. This happened mainly at the local church level, where outlandish lies could more easily be checked and the deceit exposed.

Christians who deny that there are supernatural miracles insist nevertheless that nature already contains an astoundingly rich reservoir of curative properties to be explored. The challenge is to study the "Book of Nature" rigorously and to pay heed to its patterns and laws, for they are God's orderly way of manifesting himself. According to this way of thinking, if each human body is a part of nature, then to say that the body is working to heal itself is to say that God is working to heal it. To take care of the body through proper diet and exercise is to cooperate with the Creator and Sustainer of life. In prayer, believers can commit themselves to working with God in the interest of health.

For those who think this way, prayer is many things, including the expression of hope and the renewal of the heart and mind. When the sick know that others care enough to pray for them, this knowledge is itself a healing influence—as important to them as the medication given by physicians. To these people, loving deeds and words are not ethereal, spooky phenomena, but *literal* medicine entering the body and working its healing ways.

People often use the word "miracle" to refer not to supernatural disruptions of natural order, but to the joyous surprises that sometimes happen in the area of hope. Theists and atheists alike can share together in this joy, hope, and love. One group calls the healing process nature, another calls it God working through nature. Both agree that hope and kindness are an essential part of the healing process.

Considering that the views of Charismatics are the complete opposite of those of fundamentalists in many areas, the question remains: Why didn't Jim Bakker turn the reins of PTL and Heritage USA over to a fellow Pentecostal or Charismatic in the first place instead of to Jerry Falwell, a Baptist?

First, Bakker knew that Jimmy Swaggart exerted considerable influence among Assemblies of God leaders. He knew of Swaggart's hostility toward the very concept of Heritage Village as a vacation land. Bakker feared that if he left the reins in the hands of a fellow member of the Assemblies of God, that person would fall under the influence of Jimmy Swaggart. Knowing that he would leave Heritage USA deep in debt, Bakker had good reason to fear that Swaggart could inspire a movement among the Assemblies of God potentates to sell Heritage USA and thus end Jim Bakker's dream of a decade.

That Swaggart had conscious plans to take over Bakker's organization seems to have been a figment of Bakker's imagination. That Swaggart had enough influence to cause Heritage USA to be auctioned off or sold was not a figment of Bakker's imagination. Whether or not Swaggart would have actually used his influence is a question that no one can answer. Bakker, not wanting to take the risk, went outside the Pentecostal fold to a Baptist whom he knew could handle the organizational details. Bakker had reason to think that a Baptist would not suffer intimidation from Assemblies of God leaders when the time came to turn the business back over to him. What Bakker did not, of course, count on was Falwell's absolute refusal to give him back his ministry. There is little basis for believing that Falwell set out from the start to kidnap a ministry and all the considerable assets that would remain after the creditors were paid. It would be naive, on the other hand, to think that Falwell did not very quickly realize that he had stumbled onto a potential windfall despite the debts to be paid off.

There is a second reason for Bakker's turning his organization over to Falwell. At least as far back as his days in Los Angeles in the early 1970s, Bakker had in mind "to work with all the churches and favor none." In November 1973 he resigned from the board of his television ministry because, he said, the other board members proposed "to put the ministry under the umbrella of a single church."[4] By turning to a Baptist and giving him a board of directors consisting mainly of Charismatics, Bakker theoretically had a check-and-balance plan to prevent PTL and Heritage USA from becoming the arm of one denomination only. Despite Falwell's success in getting Charismatics off the board and stacking it with anti-Charismatic fundamentalists, Bakker's plan to keep his organization somewhat ecumenical had worked so far.

16

Soap-Opera Realism

On the Bakkers' "PTL Club," two messages came across persistently. The first was that by being born again and filled with the Spirit, life could be victory on top of victory. A parade of celebrities, including born-again singers and athletes, passed before the PTL cameras. All gave testimony as to how the Lord had helped them make it to the top. It was a staged production of rose-colored lights, oozing testimonials, and splash-dash commercialism about the Christian life. In short, it was a cosmetic version of the Christian's earthly journey, far removed from John Bunyan's *Pilgrim's Progress*.

The implicit message of the "PTL Club," in contrast to the explicit message, suggested that Jim and Tammy were having emotional problems, that not all was perfect in Candy Land, that Christians were still made of flesh and blood. In many ways Tammy was always letting the cat out of the bag by demonstrating her human frailty on TV and speaking almost inadvertently of her own human weaknesses. Still, she was able to conceal her drug dependency problem for several years. This concealment in itself would have been perfectly justifiable if only she and Jim had not tried to set forth their idealized, commercialized, and romanticized image as the reality.

Except for the irresponsible tales of so-called faith healing and prosperity, Jim and Tammy's books are more realistic and moving than their TV shows. Their shows are in some ways a mingling of entertainment and commercial messages, which may very well be necessary for keeping the wheels of daily televangelism rolling.

Some critics have compared the "PTL Club" to a soap opera series. "What will Tammy say on the next show?" is a question that seemed to drive many people to bring the show into their homes every week. Ironically, there was a battle at Pat Robertson's CBN as to whether to create and produce Christian soap operas. On March 2, 1987, Stephen Winzenburg, Anson Shupe, and I spoke to an annual meeting of the Broadcast Education Association in Dallas on the topic of TV evangelism. We had the good fortune of talking privately with two professionals from CBN who were attending the meeting. One of them shared with me three of the reasons given at CBN for producing Christian soap operas. First, it is a fact that a lot of people—Christian and non-Christian—watch soap operas. The market is already there. Second, Christian soap operas provide a powerful medium for presenting the Christian life realistically and honestly. Third, good drama offers an effective mode for spelling out the distinctive Christian message and values in a concrete manner that will make a lasting impact on the viewers.

As it has turned out, the Bakkers' ups and downs have turned into a real-life soap opera, truth stranger than fiction. The hard-jabbing infighting over the control of the PTL Broadcasting Network and Heritage USA brought forth charges and language more colorful and stinging than anything found in the *Charlotte Observer* editorials. Even Ted Koppel was surprised at the bluntness of Falwell's language in leveling charges against Jim Bakker. Scarcely a political babe in the woods, Koppel confessed that he had never witnessed a political hit man go beyond the extremes that Falwell had gone to in his expose of Jim and Tammy.

Evangelist Jimmy Swaggart was one of the first to refer to the Bakkers' troubles as a soap opera. There are soap opera themes in most people's lives, including that of faith healer Oral Roberts, who perched prayerfully in a Tulsa tower, waiting for God to zap him unless millions of dollars rolled in. To the surprise of many, a Florida gambling man in the dog-racing business proved to be the agent of Oral's temporary stay of execution.

When TV evangelists recruit believers to offer publicly what can only be described as before-and-after commercials, they create a distorted picture of Christian life on earth. Even worse, they entice many decent Christians to participate in the distortion. Whatever the motives of the evangelists, the gushy testimonials function as a device for soliciting money for the TV programs. The hard-sell message is brazenly simple: If you viewers want your lives to be filled with happiness and victory day after day, you must have more faith. Show that you have more faith by sending in money.

One of the more disturbing attempts to manipulate people in the name of God is to be found in Oral Roberts's words to his son Richard and to Richard's bride Patti. The wedding cake had been cut, wedding pictures made, and congratulations offered. Richard and Patti slipped away to change clothes and to prepare for their honeymoon escape.

Suddenly, Oral appeared and called the newlyweds into his office. It was supposed to be a time of celebration and joy. But Oral had what he regarded as more important matters on his mind. Without warning, he broke out in tears and after an unnerving period of uncertainty in the office, Oral explained his strange behavior. He had had another one of his dreams. Addressing his son, Oral revealed the content of his dream. It was simple and chilling, and its intent was unmistakable. If Richard and Patti were to leave Oral's ministry or turn their backs on God, they would be killed in a plane crash. After delivering his shocking revelation, Oral then told his son and new daughter-in-law how much he loved them and finally wished them a happy honeymoon.[1]

When TV evangelists denounce humanists, the impression is sometimes left that were it not for humanists, America would be a virtual paradise. In her sometimes disarmingly honest way, however, Tammy Bakker revealed incidents about herself and her coworkers that make it clear that Christians alone, without the aid of others, are quite capable of generating their own battles and soap-opera scenarios.

When people first go to work at CBN or in a similar Charismatic environment, they often have high expectations that the meaner side of human nature will somehow have been washed out. It does not take long for more realistic expectations to replace the delusions. During his final months at CBN, Gerry Straub believed he was followed almost everywhere he went by a CBN staff member appointed to secretly monitor his conduct.

Extramarital affairs at CBN happened despite the Charismatic surroundings. When Pat Robertson learned of one of them, he instructed the man to go to the husband of the woman to seek his forgiveness, though the affair had been over for some time. It apparently did not occur to Pat to ask the woman if *she* wanted her husband to know about the unfortunate affair. As Christian counselors have stressed repeatedly, this kind of decision is exceedingly delicate and personal and the situation potentially explosive. Some marriages would be destroyed if the ended affair were confessed. Pat Robertson did not take this into consideration, perhaps because he considered a woman's affair to be a form of stealing property from the man.

At CBN Tammy felt that one woman in particular took every opportunity to say cutting things to her. Once Tammy walked into a meeting of women who called themselves counselors. The woman, who Tammy believed hated her, turned and said, "Tammy, you have not been invited, and you are not welcome." No ethologist was needed to diagnose what had transpired. Among almost all animal species there is a territorial imperative that appears as jealous protectiveness of home territory. Tammy was perceived as an intruder, and the fellow Christian woman simply reacted with primitive jealousy toward Tammy.

In an attempt to deal with the woman who seemed always to see her as an intruder, Tammy prayed, "God, bless this woman. Lord, help her to change. Lord, help me to love her. You bless her and make her a different person."

But Tammy confesses with astounding and admirable honesty that what she was really saying secretly was, "I despise her. I wish God would do something mean to her."[2]

People often find it difficult to admit that the ancient weaknesses of common envy and jealousy exist among them. They like to believe that these weaknesses are a trait of pet dogs and perhaps their less civilized neighbors. The truth is that jealousy exists in every profession and area of human life. In *The Brothers Karamazov,* Dostoevsky gives a brilliant and accurate description of intense envy and jealousy that often developed inside Russian Orthodox monasteries. Usually these emotions had to do, paradoxically, with spiritual status and prestige.

Tammy was keenly aware of the jealousy around her at CBN, and it sometimes made her bitter against those who let their jealousy show. Some Holiness Christians believe that it is possible for individuals to attain on earth a state of perfect love. But no one familiar with the interaction between the Bakkers and some of their co-workers can easily subscribe to the doctrine of moral perfectionism.

In a May 1987 TV interview, Charles Colson, who was involved in the Watergate scandal, told of becoming born again. In discussing the Iran scandal, he said that corruption in government will continue until Christian people whose hearts are regenerated are put into office. Unfortunately, there is enough known about the shady side of tel-evangelism to make Colson's comment seem either naive or circular. In his new book *Kingdoms in Conflict,* Colson shows a more balanced approach. As the founding fathers of our country realized, there must be overt checks and balances. The "good guys" can become corrupt when they are not held accountable to others.

Andrew Greeley, the noted Roman Catholic priest, contends that unfortunately his church has developed a system that scuttles overt accountability and generates envy and jealousy among the priests. This process starts, he says, in the seminaries, which Catholic boys frequently enter as teenagers. The worst effect of the seminary that Greeley attended "was that its exploitation of envy and mediocrity as instruments of social control deprived the Church of talent it would need desperately in the coming crisis."[3]

Greeley, a member of the University of Chicago faculty, writes, "Academics are remarkably envious people. Journalists are even more so. And priests make professional journalists look envy-free."[4] Instead of saying that priests are inherently more perverse than the general public, however, Greeley insists that the structure in which priests are trained literally teaches young candidates to be envious. He asks his readers to perform a little experiment: go to a local priest of their choice, praise in his presence something another priest has done or is doing, then listen to the reaction. There are, to be sure, many exceptions. But Greeley contends that for most priests envy has become "a built-in character trait." Furthermore, if Greeley's analysis is ac-curate, the system is growing worse rather than better.[5] People who claim to be sanctified, baptized with the Holy Ghost, slain in the Spirit, or blessed with some other supernatural religious status turn out on the whole to be morally pretty much like their neighbors. Some are the salt of the earth, a few are crooks, and most are struggling along trying to make a living while showing respect and kindness toward other people. The pettiness that plagues Catholics and Jews also plagues Baptists, secular humanists, and Pentecostals. Jimmy Swaggart's distrust of some of his fellow Pentecostals, and their distrust of him, is nothing extraordinary or surprising. Those who talk at length about holiness are mistaken if they believe they have soared to a moral stratosphere far above most of their neighbors.

Reading Greeley's analysis, one can hardly help but ask why even in heaven's name a good Catholic in North America or Europe would want to become a priest. The rewards seem few and the conflicts destructive. In fact, except in Third World countries, there is a serious decline in the number of candidates for the priesthood. Between 1970 and 1985, the number of young men studying for the priesthood in North America dropped by 43.7 percent, according to a study published by *L'Osservatore Romano,* the Vatican newspaper.

At a recent New York City meeting on the scientific study of religion, I was apparently the only non-Catholic at one of the sessions. I had been invited to present a paper in response to the Catholic scholars' papers. The meeting was for me very enlightening. One point stuck out above all others. The Catholic scholars were deeply concerned with anticipating the structural changes that were going to take place within the Catholic church in North America and Europe. The changes would come because the supply of priests for local parishes was seriously and steadily in decline.

If Andrew Greeley's report is correct, the climate of envy and jealousy within the priesthood is so disheartening that it is unrealistic to expect young men to be strongly attracted to the vocation. Even the grudges that bishops have against individual Curial bureaucrats who harass them are common knowledge among Vatican-watchers. The unfairness and humiliation that the curate must suffer in the pastor-curate relationship provides enough material for numerous novels or clinical studies. Many Catholic priests and scholars are convinced that their church is supporting a corrupt and perverse system that cannot be reformed without "some kind of permanent abolition and the establishment of a different kind of government structure for the central authority of the Church."[6]

The political intrigue in Rome, the death of Cardinal Danielou in a Paris whorehouse, and the mysterious disappearance of tens of millions of dollars of Roman Catholic money, involving, among other institutions, the diocese of Reno, Nevada—these and similar stories need not be explored here. But the corruption of the Catholic church indicates human weakness in a totally religious environment. Anyone who talks, as Jim Bakker once did, of a "total Christian environment" is unrealistic, to say the least. On earth, a Christian community having no contact with the rest of the world would not be wholly free of human conflict, jealousy, envy, and other weaknesses of our finite species.

Jerry Sholes, former television writer and associate producer for the Oral Roberts Evangelistic Association, is convinced that big-time evangelists are strongly tempted to play fast and loose with the truth. Sholes claims to know first-hand that Oral Roberts "misused his public trust, abused the sanctity of his purported relationship with God, and deliberately misled millions of his partners and the public with at least two outright lies."[7] In his important and informative work entitled *Oral Roberts: An American Life*[8] David Harrell, Jr., trying to soften Sholes's charge, succeeds at best in obscuring it. He suggests that Oral Roberts's claims (which Sholes brands as lies) are in keeping with the tradition out of which Roberts comes. This comes close to saying that lying is not really lying if it is done within a tradition of lying. In other words, Oral Roberts belongs to a religious tradition that allows preachers a free hand in reworking certain facts by casting them in imaginative and highly dramatized form. Hence, while the content of the story is not to be taken literally, its general message and intent is to be taken to heart by those impressed by the message. Oral Roberts seems to want it both ways, mingling fact and fiction and then presenting the fusion as pure fact. In the case of Oral's claim to have seen a 900-foot Jesus, the dramatization crossed the line into the sensational and bizarre.

Early in 1981 Jerry Falwell told an audience in Alaska about a meeting at which he and Jimmy Carter exchanged words about homosexuals. Falwell later tried to use the exchange to make a negative comment about Carter. When the White House produced a transcript of the meeting, it was obvious that the exchange had not in fact taken place. Jerry had concocted it. Instead of admitting that his imagination had played tricks on his memory, Falwell concocted another fabrication, claiming he had not meant the story he had told in Alaska to be taken literally. How it was supposed to be taken remained unclear.

The point is not that TV evangelists ought to be free of all verbal slips and mistakes, but that televangelism *as an institution* exerts enormous pressure on the evangelists to confuse their own earthly drives and ambitions with divine impulses.

The war model that seems to determine to a great extent the

hyperfundamentalist perception of the world is largely responsible for some TV evangelists' practice of systematically misrepresenting ideologies with which they strongly disagree. Tim LaHaye's book *The Battle for the Mind: A Subtle Warfare*[9] is a popular example of how the war model creates pressure on a writer to systematically misrepresent his opponent's view (in LaHaye's case, humanism). In living out the scenes of his own soap opera, Jerry Falwell frequently speaks as a man under the control of the war model. "The Sunday School is the attacking squad," he said. "The church should be a disciplined, charging army . . . . Christians, like slaves and soldiers, ask no questions." In one of his sermons, he made it clear how thoroughly the war model shapes the evangelist's perception of the world and his role in it:

> Radio became the artillery that broke my fallow ground and set me to thinking and searching, but the local church became the occupation force that finished the job and completed the task the artillery had begun. It is important to bombard our territory, to move out near the coast and shell the enemy. It is important to send in the literature. It is important to send that radio broadcast and to use that dial-a-prayer telephone. It is important to have all those external forces being set loose on the enemy's stronghold.
>
> But ultimately some Marines have to march in, encounter the enemy face-to-face, and put the flag up, that is, build the local church.
>
> I am speaking to Marines who have been called of God to move in past the shelling, the bombing, and the foxholes and, with bayonet in hand, encounter the enemy face-to-face and one-on-one bring them under submission to the Gospel of Christ, move them into the household of God, put up the flag and call it secured. You and I are called to occupy until He comes.[10]

In this particular sermon the enemy is identified as all those human beings who do not accept what Falwell regards as the essential features of Christianity. There is a certain hardness in the military model that says if you aren't with us, you're against us. Outsiders are enemies. Of the Metropolitan Community Church (a network of 250 multidenominational churches that welcome homosexuals to the church services), Falwell declared that it is a "vile and Satanic system [that] will one day be utterly annihilated, and there will be a celebration in heaven."[11] There are less vicious ways of dealing with rival views and lifestyles.

A spokesman for the Santa Clara chapter of Falwell's Moral Majority, Inc. suggested that homosexuals be put to death: "I agree with capital punishment, and I believe that homosexuality is one of those that could be coupled with murder and other sins."[12] This is not Falwell's personal view, although he did classify homosexuals as "brute beasts."

Falwell believes that abortion is premeditated murder and that murderers should be executed by the state. He has not, however, publicly drawn from his premises the required conclusion that anyone deliberately and directly involved in bringing about an abortion should be put to death as either the perpetrator or the accessory. Fortunately, some people's actions are morally superior to the doctrines and premises that they preach.

What is often branded hypocrisy among some Christians is in reality ordinary inconsistency and human finitude as individuals try to live out their own personal soap operas. To be truly hypocritical is (1) to profess some principle unequivocally, (2) to knowingly behave in direct conflict with one's profession, and (3) to have had the power and means to bring one's behavior in line with one's profession without violating another professed principle. Quite often we are unaware of our inconsistencies until another person calls them to our attention. Perhaps the injunction "judge not" takes on practical import if it means, "Do not judge people to be hypocrites because *you* see their inconsistencies. *They* may not be aware of them."

It is very difficult to believe that the Bakkers were unaware of the inconsistency between their profession and their practices regarding the misuse of money solicited in the name of God. The *Charlotte Observer* did the Bakkers a favor by pointing out the gap between profession and practice. The Bakkers tried to close the gap not by bringing their behavior in line with their teachings, but by revising their teachings to harmonize with their practice. This adjustment has satisfied some of the Bakkers' followers. The crucial question for the Bakkers is whether *they* will be satisfied with it in the long run. All such adjustments come with a price.

When Tammy was a child, she believed she saw in the people of her Pentecostal church a destructive inconsistency between the love that they preached and the way they treated her mother. "This hurt me so deeply," she wrote, "and there was almost an undercurrent of hatred in me toward those church people."[13]

When evangelists came to town, Tammy's mother would give her time and money to feed them and to do things to make their stay more comfortable. According to Tammy's memory, the pastor's wife would spread vicious gossip about Tammy's mother, shout at her, and make her life miserable. A psychoanalyst might suggest that as an adult Tammy has an ambivalent feeling toward church people. She both loves them and hates them. If she has misused some of their money, then perhaps it was the child in Tammy getting even for what was done to her mother. As Freud noted, the id knows no time. It patiently waits for its day of revenge. I do not, of course, know that Tammy was unconsciously getting sweet revenge on the church people. It is unlikely that even Tammy knows. But it is important to raise the question, because Tammy and Jim will probably seek a position of power if Jim does not go to prison.

PART VI:

Unanswered Questions About Faith Healing

17

Raising Money and the Dead

In November 1985 The Amazing Randi and I met in St. Louis to witness the faith-healing crusade of TV evangelist W. V. Grant. Arriving well over an hour early at the auditorium, I succeeded in getting appointed as an usher, which gave me what I wanted—complete freedom to go anywhere in the auditorium and to talk to anyone. Grant had a large repertory of tricks, including receiving direct communication from heaven about the names and diseases of people in the audience. As a trained and remarkably skilled illusionist and stage performer, James Randi succeeded in covertly uncovering a number of Grant's performance tricks. As usher, I talked to several people in wheelchairs and discovered the first stage of what I later dubbed the "wheelchair fraud."

In addition to professing to be God's instrument for making chairbound people walk, Grant claimed that through him the deaf have been made to hear, the blind made to see, and the cancer-infected made whole. Randi and I watched Grant take walking canes and crutches from people and break them over his knee. We recorded the evangelist's attempt to convince a woman that the lump on her breast would disappear, and we watched him place his hands on the deaf ear of an elderly man. On the next day, we talked to some of those whom he professed to heal. The woman with the lump said it was still there but was pleased that it had not grown larger.

My first clue that W. V. Grant was not all he professed to be came in talking to people who were sitting in wheelchairs on the preacher's extreme left in the auditorium. Casually I began a conversation with a woman who responded freely to my questions. Before the service began officially, I learned that she had arrived on foot

197

before my arrival. Because I was an usher and perhaps because she assumed I was a part of Grant's evangelistic team, she revealed how she was offered a wheelchair *after* her arrival. The wheelchair did not belong to her but to Grant. As I later realized, it served as a prop for his staged production.

The healing service in the auditorium began with considerable singing and band music, then W. V. Grant described how people in other cities where he had preached had stood up from their wheelchairs and miraculously walked. After a brief sermon that served to raise the audience's expectations of miracles, Grant moved up and down the aisles, laying on hands and pretending to have God-given information about his followers. A similar trickster-evangelist, Peter Popoff, actually concealed a small electronic listening device in his ear. From backstage, his wife communicated to him information about certain individuals in the audience. Stepping up to these individuals, Popoff repeated the information to the astounded audience, which seemed to believe that the information came from God in heaven rather than from Mrs. Popoff backstage. Popoff, of course, came across to the audience as a whiz-bang man of God. As Randi later showed, however, Popoff was a charlatan, getting his information through his small electronic receiver. W. V. Grant uses an old mentalist trick without resorting to the electronic device. Randi succeeded in uncovering Grant's method of deceit, too, and discusses it in *The Faith Healers*.

Needless to say, the sincerity of evangelists like Grant and Popoff comes into question. But the question of sincerity is not as simple as some think. To expose fraud and dishonest methods is one thing, to conclude that deceitful evangelists believe little or nothing of what they preach is quite another.

Jim Bakker learned early in his ministry that he did not need all the tricks of illusionists and so-called mind readers to convince his audience to send money. He knew he could perform miracles despite the ease with which the word flowed from his lips. Although he could not raise the dead, he could raise money from the living and thereby keep his organization alive. Unlike some of the more gutsy, old-line Pentecostal faith healers, Jim Bakker's style of healing protects itself in vagueness and hides safely in untestable allusions. Bakker is too shrewd to become definite in his promises to heal.

While all the faith healers profess to believe that nothing is too difficult for the all-powerful God, none of them claims to have a documented case of a real miracle such as causing a new limb to grow in the place of a severed limb. W. V. Grant claims to make short legs grow longer, but it is mostly an expression of his willingness to pull the leg of a gullible audience. Tricks and gimmicks can be learned, but the performance of real, hard-core supernatural miracles is not in the repertory of men like Jim Bakker, Oral Roberts, and W. V. Grant.

When Grant, microphone in hand, walked across the front of the auditorium and stopped in front of the woman I had quietly interviewed earlier, I listened and watched. Would the evangelist actually claim to heal this woman of a handicap she did not have? Would he raise her from the wheelchair that belonged him? I waited and listened to the long dialogue between the preacher and the woman. Grant was a clever manipulator of his audience. The people exploded when he commanded the woman "in the name of Dr. Jesus" to get up out of her wheelchair. Grant had created the impression that she had been confined to the wheelchair for years, and now she was standing on her own two feet. "It's a miracle," someone behind me exclaimed in an awed whisper.

By now, Grant was riding high. He next commanded the woman to walk up the aisle. She complied, praising Jesus all the way. "Run," Grant commanded, and she did, grinning heavenward and conspicuously enjoying her command performance. I could not help but feel compassion for her. She knew she had not been confined to the wheelchair. She knew it was all an act. But at least for one glorious moment she was somebody important—a star. She was happy, and the crowd was ecstatic.

On the following day, Randi and I visited an elderly man who had performed in a similar manner for W. V. Grant. We learned from his landlady that he lived on the second floor of her house and that he regularly walked up and down the stairs. He had never owned a wheelchair. It had all been an act, and he seemed embarrassed at having been found out.

"Faith is a wondrous thing," said novelist Arthur Koestler, who had once been a true-believer in Marxism, "it is not only capable of moving mountains, but also of making you believe that a herring is a race horse."[1] In the auditorium, it was easy to believe in sensational healing miracles and in fish turning into horses, but the next day reality returned—at least until that night's performance.

One conspicuous audience member was a teenage boy in a wheelchair who looked as if he might be the victim of a congenital disease. His head hung to the side and he appeared almost emaciated. It was obvious that this frail, lifeless boy could not possibly walk. While Grant did his act, walking up and down the aisles, he did not approach the boy who had come to the service in his own wheelchair. It became obvious to me that Grant avoided walking up to talk with him during the service. When the service ended, I could not help wondering how the boy's mother felt as she quietly pushed the wheelchair out of the auditorium, taking her afflicted son home in disappointment. All around her, people seemed to have been healed. Why had her son been denied a miracle when the preacher had earlier said that God wants to heal all the afflicted?

Tulsa, Oklahoma, and the farming village of Medjugorje in Southwestern Yugoslavia have something in common; each is said to be the site of a miraculous vision. In Tulsa, Oral Roberts claimed to have seen a 900-foot Jesus who had a message for him and his faithful supporters. The message said in essence that Oral was to continue building his City of Faith. In Medjugorje, six youngsters claimed to have witnessed several appearances of a beautiful woman with blue eyes, black curly hair, and a shiny face. She was, they still insist, "The Blessed Virgin Mary." Her message had nothing to do with Oral's City of Faith or any personal project of a member of the clergy. Rather, the message was simply *"MIR,"* the Serbo-Croatian word for peace. Catholic physicians are already studying almost 300 affirmations of miraculous healings that purport to be connected with the appearances of Mary. The Yugoslav visionaries insist that the Virgin told them that her appearances at Medjugorje would be her last on earth. A number of excited Charismatic Catholics have taken this to mean that the end of the world is near.[2]

The pope's investigative commissions will eventually have to report back to the Vatican and recommend that the Catholic church either give its official seal to the visions or condemn them. This process could take years. An ironic political controversy over the appearances has already begun, with the Croatian Franciscans lining up in support of the visionaries while the local bishop charges that the visionaries are at best hallucinating and at worst lying. As the year A.D. 2000 approaches, Catholics and Protestants will witness among their members a sharp increase in the number of predictions of the Second Coming and the end of the world. Catholics all over the world will be tempted to report visitations from Mary. If the recent appearances in Yugoslavia are labeled as genuine, however, they may be used as a tool to restrain the expected increase in the number of subsequent visits from Mary. Confronted with the official pronouncement that the appearances in Yugoslavia were absolutely the last on earth, all future visionaries face the option of having their own experiences of the Virgin branded counterfeit.

Jimmy Swaggart, who believes that Jesus talks to him, does not believe that the Virgin Mary appears or talks to anyone on earth. His theological frame of reference allows him to come to any of three conclusions regarding the visions in Yugoslavia: they were supernatural phenomena inspired by Satan; they were hallucinations or some form of natural illusion; or nothing in fact happened and the so-called visionaries were lying all along.

Fraud in the miracle-and-faith-healing business is nothing new. Paradoxical as it may seem, intensely religious people are often both the most gullible and the most skeptical on earth. One reason for their skepticism lies in the seemingly endless proliferation of miracles. Not even the most gullible believer could possibly accept as authentic all the alleged miracles around the globe. In order to select some and reject others as genuine miracles, however, some standard for discriminating has to be invoked.

Pentecostal and Charismatic Christians are quite skeptical of claims of miracles mediated by Hindus, Buddhists, and other non-Christian believers. Even though most followers of Islam regard their sacred scripture, the Koran, to be the supreme miracle, most Christians remain unshakably skeptical of the claim. Many fundamentalist Christians believe that while supernatural healing miracles occurred in biblical times, they do not occur today at the hands of faith healers. The claims of miracles made by Jim Bakker, Oral Roberts, and Pat Robertson are met by a wall of skepticism erected by most Christians in America and Europe. Some faith healers angrily charge that the general skepticism that presumably thrives in America has so infected many American Christians that they can no longer recognize a genuine miraculous healing when it stares them in the face. These same faith healers, nevertheless, are often bluntly skeptical of the claims of non-

Christians to heal in the name of their gods.

One Pentecostal preacher told me that the apparent miraculous healings in India and other pagan countries were done by the devil. When I asked why his devil would want to heal anyone, he replied that Satan always likes to imitate what Christ does in order to mislead people and to keep them from finding Christ. Some Pentecostal preachers have become skeptical of rival Pentecostal faith healers.

Charismatics and Pentecostals like Jim and Tammy Bakker use the word "miracle" so frequently that, for many Christians, miracles have become trivialized and commonplace. Millions of people walk across the street every day. Only a few are hit by cars. Is it a miracle when some who are hit do not die? Is it a miracle that millions of people do not get hit in the first place?

The radical Deliverance Theology of Jim Bakker, Oral Roberts, and Pat Robertson comes close to turning God into a genie on call round the clock. By contrast, for conservative folk theology, miracles are never everyday occurrences, but rare rescue measures taken by God during dire emergencies with consequences of sweeping historical significance. For them, a miracle is God's saving grace in rare, colossal emergencies that would certainly end in disaster unless the natural course of events were supernaturally interrupted.

The seed for the idea of miracles is found in the childhood experience of getting into serious trouble and having a parent who intervenes to save the day. Hence, the chief gods have traditionally been called Father or Mother.

It is not an uncommon experience for many Christians and Jews, however, to go through crises and defeats with no belief in any special intervention from heaven. When death unexpectedly strikes a loved one or a tragedy happens without warning, believers ordinarily suffer doubts about the claim that the universe perfectly demonstrates the loving care of divine providence. The need for a miracle in the first place suggests that the Creator's control of events might be less then perfect. Miracles are therefore perceived as God's way of gathering events back under his control. If the longed-for miracle fails to come, disappointment sometimes turns faith into prolonged doubt.

The occurrence of apparent miracles for the benefit of unbelievers or even for the wicked has traditionally been the bitterest pill for believers to swallow. In his brilliant study of the development of theology among the early Hebrews, Dan Jacobson shows how the prophets in particular seemed compelled to revise Hebrew theology more than once in desperate attempts to find some residue of meaning in the stream of disasters that befell "the Chosen People."[3]

The Holocaust, in which over six million Jews were sytematically exterminated by the Nazis, has generated what has been called after-Auschwitz theology. The question of why the God of Israel failed to come to the miraculous rescue of the innocent victims of the Nazi death camps has caused many Jews and Christians to rethink the entire question of miracles. To many, it seems absurd if not obscene to claim that while God miraculously caused $8 million to flow into the coffers of PTL and Heritage USA during the month of May 1987, he refused to intervene on behalf of six million Jews during the 1930s and 1940s.

Adolph Hitler narrowly escaped being assassinated. If there had been only a slight difference in circumstances, the Nazi leader would have been killed by fellow Germans. Was his narrow escape a miracle? If not, what was it? Calvinist Christians do not hesitate to say that God in his providence spared Hitler's life at the time of the attempted assassination because his purpose for Hitler had not yet been fulfilled. God raises up individuals like Hitler, Pharoah, and Judas in order to carry out wickedness and subsequently to suffer damnation—all to the glory of God. Quoting the chilling Romans 9:11–22 passage, Calvinists not only allow but insist that God wills evil to come into existence. By putting a lying spirit into the mouths of his prophets, God caused the prophets to lie (II Chronicles 18:22). Satan is kept alive, according to John Calvin, because he serves as God's minister of wrath, disease, and destruction. God through Satan hardened the heart of the king of Sihon because God had already willed his destruction. The predestined rebellion in the king's heart was therefore merely divine preparation for his final ruin.[4] Calvinists do not hesitate to say that the ultimate reason for the extermination of six million Jews at the hands of the Nazis was God's will. God *wanted* Auschwitz, Buchenwald, and the other death camps. And that is what he got.

In reading the following true story, certain inescapable questions will emerge for theists: Was God in control of all the brutal details that happened? If not, did he lose control? Or did he surrender it? How much control can he give up and still be regarded as Sovereign Lord of the universe?

On Friday the thirteenth, June 1980, an ax murder involving a case of adultery took place less than an hour's drive from my house. It happened close to Southfork, the setting for the "Dallas" TV series. Months after the slaughter of Betty Gore, I sat with my wife at our dining room table and listened to a woman who knew well both Betty Gore and her killer, Candice Montgomery. We listened to the shocking turns in the macabre story. A few years later, the story appeared in a carefully written book under the ironic title *Evidence of Love*. There was lawyer-talk of transferring the trial to Denton, Texas, where it was said a fair trial could be held. My family and I had moved to Denton in 1967, when it was a pleasant little town with a quaint train stop. It was a suitable place to raise kids—except for an occasional murder or rape. I was somewhat relieved to learn that the trial would not come to Denton. My daughter and I had witnessed a similar trial in a downtown courtroom. We had listened to two skillful lawyers defend a mother who had recently pierced her baby's heart with a kitchen knife. The jury decided that the woman was insane at the time. She claimed she had seen a horror film at the theater and had subsequently come to believe she was under the power of a demon telling her to kill her child.

The ax-killing trial would take place in neighboring Collin County. That was close enough as far as I was concerned.

The circumstances of Betty Gore's brutal death caught my attention, nevertheless, because of a seeming inconsistency in the story. As Candy Montgomery's Methodist minister said, "She's a very pleasant, very loving sort of person. She's not capable of committing murder. . . . There's not a person out here who believes for a moment that she's guilty."

The trouble was, Candy was guilty. She drove the ax blade over forty times into the body of a woman whose husband she had known intimately. According to one report, Betty Gore's heart continued to beat while Candy Montgomery delivered most of her blows of fury.

Less than an hour earlier, Candy had been at the Lucas Methodist Church to help her church friends on the last day of Vacation Bible School. Standing before the children, Candy Montgomery appeared to have no plan or scheme to kill anyone. No murderous thoughts tormented her mind. In fact, she told the children a story called "The Three Trees" and led them in prayer. Candy had been the lay delegate from her church at the Methodist Annual Conference in nearby Dallas, where she had first heard the story of "The Three Trees." The children were captivated by the story, which closed with a little moral lesson about God's having a special plan for every individual's life. Candy almost certainly did not believe that God had in his plan for her the brutal slaughter of Betty Gore.

Billy Graham is right about sex. It is like dynamite—or it can be. And who can know what will set off an emotional explosion if sex is connected to the fuse of jealousy? On that Friday the thirteenth during the hottest, most punishing summer in modern Texas history, Candy Montgomery left the church, promising to return shortly after running a few errands. She also needed to drop by Betty Gore's house to pick up a swimsuit for Alisa Gore, Betty's daughter. Alisa planned to spend the night at the Montgomerys' house.

When I was a boy growing up in the South, I used to hear tales of strange and horrible things happening during "dog days." Something happened to Betty Gore during the dog days of 1980, something that made her pick up a curved three-foot ax while she talked to the woman with whom she had sung hymns in the choir at Lucas Methodist Church.

The case of "Tex" Watson also raises questions of divine providence. Only a few miles across the flat prairie land, in Collin County, Charles Denton Watson had grown up to become a local football hero. He attended North Texas State University in Denton, but left without graduating to live in California. It was there that Charles, now called Tex, met Charles Manson and became a member of his murderous circle. Fifteen detectives were searching for Tex in connection with the Manson crimes. When the sheriff of Collin County received word on the phone that his second cousin was wanted for murder, he said, "Charles is living here now. He has an apartment in Denton. I'll bring him in."

It so happened that Tex was living only a few blocks from my office at North Texas State University when he was picked up by his Uncle Maurice and returned to Collin County.

A few years later, this time only a couple of miles from my office, the police gathered up some of the pieces of a woman's body and put them into a bag. A compulsive murderer named Henry Lucas had passed through town and had found another victim. Thanks to the truly competent and outstanding detective work of Phil Ryan,

Henry Lucas was apprehended. Eventually, the suspect confessed to other so-called sex murders.

A few years before these slaughters in and around Denton, Texas, took place, a savage tornado ripped through downtown Lubbock, Texas, and left enough dead people to fill a small cemetery. I can remember a worse tornado plastering Wichita Falls, a few hours' drive west of Denton. The destruction, death, despair, and heart-breaking misery that were created in only a few minutes by the roaring force of nature are still felt. Many people in Wichita Falls will never fully recover emotionally or financially from the devastation.

The question that many sensible theists ask when their lives are touched by horrors such as these is: Did God will this?

"Yes," reply the Calvinists unhesitatingly.

Some Charismatics and Pentecostals think that Satan somehow causes tornados, although they are seldom clear as to how their Satan wrested control from God's hands. Others say God for some inscrutable reason chose to surrender partial control of weather fronts to Satan and his cosmic criminals. When Pat Robertson rebuked the hurricane demons and prayed for God to turn the powerful force away from Virginia Beach, he was in effect urging the Creator to recapture control of weather fronts.

Slowly the logic of the faith healers and Charismatics begins to take shape. Even though diseases are caused by Satan and his vile crew, Holy Ghost-filled believers can often cast out demons if they have the heavenly gift. Diseases overpower people because of unbelief and sin in their lives. The same logic applies to the havoc wrought by tornados and floods. When unbelief and sin in a city get out of control, the invisible shield of righteousness that surrounds the city begins to weaken. This encourages Satan to mount a vicious, raging attack on the citizens. According to Charismatics and many fundamentalists, a host of demons stands ready at every moment to break through the invisible wall of protectiveness encircling a city. When sin begins to flourish among the citizens, the army of demons strikes savagely with tornado, pestilence, or disease. Pat Robertson is convinced that if evangelical and Charismatic Christianity can put their kind into office, the invisible protective shield around the country will be strengthened against the forces of evil.

Folk theology is usually riddled with contradictions or at least unanswered questions that cry out for answers. The Charismatic and

Pentecostal theology of the Bakkers and the Swaggarts is in many ways a return to pre-scientific animism, which populates the universe with spirits everywhere. Everything that happens in the universe is, furthermore, said to be the product of supernatural beings—good and evil—working sometimes through earthly mortals. The Pentecostal's God has his hands full trying to keep Satan and his army from turning his heaven-bound parade into a bloody free-for-all. In the final analysis, the real troublemaker is mankind. Earthquakes, diseases, droughts, floods, horrible accidents—these phenomena would not even exist on earth were it not for sinful human beings. According to most Pentecostals and Charismatics, there were no mosquitoes or poisonous spiders in the Garden until Adam and Eve rebelled. In short, the human species has come close to turning God's whole plan into a debacle. In fact, Charismatic/Pentecostal theology maintains that mankind ruined most of God's plan because most people will end up in hell, which is not what the Creator originally planned.

By contrast, modern Christian followers of John Calvin do not flinch when they say confidently that God is in absolute and full control of every detail and that everything is developing precisely on schedule as God originally intended. Nothing that has happened on earth or that is happening now is anything other than what God wanted it to be. One modern follower of John Calvin sums it up: "I wish very frankly and pointedly to assert that if a man gets drunk and shoots his family, it was the will of God that he should do so."[5] Since God wanted Candice Montgomery to ax Betty Gore to death, he arranged all the circumstances to bring the foul deed about.

The Calvinists say that either God is running things or he is not running them. If he is, then he has to be in charge of every detail. He has to be the cause of everything, including tornados and volcanic eruptions. Suffering, disease, retardation, murder, and bitter jealousy are all part of this world. And God knowingly caused all evils to come about. He created men and women to commit atrocities so that the atrocities would come about. After all, God has a place for atrocities in his plan. Everything, say the Calvinists, fits into God's overall plan and therefore everything is precisely as God intended. Since he is all-knowing and all-powerful, there are no flaws in his plan or its execution. If he had wanted a different version of the world—with no Hitler, Judas, cancer, AIDS, all other diseases, poverty, moral corruption, jealously, or murder—God could have made that world instead of this world. But God created what does in fact exist because it is precisely what he wanted down to the last detail. To say anything short of that, the Calvinists insist, is to deny the Creator's sovereignty. "Every detail of history was eternally in his plan before the world began; and he willed it to come to pass."⁶ God wanted drought and massive starvation in Africa, and that is what he got. He wanted a new hospital built in Tulsa, Oklahoma, and that is what he got. God wanted the vibrant forty-one-year-old mother to suffer and die. Consequently, she died slowly under the attack of cancer cells, which carried on precisely as God desired and directed.

Jim and Tammy Bakker are among the champions of the radical folk theology that shakes its fist in the face of Calvinism. Passionately, Jim Bakker and other folk theologians denounce as coldblooded the Calvinists who smugly say, "Yes, of course, God could heal everyone today if he wanted to, but he doesn't want to." In the sixteenth century, John Calvin himself had already said that while God could have caused everyone to go to heaven, he chose to send great hordes to eternal damnation. Why? Because it pleased him to do so. God simply did not want everyone saved. In fact, said later Calvinists, God actually wanted and predestined a great number to suffer everlasting torment in hell. This icy doctrine of predestination so horrified and infuriated John Wesley in the eighteenth century that he unleashed a scathing verbal attack against it, charging that it represented "the Most High . . . as more cruel, false, and unjust than the devil."⁷ By contrast, the American Calvinist Jonathan Edwards said he found warmth and comfort in the doctrine.

Although Wesley desperately desired to get the Creator off the hook, he failed. He had already walked too far down the road with Calvinism before turning away from it. Like John Calvin, he had come to believe that perhaps most of the human race will end up forever damned to hell. Unlike Calvin and Edwards, Wesley could never bring himself to believe that God actually *desired* such a macabre and horrendous outcome. Hence, in order not to blame the all-powerful God for the wretched outcome, Wesley chose to dump all the blame onto the human species. Having branded as absurd the Calvinists' claim that God desired that hordes of his creatures suffer endless and hopeless torment forever, Wesley leaped to the equally absurd conclusion that the people who go to hell to suffer endlessly do so because they *earnestly desired* to be in hell forever.

Today, the proponents of the Gospel of Health and Wealth throw down the gauntlet by asking Christendom a seemingly innocent question that turns out to be anything but innocent: Does the all-powerful Creator of the universe *want* his children to be deprived of their physical and mental health? With this one simple question Jim Bakker, Oral Roberts, and Pat Robertson thrust upon Christians outside their camp an agonizingly severe dilemma that Christians for centuries have tried to put out of sight. The question, like the insane wife in *Jane Eyre,* was locked away in the attic. But the faith healers have now brought it out into the sunlight with a vengeance, not aware that in doing so they compel Christianity once again to face the old and unnerving dilemma with which it has been cursed for centuries but which it has never been able to resolve.

Voltaire, the French skeptic of Wesley's time, wrote a biting satire, *Candide,* to expose what he took to be the cruelties and absurdities entailed in this dilemma. Rabbi Harold S. Kushner has come to see clearly that Jews who believe that a loving Creator governs the universe are cursed by the same dilemma. His 1981 book *When Bad Things Happen to Good People*[8] became a best seller largely because many thinking Christians and Jews who believe in divine Providence were searching for plausible answers to tough questions posed by the ancient dilemma. While speaking of a loving Creator who rules the universe, morally sensitive Jews and Christians keep discovering widespread suffering imposed by the seemingly impersonal forces of nature and cruelties imposed by some human beings on others around the globe.

TV evangelist John Ankerberg, of Chattanooga, invited Rabbi Kushner to be a guest on his show. They discussed the infamous dilemma of why there exists so much suffering in a world that is supposed to be governed by an all-powerful and loving Creator. Disagreeing with the rabbi's answers, Ankerberg brought in a Falwell-type fundamentalist theologian who tried to set the rabbi straight. In the process, the fundamentalist succeeded in turning the dilemma into a hopeless muddle.

Unwilling to blame themselves or their God, faith healers instead blame the victims for their disease and misfortune. "Don't blame God for your failure," Jim Bakker writes. "He's given you all you need to be a winner."[9] The cruelty of so-called faith healers is twofold. First, despite their claims, they do not serve as agents of supernatural cures but simply take the easy cases and ignore the difficult ones. Second, they often lay an additional burden upon those who are truly afflicted and diseased. In addition to suffering their infirmity, the unhealed are frequently made to feel that they have been denied the heaven-promised healing because their faith is weak. Not only do they feel physically inferior, they come to feel spiritually and morally inferior. "Rarely does sickness glorify God," Oral Roberts writes. Sickness is the rare exception. The rule is full health. If there is sickness, Oral explains, it is because barriers exists between the sufferer and God.[10] God did not erect the barriers, both Oral Roberts and Jim Bakker agree. In Jim's words, God has already given us the key to victory. "He has defeated our foe, Satan, the enemy of our soul. . . . God has already done all He can do for us until we begin to take action on our own!"[11] The conclusion is inescapable. As a rule, where there is sickness, the patient is spiritually at fault and has erected barriers. God wants to heal every disease, but the patients block their own healing. Oral and Jim do their best. So, the blame inevitably falls on the afflicted. Jim Bakker has it reduced to a simple formula: "There are certain principles in the Bible so powerful that putting them into practice will literally guarantee success."[12] The poor and the afflicted are judged as having failed to apply the biblical principles. The logic of this view is that if the citizens on the streets and in the gutters of Calcutta, India, were to convert to Christianity and start living by biblical principles, including sending seed-faith money to someone like Oral or Jim, they would rise up out of their poverty and their withered limbs would be made whole. As long as they remain non-Christians, however, and fail to sew seed-faith money, they get only what they deserve.

Pentecostals and Charismatics tend to turn the entire universe into something of a morality play. If anything bad happens to anyone, Pentecostals seem driven to believe that someone has to be blamed. Pentecostals insist that even though there are hostile forces in the world that are out to destroy or corrupt people, God provides defenses for those who make a moral commitment to Christ as the true Messiah and turn to him for protection.

Bailey Smith, one of Jerry Falwell's appointees to the new and now defunct PTL board, said in public in 1980 that Almighty God does not hear the prayer of a Jew. Despite criticism, even from some of his fellow Southern Baptists, Smith reaffirmed his stand in St. Louis in 1987. "Unless they [the Jewish people] repent and get born again, they don't have a prayer."[13] Jimmy Swaggart appropriated

Smith's premises for his own statement about Jews perishing in the Holocaust because they were not Christians.[14]

The question of sincerity eventually emerges when the faith-healing business is explored in depth. As suggested earlier, it is too simple to say that if faith healers practice deceit and fraud, they do not believe what they preach. G. H. Montgomery, one of the most prominent Pentecostal leaders of the 1950s, believed in faith healing and at the same time pointed out yawning gaps between certain faith healers' preaching and their lifestyles. With an insider's instinct for the jugular, he cited in addition the exaggerated claims of the evangelists and raised the key question of fraudulent miracles. He charged that many of his fellow Pentecostal preachers had padded their reports of healings and conversions in the attempt to look better than their competition. Because their audiences would not "pay big money for straight honest work," Montgomery wrote, the evangelists resorted to "great swelling words" as they embraced the principle of "the bigger the report, the bigger the collections." Condemning what he called dishonest psychology and gimmicks to make merchandise of the people, he listed twenty-three distinct commodities hawked by various evangelists—including drops of water from the River Jordan and pieces from a noted evangelist's tent.[15] W. V. Grant offered his financial supporters a little relic made out of wood from the Holy Land.

Oral Roberts and G. H. Montgomery were close friends for years. For nearly a decade he served as editor of Oral's magazine. Before that, he edited the magazine of the Pentecostal Holiness Church. In 1961, however, he and Oral had a bitter quarrel and broke off their friendship, Montgomery later threatening to release a file that would discredit Oral. In an article entitled "A Lying Spirit in the Mouth of the Prophets," he called attention to the fact that for a two-year period the evangelists reported over three million converts in Jamaica, which had a population of only a little more than half that number. Pulling no punches "to illustrate the lying practices of men who pad their reports to get gain and glory," Montgomery unleashed the fullness of his moral outrage against the alarming rise of deceit among those who professed the Pentecostal faith:

> Some of these evangelists reported that literally hundreds of
> deaf people were healed and received their hearing in Jamaica

meetings. Now, it so happens that we have a missionary daughter in Jamaica who works exclusively with deaf people. In five years of work with these people, neither she nor her colleagues have ever found so much as one person who was healed of total deafness.[16]

The above admission, coming as it does from a believer in faith healing, deserves to be treated with respect. What Montgomery did not clearly see, however, was that the faith-healing business by its very nature breeds exaggeration, deception, and fraud. What begins in deception will, when turned into a business, end in fraud and exploitation.

Assemblies of God faith healer Jack Coe provided perhaps one of the most fascinating and tragic examples of how complex and complicated human nature can be and how an evangelist's sincerity can be severely tested. In my opinion Coe practiced great deception and yet mingled his deception with earnestness and sincerity. Without question, Jack Coe was one of the most audacious of the faith healers in America. He played brilliantly to the crowd, with claims to miracles more daring and extreme than those of his colleagues.

He was for years one of the old-line faith healers who thought that going to a physician for treatment showed a lack of faith or a poor relationship with God. Eventually, he was brought to trial in Florida on the charge of practicing medicine without a license. Always preaching frenetically and thriving on controversy, he did not hesitate to warn that those who openly opposed his work stood in danger of being struck dead. Fiercely competitive and self-assured, this big, heavy-set man looked upon himself as the world-champion healer. While denying that he was in competition with Oral Roberts and other faith healers, he never tired of boasting that he owned the biggest tent in the world, larger than Ringling Brothers'. Some people said he put on a better show than the Ringling Brothers as well.

Like Jim Bakker, Jack Coe came under fire from his fellow Assemblies of God ministers. When his ordination was revoked, never to be restored, Coe elected to go his own way. In 1954 he completed building the Dallas Revival Center. Within two years it was one of the largest churches in Dallas, a city known for its huge churches.

In 1956 the Florida court case against Coe was dismissed after a two-day trial. In December of that same year, however, a disease attacked the flamboyant Coe and did to him what his opponents could not do in court. Critically ill, he finally gave his pleading wife permission to take him to a hospital despite the fact that for years he had denounced doctors and hospitals as agents of unbelief.

The tests at the hospital revealed that the faith healer had been stricken with polio at the young age of thirty-eight. This news was perhaps the greatest trauma in the history of faith healing. A friend wrote of Coe in the hospital: "He is unconscious part of the time, but occasionally he rallies and makes known some desires. He cannot speak . . . but we know God can and *will* deliver him."[17]

Despite all the prayers and bold prophecies of his recovery, Jack Coe died early in 1957. Evangelist O. L. Jaggers scolded Mrs. Coe for failing to call him to Jack's side. The doctors had quarantined Coe. Undaunted, Jaggers insisted that he could have raised Coe from the dead if only Mrs. Coe had requested his aid.[18]

After researching the faith-healing claims of modern Charismatics and Pentecostals, I found it impossible to limit to only a few succinct pages the subject of the sincerity of faith healers. The following comments will serve as a brief summary of my conclusions.

First, it is a disconcerting paradox that our human propensity for embracing delusions actually increases our ability to remain sincere. When opponents detect a fundamental inconsistency or severe weakness in the claims we make, they are tempted to regard us as insincere or hypocritical if we persist in our claims. In reality, however, we might not see the inconsistency. Or if we do see it, we might have an explanation that purports to resolve it. If our opponents think our explanation is flimsy, they will be tempted to regard our insincerity to be so deeply entrenched as to be perverse. In order to avoid concluding that we are insincere or hypocritical, they must come to believe that we are simply *deluded* about the power of our explanation.

Second, under certain conditions, lying itself can be done sincerely. It is quite likely that some faith healers know that they often lie to deceive their supporters. They can remain sincere, however, if they are committed to a goal that they regard to be sufficiently high in value to justify the lies and the fraud.

Jerry Falwell apparently thought Jim Bakker's goal of building the Towers Hotel failed to justify his deceptive practices in raising money, especially since Bakker apparently was committed to the less-than-worthy goal of making himself exceedingly wealthy. At the same time, however, Falwell had nothing but praise for Lt. Col. Oliver North after the Iran-Contra hearings. Falwell called him a hero and offered him a job at Liberty University in Virginia, despite the fact that North practiced deceit and told a long series of lies, including some to Congress.

Jimmy Swaggart told interviewer Larry King in August 1987 that Oliver North was a man of "honesty and integrity." It seems that both Falwell and Swaggart hold that a Christian like North might justifiably lie if he thinks his lies are an essential part of his chosen profession in national defense. In short, Christians may sincerely become professional liars in some situations. This raises the question of whether prostitutes or professional killers can also be sincere in service of a higher cause.

Ironically, the author of I Timothy 1:10 places liars and perjurers in the same group as sexual perverts and sodomites. Again ironically, the biblical passage that Swaggart bends over backward to interpret as a condemnation of oral sex between husband and wife condemns deceit in the plainest language and offers no exceptions or exemptions (Romans 1:24–32).

Apparently, Falwell believes that lies and deceptions are justifiable only if carried out for a higher cause. Thou shalt not bear false witness except for a high and holy purpose. He certainly holds that killing for a higher purpose is sometimes justifiable. He has not made it clear, however, whether he thinks a woman could justifiably commit fornication or oral sex as a CIA covert agent assigned to steal critical documents from the Soviets. In order to be effective in undercover activities in the line of duty, the patriotic agent must practice deceit, other questionable acts, and numerous forms of insincerity. (Esther in the Hebrew Bible practiced both deceit and adultery in order to save her people.) Paradoxically, an agent in the line of duty may *sincerely* engage in numerous acts of insincerity. Lower purposes or goals may be justifiably subverted through deceit only if done in service of higher goals or purposes.

Regarding sincerity, the big question about faith healers can be stated in this way: Are they aware that they are making outlandish promises that do not come close to being fulfilled? This question is not always easy to answer. If the faith healers are not aware of the gap, they might be regarded as sincere. But, in this case, their sincerity might itself signify a more severe character flaw. If a faith healer engages in numerous acts of deceit, it is important to uncover his higher goals and purposes. They might turn out to be high in his estimation but low in the eyes of others. The collapse of character comes when deceit is no longer perceived as needing justification even in one's own eyes.

In many respects, the phenomenon of faith healing is the very opposite of science. In science, the existence of an apparent contradiction in a theory suggests that something might be wrong with the theory. Various ways of dealing with the contradictions are activated. Eventually, however, if enough severe contradictions pile up against a theory, science begins to generate a revision of the theory. If this fails to work, a substitute theory emerges. This process of revising and replacing the prized theory may take years or decades, but it is absolutely essential to the growth of scientific knowledge. In fact, scientists often attack a theory in order to expose its weaknesses. This is why science has over the centuries witnessed the death of many old theories and the birth of new ones.

In the faith-healing process, the situation is quite reversed. Very little reward comes to the preacher who openly admits to contradictions in the faith-healing theory that God not only can heal all sickness on earth, but would cure them instantly if only the diseased would remove the barriers that prevent healing.

Whereas in science the goal is to press the theory for all it is worth and to create a better theory if possible, in faith-healing circles the goal is to keep the theory (i.e., the central belief) intact and protect it against all open criticism. Every attempt to expose a contradiction in the central belief is denounced as skepticism, unbelief, or something worse. The professed concern is that the central theory itself not be changed. The change that is permitted and even encouraged is a change in the people themselves. To be more precise, the assigned role of the faith healer is to generate not a better theory, but more faith in it among the people. The evangelist's publicly acknowledged role is to call attention to flaws in the people, not in the central theory. It is not the theory that is tested, but the people's faith. Faith healers insist that the lack of faith is a barrier and that the possession of faith tears down the barriers that deny the diseased and afflicted their promised healing.

Faith is a synonym for "right relationship with God." The catch comes in defining faith in concrete, practical terms. If it is a purely private, subjective feeling, it has no common meaning that the evangelist and his audience can agree on. Jim Bakker and Oral Roberts succeeded in convincing a large portion of their TV audience to label and accept money as an exemplification of faith. Every month the viewers send money or pledges as seed-faith. Jim and Oral have convinced their followers that by doing this they help break down barriers that prevent God's promised health and wealth from coming into their lives. "And remember," Jim Bakker says, "that the single most important item on your budget is the tithe. . . . If you are faithful to give the first fruits of your income to God, He has promised to *open you the windows of heaven, and pour you out a blessing, that there shall not be room enough to receive it* (Malachi 3:13)."[19]

There is no supernatural miracle in any of this. Faith for Jim and Oral is largely a TV and mail-order business. Its denominations are tens, twenties, and hundreds. Bankers are the ministering angels. The money sent in is not a sign of faith, it *is* faith. It is not the whole of faith, but it is the part that keeps the machines and computers of the faith-healing business moving. Stated in simple English, from the viewpoint of Jim and Oral, healing does not come free of charge. It comes only with faith, and money sent to Jim and Oral is the hard currency of faith.

According to the teaching of Jim and Oral, God does not collect faith directly from people. He has appointed collecting agents who receive the seed-money on God's behalf. The money never goes directly to God. Agents like Jim and Oral invest it and use it, they claim, both on God's behalf and on the contributors' behalf. Apparently, in the case of Jim and Oral, God has given considerable discretionary power to his agents in the use of his money.

Given this way of looking at faith, people have a right to know what to expect to receive for their seed-money. Oral sometimes replies, "Something good is going to happen to you."

Is there anything more definite?

One point can be made with crystal clarity. When the TV viewers send in their checks, something really good is going to happen to Oral Roberts, his wife Evelyn, and their son Richard. Jim Bakker promised his supporters that the windows of heaven would open and blessings would pour out if they planted seed-faith in an envelope and mailed it. The *Charlotte Observer* has been recording faithfully

over the years the good material blessings coming to the Bakkers—
the finest clothes, expensive houses, top-of-the-line cars, costly trips
abroad, and enough pocket change to keep Tammy from being
embarrassed at the checkout line.

It is fair to ask what the paying customers received for their
money. The Bakkers have no records of helping totally blind people
to gain their sight, amputees to grow limbs, or Kevin either to grow
longer than twenty-nine inches or to stand up and walk. Science
keeps careful records, which helps to monitor flaws in the major
theories. Records are also important in medicine. If there are any
records more shoddily kept than the Bakkers' financial records,
however, they are the records of their reported healings. Indeed, a
careful scrutiny of the Bakkers' messages over the years suggests that
Jim and Tammy phased out supernatural faith healing except in the
most general and untestable terms.

On June 25, 1987, at a Charismatic Bible Ministries Conference,
Oral Roberts mentioned that he had once raised an infant from the
dead. Later, he explained that it looked dead to him, although now
he is not sure, since there are various medical definitions of death.
There is, however, another case of an infant's dying that Oral does
not invoke as a testimonial. It happened on his home territory at Oral
Roberts University. One of the faculty members and his wife watched
their baby grow ill. Taking seriously some of the Deliverance Theology
that speaks of God's willingness to heal everyone on earth, the faculty
member prayed for the child rather than taking it to the hospital. When
the baby died, the couple began praying and fasting to bring the baby
to life. They requested Oral's presence to pray for the dead child in
their home. One of the university's vice-presidents responded as follows
to the request: "[Oral] wouldn't touch that with a ten-foot pole. That
dead baby was in their home for three days before I could get a doctor
in there and get the baby out of the house. A story like that would
ruin Oral. The press would crucify him."[20]

Why would the press crucify an evangelist for bringing a child
to life after it had been dead for three days? The answer is that
it wouldn't. But the spokesman and Oral knew better than to take
this clear, unambiguous test case. They knew the baby would not
come back to life. Recently, Richard Roberts was quoted as saying,
"There are probably dozens and dozens of documented instances of
people who have been raised from the dead." Richard presented no

documented cases, especially of people who have been incontrovertibly dead for two or three days. Richard Roberts's claims seem to thrive best in a cloud of ambiguity and equivocation.

According to John 11:44, Jesus raised Lazarus after he had been dead in the tomb for four days, so dead that his sister Martha was reluctant to open the tomb-cave for fear there would be a foul odor. Oral Roberts has never claimed to raise anyone who has been dead for four days even though according to John 14:12, Jesus said to his disciples, "Truly, truly I say to you, he who believes in me will also do the works that I do; and greater works than these will he do . . ." (RSV).

"Be like Jesus," Oral urges his ORU students. According to Luke 8, Jesus brought a girl back to life; and according to Acts 9, the apostle Peter is said to have raised the kindly Tabitha from death. But Oral Roberts did not even try to bring to life the baby of his own faculty members. Why? For the same reason he does not part the Gulf of Mexico or perform any other supernatural miracles. He cannot pull them off. Knowing he could not heal the afflicted teenage boy who had come to the service in his own wheelchair, W. V. Grant did not walk down the aisle and try to become the agent of a real supernatural miracle.

If Jim Bakker, Oral Roberts, W. V. Grant, or Pat Robertson had raised even one person to life after he or she had been dead for several days, the public would never cease hearing about it. The event would be written up by the evangelist himself and millions upon millions of copies of such a book would sell. The evangelist would simply not let his audience forget that he had been the instrument of a genuine, publicly witnessed resurrection. Today, no one is going to find these so-called faith healers visiting cemeteries for the purpose of bringing someone's child or parent back to life. They can raise dollars by the millions each year, and that is no miracle. But they cannot raise one truly dead body from the grave, and they know it.

In the 1960s, when the Bakkers were still at CBN, pretty, six-year-old Susie became a regular part of the "Jim and Tammy Show" audience. The Bakkers' hearts sank when they received the news that healthy-looking Susie had just died in her father's arms on the way to the hospital. A friend of the parents phoned to say that Susie was a hemophiliac. It apparently never occurred to the Bakkers to drive to the hospital and attempt to bring the child back from the dead.[21]

The burning question remains: Did God want little Susie to die at the age of six? Only a Calvinist could answer yes. The Pentecostals and Charismatics insist that God wanted her to live a full life. She didn't. Why? Deliverance Theology insists that someone is to *blame*. As if the death of a child does not create enough suffering, Deliverance Theology tends to add the pain of *guilt*. There is clearly a cruel side to this Charismatic folk theology.

A tragic case in which the world of make-believe miracles collided with the real world happened on Wednesday, January 7, 1987, in the Southern Louisiana town of Jeanerette, near Jimmy Swaggart's home. Eight-year-old Takietha Phillips suffered from Down's Syndrome. Her mother and other residents of Jeanerette believed that the little girl was possessed by demons that had caused the disease. An exorcist squeezed the child's neck repeatedly while assistants held her down. According to District Judge Richard Haik, who presided at the arraignment, this was an effort "to remove the demons from the child's body and make her normal." The exorcist succeeded not in curing the disease, but tragically in strangling the girl to death.[22]

The following is an observer's report of a blind girl attending one of Aimee Semple McPherson's healing services. No comment is necessary.

A little girl wore a pair of glasses, one-half of which was entirely black. I gathered that she was totally blind in one eye and almost blind in the other. I sat upon the stage very close to the whole procedure. While prayer was being made for her, the little girl, who appeared to be about 11 years of age, wept and sobbed and writhed in her eagerness to secure the help that she had been led to expect. She left the platform and public claim was made by one of the workers that she had been healed, and the little girl verified the claim by a nod of the head given in reply to the question of the workers. An hour later, when the meeting was out, I noticed a small cluster of women near the platform. I thought I saw the blind little girl in their midst, so I asked my wife to go over and investigate and talk to her if necessary. She found the erstwhile "cured" girl flat on her face on the floor, sobbing, with shattered hopes and a breaking heart. Her disappointment was complete, and so was her disillusionment. The improved

sight that she seemed to have had in the midst of the excitement
on the platform had disappeared, and with it the hope of
the little girl.[23]

It would be inaccurate to conclude that evangelists' customers
receive nothing for their money. They receive what they would normally
get if they took their checkbooks and flew to Las Vegas for a few
days. They are entertained. In the highly emotional healing services
that transform the entire auditorium or big tent into a vast stage
on which everyone has a role to play, the entertainment is usually
at the expense of the truly afflicted and diseased. Those who take
on only a temporary role of illness (i.e., fake a disease for the sake
of the performance) gain a great deal of attention and become for
one brief, shining moment a star in the theatrical production. Unlike
the big tent or the auditorium, the television tends to be a cool medium, which loses much emotional intensity. Consequently, the TV
viewers become more like entertained spectators than actors on the
stage or set. If one of the Bakkers' customers mailed in $30 each
month for a year, she would spend less money on the Bakkers'
entertainment than many people spend on a trip to Las Vegas.
    In many ways Jim Bakker understood early in his ministry that
he would become a TV entertainer. In the mid-sixties, about the
time that Oral Roberts was thinking more of a TV musical show
than healing services, Jim Bakker shouted to Tammy, who was in
the kitchen of their second trailer: "Why can't Christians have talk
shows, too?"
    Tammy came to the doorway. "What are you talking about?"
    Jim pointed to the TV set. "For years I've been coming home
from meetings at night when these shows are on with movie stars
talking about their latest love affairs."[24]
    Without apology, Jim deliberately set out to offer his audience
a grand dose of entertainment, beginning with the children's show.
Throughout his entire ministry he moved steadily in this direction.
Ironically, he could have had more than enough support from his
followers if he had been perfectly up-front with them. Furthermore,
he could have become fabulously rich without having to either juggle
figures or break the law. The point is that Pentecostals, Charismatics,
and many other types of Christians are more than eager to pay for
what they regard to be Christian entertainment mingled with a little

preaching and even indoctrination. The market was there and still is. The Bakkers did not create the demand; they supplied it.

The appeal of old-line faith healing on TV is limited, especially if the evangelists become so specific that they make claims that can be carefully documented or tested. Oral Roberts has discovered that it is safer to promise psychological and spiritual healing, the kind that swims in ambiguity and vagueness.

Healing bank accounts has become the TV Charismatics' new fad. Healing broken marriages is also popular. Encouraging people to find better jobs or to feel better emotionally about themselves are all a part of the new healing. Jim Bakker very frankly reveals that he borrows from secular success motivation seminars.[25] Many TV evangelists' shows have begun to resemble Power of Positive Thinking rallies, salespersons' pep talks, and get-ahead success videos.

In short, the old-line supernatural healing claims have definite limitations on TV for the simple reason that the faith-healing evangelist cannot do anything more than what the secular pop psychologist or the everyday, hard-working preacher of inspiration can do. Miracles have become a dime a dozen, every Charismatic preacher claiming to be a worker of supernatural wonders but none producing a healing that an inspirational non-Charismatic minister or an atheist doctor or counselor cannot duplicate.

PART VII:

The News Media and Televangelism's Future

18

PTL Versus the
Charlotte Observer

An entire book could be written on the twelve-year war of
words between PTL and the *Charlotte Observer*. In fact,
it was more than a confrontation of words. On November
8, 1984, PTL President Jim Bakker and *Observer* publisher Rolfe
Neill met like two heads of state trying to learn more about each
other. The meeting took place on PTL territory, in a private mirrored
dining room.

Bakker informed Neill that PTL had hired a private detective
to follow and investigate him. It might seem odd that an organization
professing the Golden Rule would hire a detective, but Jim Bakker's
idea may have come from the eye-for-an-eye principle: "If you
investigate and shadow us, we will investigate and shadow you." In
his excellent report on the struggle between PTL and the *Charlotte
Observer,* Charles Storch of the *Chicago Tribune* (August 23 and
24, 1987), raised the question of newspaper bias. He also pointed
out that in retaliation for coming under perpetual investigation, Jim
Bakker waged his own TV campaign against the newspaper in April
1986. The campaign had its own title: "Enough is Enough!" On
television, Bakker promised that a book would be written to document in detail the bias and smear tactics that, he charged, the *Charlotte Observer* had employed. The title of the book had even been
selected: *Anatomy of a Smear.*

The book was never published and Bakker did not make clear
whether it was completed. Don Hardister, who was Bakker's bodyguard, went so far as to shadow both the editor and the publisher

of the Charlotte newspaper and to prepare a dossier on them. Later, in the summer of 1987, Hardister told the *Chicago Tribune* that he failed to find damaging material or documents that PTL could use against them.

The question must be raised regarding newspaper bias throughout the long battle between PTL and the *Charlotte Observer*. When examined from one angle, the war was not so much a confrontation of personalities as a confrontation of institutions. The newspaper represented a conservative, traditional style of communication in the Charlotte community. Bakker's television station represented a radical style of communication thrusting itself into the Charlotte establishment. In some ways, the newspaper and the TV station were and are natural enemies, or at least opponents.

The *Charlotte Observer* was, therefore, not without profound self-interest in its investigation of PTL, a self-interest which it protected uncompromisingly. The stakes were extremely high because the TV station and the newspaper were institutions not only of communication but of influence and power. To say that the newspaper was biased in favor of securing its own influence is not to say, however, that it was unfair in its treatment of PTL. If being unbiased is a requirement of fairness, then there exists no fairness in any human activity, a conclusion that might seem to some to be unwarranted.

To assert that the Charlotte newspaper acted out of self-interest without compromise is not to imply that it did so irrespective of the cost. It maintained itself as an investigative newspaper and did not become a scandal sheet of the kind to be found in supermarkets.

Looking back over the years, the publisher of the newspaper, Rolfe Neill, charged that some of his own staff had come off "very smugly" in the January 1986 series of articles about the FCC files on PTL. He charged further that his newspaper had a told-you-so tone. Not all of the newspaper staff would agree with this, however. What Neill may have overlooked was the fact that it was the *Charlotte Observer* and not the FCC who kept after the story. As the newspaper's metropolitan editor Ken Friedlein pointed out, since no government agency regularly watches over the shoulder of the big business of TV evangelism, it is not only the option but the duty of the local newspapers to keep the vigil. The FCC was inexcusably lax in reporting its investigation, and editor Rich Oppel was perfectly justified in reporting that it was the *Charlotte Observer* and not the FCC who had carried out its responsibility, sometimes in the face of organized opposition.

My own criticism of the *Charlotte Observer* is not that it was persistent and uncompromising, but that it has not gone further into investigating the claims of faith healers. It might be that newspapers are reluctant to move in this direction because they are nervous about probing into people's religious beliefs and claims. Or it might ʰ⸱ that they are reluctant because investigative reporting of this type is ᵤⱼyond the skill and training of their current staff members. In the future, a bold and daring newspaper editor and publisher will perhaps develop the conviction that the faith-healing enterprise needs investigating in an uncompromising pursuit for truth (or "facts," as newspeople are prone to say). If such an editor and a publisher become so convinced, then perhaps they will see the wisdom of employing a James Randi to teach a few of the newspaper's investigative staff some techniques for exposing fraudulant faith healers.

Newspeople usually do not like to admit that their treatment of religion is biased. When some of them attempt to deny their biases, they usually succeed in revealing them all the more. Some editors appear chagrined when questioned about the topic. They know they have been found out and seem embarrassed, as if having a bias were in the same category as misappropriating funds. Other newspeople seem to look upon bias as something like lusting for their neighbor's spouse. It is a weakness, they confess, and they wish they could rise above it. It is not a topic they enjoy talking about in public.

By contrast, other newspeople take the easy way out. They say, in effect, that to keep any bias they have from showing through they are entitled to treat the subject superficially.

The popular TV series "Lou Grant" was about a newspaper staff and the problems they encountered in getting the news out. It was a running joke in the series that an assignment to report religion was a low-status job. The not-too-subtle bias behind the joke was that religion is neither exciting nor important. It is a cliché among many newspeople that religion is wholly a private matter between the believer and God, that is, the *alleged* God. After all, neither the news photographers nor the TV camera crews have ever succeeded in getting a close-up of God. The other side of the moon finally became newsworthy when satellites photographed it. Apparently, if there is nothing materially observable about God, he is not a news event.

Some newspeople will insist with Cub Scout innocence that they write from a *neutral* point of view, which they imagine to be synonymous with objectivity. Many are uncomfortable about this boast. A twinge of guilt suggests that they are not yet cleansed from the "stain" of their own biases. There is even the fear of being exposed.

Almost comically some reporters indicate a need to go through a purification rite that will purge them of their strong biases so that they may become pure-hearted news investigators. Too honest to deceive themselves into thinking they have succeeded in the purge, however, they try what they think is the next best process. If they cannot wash away all their strong biases in the baptism of neutrality, they can perhaps transform them into weak biases. They can be cool. Detached. Disinterested. Passionless.

The fact is that members of the news media do not go to church as frequently as most Americans and are not as interested in religion, or at least the standard organizations of religion, as most Americans. Confusing indifference with objectivity, some point out that it is difficult to do news reports on religious topics because there is so much diversity of conviction among believers. This explanation will not do, however, because despite the fact that politics contains a staggering diversity of conviction, political topics dominate the news.

In the past, newspeople tended as a group to be so poorly trained in the field of religion that they knew they would embarrass themselves if they tried to write with any depth about the topic. If sportswriters were as naive, ill-informed, and high-handed as some of the reporters who dabble in religious topics, they would be drummed out of the business with ridicule. Fortunately, a number of newspapers in particular have appointed to their staffs men and women who have studied intensively the field of religion (e.g., Thomas Morton of *Beaumont Enterprise*).

Some naive reporters think that if they are not "contaminated" by any particular religion, they will be more objective, as if having no prior convictions on the subject is a virture or advantage. They go so far as to believe that to be *dis*interested investigators they must be *un*interested in the subject matter. If they looked carefully at sportswriters, however, they would see that those who excel in their work are passionately interested in the game. A staff writer who did not care deeply about his field of investigation would have little motivation to probe.

If there is an area that is treated with less respect than religion in the newspaper business it is science. News journalists tend to be in a state of intellectual poverty regarding science, making little distinction between science and technology. Their newspapers reflect this poverty. With some outstanding exceptions, the journalistic art of making scientific and theological news interesting is not in the repertory of most of the nation's news rooms. Articles on Shirley Maclaine's latest balmy excursions into Woo-Woo Land are easier to write, requiring minimum discipline and no scientific training at all. The argument that stories on Shirley and on Nostradamus sell copy is the same argument used by *National Enquirer* in reporting the bizarre and the zany.

As Cecile White of the *Houston Chronicle* pointed out, editors and their staff writers sometimes work under almost unmanageable pressure. The added nagging feeling that they are not living up to the standard of intellectual neutrality does not help them become better newspeople, especially since neutrality is not so much an ideal as a mirage. The quest for a pure heart free of biases is a holiness trip that is misconceived from the start. It seems obvious that many in the news-gathering business take their model from the seventeenth-century philosopher John Locke, who imagined that the mind in its flawless state was an innocent, uncontaminated blank tablet. Locke's followers went further to suppose that intellectual integrity meant keeping all biases locked out and letting in nothing but facts unspoiled by theories.

News reporters who think they can be purified of biases not only are letting the ghost of John Locke haunt them, but are beating themselves down for nothing. Instead of looking upon biases as the scarlet-letter sin of the news business, some reporters are fortunately able to see that bias is a positive value in their profession. Far from functioning as the news reporters' equivalent of original sin, biases make thinking possible. It is by leaning in one direction rather than another that a bias becomes an ingredient of thinking. Thinking cannot come about apart from making judgments. When judgments form a pattern, they influence thinking primarily in one direction, thus becoming a bias. A reporter whose thinking goes off in all directions is not thinking. Biases give focus. Because they are not infallible, however, they will doubtless be revised or even replaced. A mind free of all biases has not reached the first base toward objectivity. Rather, it has been disqualified from the game.

When preachers or others charge that newspapers are biased, editors have no need to deny the charge. The critics are biased too. That is not, however, similar to saying that unfortunately everyone is morally flawed. To have a bias is not a flaw or a misfortune, and that is how it differs from, say, embezzlement. It would be odd to say to an embezzler, "Look, you must try to improve your embezzlement." But it is appropriate to put one's biases to use in the thinking process with the goal of improving them.

To try to purge the mind of all biases is to confuse an open mind with an empty mind. Biases are one's intellectual fortune— inherited and earned—and are the starting points of all rational inquiry. The goal is to arrive at biases that have been well-formulated, tested, and corrected.

In the Jim and Tammy Bakker story, the *Charlotte Observer* has been strongly biased from the very start. It is a bias that not only has been tested over the years, but is very likely embraced by the majority of Charlotte's citizens. It can be formulated as follows. *Anyone who sets up an organization that raises millions of dollars in the name of Jesus or any other religious figure should not be a crook or con artist.* Not only is this view a bias, it is a *moral* bias. Anyone who claims that newspapers just report the facts and do not become involved in making moral judgments is incredibly naive. The impetus of the twelve years of investigative reporting by the *Charlotte Observer* is a strict, uncompromising moral judgment. In this sense, the editors and reporters were inescapably a part of the news from the start. Far from being a flaw or a weakness, however, their moral bias was absolutely essential to the investigation. Editor Rich Oppel spoke softly, but there was quiet conviction in his manner when he looked straight at me and said, "If a con man claims to talk to Jesus, it doesn't make him less a con man."

There is another bias that most news-gathering agencies seem to share with a large portion of the viewers and readers. It may be called the bias of spatial and temporal existence. For the purposes of news reporting, whatever is real must exist in space and time.

Reporters ask *where* and *when*. When asking *what happened,* they are searching for an account of the trail of events in definite space and time. For them, the person or persons *who* did it must be embodied in space and time. If a witness to an accident tells the reporter that it was demons or invisible Martians who caused the accident, few reporters will believe it. They will, instead, search for clues to the causes that their bias tells them existed in space and time. Reporters like to see themselves as servants of the quest for facts. But a bias often determines what can and cannot be regarded as a fact.

Consider the following stories: (1) when the Mormons settled in Utah, God sent seagulls inland to devour the millions of insects that were in process of destroying the Mormon's crops; (2) an angel named Gabriel gave to Muhammad the Koran as Sacred Scripture; (3) Sun Myung Moon's sermons, collected in a book called *Divine Principle,* are God's special revelation to the Reverend; (4) a statue, erected in honor of Roman women, suddenly began speaking as it was being set up (Plutarch reports that the alleged words were: "Dear to the Gods, O women, is your pious gift of me"); (5) there were miraculous signs of God's sorrow at the death of Julius Caesar (at the first games established in his honor by his heir Augustus, a comet shone for seven consecutive days and was believed to be the soul of Caesar received into heaven); (6) a Hebrew named Balaam engaged in a two-way conversation with his donkey, who saw the angel of the Lord standing in the road; (7) there was once a paradise where a woman named Eve conversed with a serpent; (8) Jesus of Nazareth rose from the grave bodily, so that had there been movie cameras in the first century, his resurrection could have been captured on film and his ascension into heaven filmed for miles, especially if a camera enclosed in a space ship could have traveled alongside him into the stratosphere and beyond; (9) the Virgin Mary is a real person who appeared to shepherd children in 1917 in Portugal; and (10) the writer Carlos Castaneda has a Yaqui Indian friend who is a genuine sorcerer.

Are these incidents factual?

Such situations are impossible for reporters to investigate. A number of reporters prefer to steer clear of an investigation that deals with the so-called supernatural.

Paul R. Waddle, Jr. (known as Ray to his friends) is the religion editor for the Nashville newspaper *The Tennessean.* In the spring of 1987 he traveled to Yugoslavia to investigate claims that the Virgin

Mary appeared to some young people in the small village of Med-jugorje. Ray sent me copies of his news articles on the happenings in Medjugorje. They were informative and artfully written. With considerable skill he succeeded in hiding from the readers his own bias. This is not to say that the articles are free of all biases. If they had been, they would be worthless. Waddle's reports were quite useful because he actively sought out and reported a variety of biases about the alleged appearances of the Virgin Mary in the little Yugoslavian village. Furthermore, he explored the biases rather deftly, showing that a considerable amount of high-powered theorizing has already been launched in the difficult task of trying to find out what is actually going on in the village.

Ray Waddle shared with me his bias on the question of what took place in Medjugorje. It is not my bias, but I am impressed with the objectivity that he achieved in his reports. My only criticism is that I wish he had in his articles given more information about his own bias because it is, in my opinion, carefully thought out and well worth considering. His articles would have been more objective, not less, had he added his own bias. Modesty probably restrained him.

There are at least five ways in which reporters can be biased regarding the supernatural. They may (a) deny the existence of the supernatural; (b) sincerely affirm the existence of the supernatural; (c) think that reality is such that no one can know if there are supernatural beings and events; (d) have no well-thought-out opinion on the subject but believe that the topic is not worth pursuing; or (e) have been able to arrive at no well-constructed theory but remain interested in the topic. Each of these above positions is a bias, which is not to be confused with a dogmatic frame of mind.

A few newspaper reporters have told me that they were not interested in theories and speculations. They assured me righteously that they were interested only in facts. They were, of course, young reporters who could still afford the luxury of naivete.

In raising the question of the role of theories in the search for facts, I offer the following hypotheses: (1) on a stormy night in March 1980 Jean Harris fatally shot her lover of fourteen years, Dr. Herman Tarnower, author of the best-selling *The Complete Scarsdale Medical Diet;* (2) Lee Harvey Oswald, acting alone, murdered John F. Kennedy in Dallas on November 22, 1963; (3) Alexander Haig was "Deep Throat" in the Watergate Scandal (Nixon's former lawyer, John Dean, thinks he was); (4) Joseph Stalin had his wife murdered; (5) Dr. John Hill in 1969 murdered his wife Joan Robinson Hill, a beautiful Texas socialite; (6) young Robert Hill was telling the truth in a Houston court in the summer of 1977 when he testified that his grandfather, Ash Robinson, caused the death of his father, Dr. John Hill; and (7) Texas multimillionaire Cullen Davis murdered his twelve-year-old stepdaughter in cold blood.

Books or articles have been written about each of the above alleged facts. In each case, there are several *theories* as to what happened. The facts that reporters are searching for have to be reconstructed, as the events happened in the past. But that cannot be done literally. What is literally constructed is a theory that is set forth as a representation of the perished fact. In order to create a fruitful theory, investigators—whether archaeologists or news reporters—use a combination of other facts and auxiliary theories. Some reporters like to imagine that they do not speculate; but the truly outstanding reporters, detectives, and archaeologists are remarkably skillful in using such essential intellectual tools as daring speculations, hypotheses, hunches, guesses, leads, and conjectures. A brilliant investigator's work is a combination of bold imagination and a willingness to criticize and test his or her own hypotheses severely in reconstructing a theory of what happened.

The Jim Bakker case provides an example of how a bold or even wild speculative venture can be woven into possibly related facts to produce a fruitful preliminary hypothesis. It is well established that David Taggart began working for PTL in 1981, when Taggart was only twenty-three. The incredible amount of money that Taggart has accumulated in so few years raises eyebrows. David's brother James, age thirty-three, worked for a while for PTL as an interior designer. He, too, has accumulated great sums of money and expensive gifts. The question is: Why would Bakker pay David Taggart what seems to be an inordinate amount of money? In a fifteen-month period ending at the close of March 1987, David received over $620,000. According to one report, the Taggarts' father was a wealthy Michigan car dealer. Legwork revealed, however, that the father, who declined comment, worked as an auto body shop manager and that the Taggarts grew up in a modest neighborhood in the Detroit area.[1]

There are some facts that suggest the hypothesis that Bakker has engaged in relationships that would ordinarily be classified as homosexual. This in turn stimulates speculation that perhaps there was a homosexual relationship between Bakker and Taggart and that the inordinate payments to Taggart were implicit hush money. The value of this speculative conjecture is that it directs a line of investigation, giving it a focus and defining specific problems to be solved or questions to be raised. The difficulty of pursuing such a speculative venture can also be appreciated.

Facts, theories, hunches, speculative leaps, and educated guesses actually feed one another. It is important to see that even when a hypothesis is made plausible, this does not mean that it has been put to serious test. How to go about putting it to rigorous test is still another side of creative and sometimes ingenious investigative reporting. In the specific speculative hypothesis suggested in the case of Taggart, the investigator does not so much suspend judgment as create other hypotheses that compete with earlier ones. The process of making judgments in this case is highly active and is not passively suspended. It is simply that none of the competing hypotheses is so compelling that it overrides the others.

Reporters provide not so much statements *of* fact as statements *about* facts. And that means that their statements are always subject to being tested, revised, replaced, or stated more profoundly. Charles Shepard of the *Charlotte Observer* has proved to be an invaluable investigator of the whole PTL phenomenon because he has acquired experience in his highly specialized ten-year investigation. Frye Gaillard of the same newspaper is a staff writer and investigative reporter who cares deeply about religion. He is also sophisticated enough to know that as a reporter his own background of experience and study often shapes what he selects as significant to report. Because he has original theories of his own and does not pretend to be invisible in his investigation, his material makes for fruitful reading.

Like Jim Jones of the *Fort Worth Star-Telegram,* Gaillard and Shepard understand that facts exist in connection with other facts and that good reporting requires a grasp of their patterned connections. No fact exists as an island to itself; and over a ten-year period, the *Charlotte Observer* has collected thousands of facts and hundreds of theories and pieced them together to give meaning and structure to what is going on inside PTL. When Charles Shepard publishes his book on the structure of PTL, it will be a formidable book because its author has learned that apart from its numerous contexts, a bare fact is virtually meaningless.

A few religion reporters, John Dart of the *Los Angeles Times* in particular, are so thoroughly versed in a special area of religion that they become scholars commanding respect from other scholars. The future of news reporting in the area of religion is bright because of newspapers like the *Charlotte Observer* and because scholars and religion reporters and editors are learning from one another.

One of Jim Bakker's biggest mistakes was to assume that because news reporters did not share *all* his biases, they were enemies determined to destroy him. Apparently before realizing what was happening to him, Bakker began regarding critics as demonic enemies and supportive letters from his fans as proof that he did not need to listen to criticism. It is unfortunate that he either had not heard or had not pondered seriously David Brinkley's sobering words about becoming a celebrity: "You could put a baboon on television and he'd become a celebrity if you kept him on long enough." Brinkley sometimes referred to a young ape named J. Fred Muggs, who not only became a regular on the "Today" show with Dave Garroway, but developed a great following of his own.[2]

A celebrity like Bakker pays a dear price when he listens only to those who praise him. This makes him even more vulnerable because he confuses reality with his popularity. Truth becomes whatever it is that motivates his fans to write and enclose money. If he exaggerates and stretches the truth unconscionably and is not called on it, he will start believing his own fabrications. He may actually take risks in seeing how far he can go in his make-believe world.

A reporter phoned a member of Bakker's staff late one night to ask some questions. It was perhaps inconsiderate of the reporter to phone so late. Bakker, however, in front of his audience (but off the air) told his fans that reporters were making threatening phone calls at midnight. In the audience at that moment sat two reporters whom Bakker knew. After the meeting, one of them approached Bakker and told him that the information he had just given to his audience was untrue and he knew it was untrue. At first Bakker invented another tale to cover up his previous fabrication. The reporter pressed him. Bakker tried still another approach rather than simply saying he was sorry. Finally, after the reporter persisted and would not ease up, Bakker admitted, "Sometimes I get carried away."

It is only human to get carried away. Bakker unfortunately has been all too human, letting himself get transported much too often into a world of his own invention. One of his first outlandish allegations was that PTL had a TV audience of twenty million viewers. Had he claimed two million he might have been exaggerating. Sometimes Bakker's touch with reality seems recklessly tenuous. He might have served himself well by learning from the *Charlotte Observer* and other respected newspapers.

19

The Past and Future of Televangelism

by Steven Winzenburg

The "electronic church" first appeared about the time that broadcasting itself began. The nation's first full-fledged radio station, KDKA in Pittsburgh, began operating in November 1920, and two months later the first broadcast was made of a church service. The pastor of the church "considered radio a passing fad and doubted that the hookup from the church sanctuary to the station would work," so he let his associate pastor conduct the Sunday evening service. The first electronic service was Protestant, and engineered by two KDKA employees: one Roman Catholic, the other Jewish. The engineers donned choir robes so their presence would not distract the congregation.[1]

The audience was so responsive to that pioneer broadcast that the station made the service a regular program. Soon other new stations began broadcasting religious services and sermons.

In 1923 the first nondenominational religious program began on station WOW in Omaha. Also that year, ten churches were operating their own radio stations, programming only their own church services.

By the 1930s, there were dozens of religious programs aired nationally, some church-produced like "The Lutheran Hour," and others nondenominational like Charles Fuller's "The Old Fashioned Revival Hour." The former bought time on CBS for $4,000 a half hour. The latter was carried on eighty-eight Mutual Broadcasting Stations for $4,500 a week. Not only were these programs good revenue for the stations, but they attracted a weekly audience of ten million.[2]

By the 1940s, there was a battle over religious air time on radio. On one side was the Federal Council of Churches (now the National Council of Churches) which represented traditional, nonevangelical Protestant congregations; on the other side was the newly formed National Association of Evangelicals. The networks were supplying free air time to the three major faiths, with Protestants represented by the Federal Council of Churches. The council refused to share its air time with evangelical churches and fought for a broadcasting policy of using sustaining time only for religious broadcasts.

The National Association of Evangelicals was formed out of a concern that their rights to buy time were being infringed upon. Because they were excluded from the network's sustaining schedule, the evangelicals had to pay for whatever time they could find. During the war years, many evangelical programs were dropped by stations in favor of "sustaining time only" programming.

If it had not been for the council's strong opposition in the early 1940s, the National Association of Evangelicals might never have been formed. The NAE was organized to keep the few successful evangelists on the air during the war years. The council's plan backfired when World War II ended and evangelicals became stronger and more successful than ever. After the war, radio advertising was at a low, and stations again began selling time to religious broadcasters. The council continued to object, as evangelicals took audiences and prime radio time from the mainline churches.

As television began its entrance into the nation's homes, a very traditional religious leader emerged as the star of the small screen, Bishop Fulton Sheen. The Catholic preacher was the only religious leader on network prime time, and after an initial unsponsored run, the Admiral Television Corporation paid $1 million in 1952 for commercials at the beginning and the end of the half hour.[3]

On Sunday mornings, the networks chose to air interdenominational programs. CBS-TV produced "Look Up and Live," in cooperation with the National Council of Churches, the National Council of Catholic Men, and the New York Board of Rabbis. CBS also presented "Lamp Unto My Feet," a program containing theological discussions, the arts, drama, and truths which underlie all religious faiths.[4]

NBC aired a number of rotating programs in the same Sunday

morning time slot: the National Council of Churches' "Frontiers of Faith," "The Catholic Hour," "The Eternal Light," and two programs a year devoted to evangelicals. ABC developed a series of religious documentaries entitled "Directions," which still air today on some of the network's affiliated stations.

Most of the network religious programs lasted over twenty years, until they were canceled in the 1970s. Now occasional specials are presented on religious topics, and services are aired during holiday periods.

While the TV networks upheld a policy of providing sustaining air time for representative church groups, evangelicals again had no choice but to buy syndicated time. The NCC "condemned the sale of TV time to religious groups or individuals," and refused to let evangelicals have a portion of the NCC's network time.[5]

Some stations were willing to sell Sunday morning air time to whoever had the money. Others followed the council's guidelines, and by the 1960s, over half the stations in the nation refused to accept sponsored religious broadcasts.[6]

Again, the National Association of Evangelicals encouraged Charismatic evangelists to get involved in the television medium. Because they were rarely allowed time on network TV, the evangelists had to find effective techniques to draw viewers and make money. That forced the evangelists to develop along the lines of commercial television with lavish sets, simplistic methods, and the hard sell. In effect, the National Council of Churches caused the evangelicals to develop the very techniques the council scorned.[7]

The early stars of syndication were Rex Humbard, Oral Roberts, and Billy Graham. Humbard broadcast a showy church service from Ohio; Roberts started by filming his faith-healing tent crusade, then changed to a classy, well-produced TV variety show. Graham has always simply broadcast his occasional citywide crusades. Other religious TV programing in the 1950s consisted of local church services and "Gospel sings."

In the 1970s, such an astounding change took place in religious broadcasting that by 1980 there was almost no free time available on commercial television for religious broadcasts. Fifty-three percent of religious TV time was paid for in 1970; a decade later it was 92 percent.[8] Most of that air time is purchased by the popular new evangelists who work well in front of the television camera.

Robert Schuller, Jim Bakker, Pat Robertson, and Jerry Falwell joined Roberts, Graham, and Humbard as the stars of the electronic church. They not only appeared on Sunday mornings, but branched out into prime time and weekday mornings, producing specials and talk shows.

The hesitancy of some television stations to sell time to preachers also led to the creation of religious television stations, beginning in 1961. Twenty years later there were thirty-five full-time religious stations in the United States, with a current average of one new religious TV station starting each month.

The religious talk show, a new format in religious broadcasting, is a product of the 1970s. Though Pat Robertson started the first religious station, which eventually evolved into the first religious network (CBN—the Christian Broadcasting Network), his "700 Club" had a miniscule following until 1974, when he began buying time on satellites to send his talk show to cable stations. At the same time, two other national talk shows began competing for the religious audience. Jim Bakker started the "PTL Club" (which first stood for "Praise the Lord," then changed to "People That Love") on his own PTL Network. Paul Crouch organized the small Trinity Broadcasting Network, which aired its own "Praise the Lord" show to the large Los Angeles market.

One reason for the success of Bakker and Robertson may lie in the fact that they had not only their own programs, but their own networks. Oral Roberts had no network. Neither did Billy Graham or Robert Schuller. But Bakker and Robertson each used the talk show as the base to support the larger network operation.

Today the secular media and other nonevangelical church members continue to be skeptical of these preachers who have been drawing audiences for over thirty years. Predicting that the Bakker scandal is the beginning of the end for born-again preachers, the skeptics fail to understand why televangelism is here to stay.

"Accountability" is the new buzz word. TV evangelists thrive on crises. If they do not have crises, they invent them and call on their faithful followers to save their partnership ministry from sinking. Swaggart told his followers that if they allowed the Bakker scandal to cause them to withhold their pledges or contributions, they would be responsible for millions of souls literally going to hell because he did not have the funds to reach lost souls with the gospel.[9]

Robert Schuller talked of accountability, assuring contributors that "your donations are in good hands."[10] His proof was not in the form of a financial statement but in bringing celebrities and business leaders on his telecast to vouch for his integrity. Claiming that the spring and summer of 1987 had been horrendous, Schuller asked guest Art Linkletter to comment on what he thought of the scandal. Linkletter responded with a well-rehearsed endorsement of the preacher, assuring the public "anything he promises he'll deliver."[11] Schuller never mentioned how much money he lost due to the scandal, but said, "I need thousands of people to say 'I'll keep you alive' to survive."[12]

Pat Robertson made the most ambitious attempt to prove his accountability by spending an entire "700 Club" program to show viewers where their money goes. Using huge pie charts and a pointer, Robertson stood in front of the camera and explained how $31 million, one-fourth of the money contributed in 1986, was paid to the CBN staff, with $1.4 million going to the top executives. He claimed that his own salary was $60,000, but that in 1986 he gave back $90,000 to CBN! Later realizing the imbalance, he explained that he has other income through royalties on books, "investments," and a position he holds on the board of a bank.[13] His frustration over the loss of millions of dollars in contributions culminated in the firing of 500 CBN employees within three months of the scandal. By early July the situation went from a "real crisis" to looking "brighter than ever."

Robertson, like most of the TV preachers, used the Bakker scandal to his advantage as a fund-raising pitch. Just as Jim and Tammy had turned their crusade against the *Charlotte Observer* into a way to raise extra money, so Robertson, Schuller, and the others took the opportunity to turn a normally slow late spring/early summer into their biggest fund-raising event of the year.

Jerry Falwell had to raise money both in his new role as chairman at PTL and on his own "Old Time Gospel Hour." PTL had its biggest fund-raising month in the thirteen-year history of the ministry when Falwell asked viewers for a "May Miracle" to keep the show on the air and they responded with $8.5 million. He followed up with a "D-Day" promotion during June on his own weekly program from Lynchburg, Virginia, where he managed to raise $5 million from viewers who would meet a matching contribution before his fiscal year ended. Amazingly, in the midst of all the talk of the scandal being "the worst thing that ever happened in the history of Christianity," Falwell managed to pull off the biggest fund-raising campaign in the history of religious television.[14] What originally was seen as the death of televised religion quickly became the rallying point to pump new financial blood into aging ministries.

Accountability was mentioned often by Falwell: at press conferences, in interviews such as on ABC's "Nightline," and on his own religious telecasts. But whenever he was asked when he would make his books public, he replied that a full financial statement would be disclosed "within weeks." The weeks turned to months before a statement was released. And, as with all TV ministries, an "audited financial statement" hardly answers questions of where money is going. For instance, in Jim Bakker's 1980 statement, which I acquired from PTL when writing my master's thesis on Bakker, "salaries, wages, other payroll costs and contract labor" are all listed in a lump sum ($9,613,079) under "expenses." Travel for guests and staff, a legitimate expense on a TV talk show, came to $880,313. "Other operating expenses" are listed as $1,641,501. Nowhere are these numbers broken down, telling exactly how much Bakker made, in salary and bonuses, or how much of the travel expenses went to Jim and Tammy's Hawaiian vacation. Audited financial statements answer few of the specific questions viewers have about how money is being spent. Most TV preachers use the statements as proof of accountability when the reports are no more than vague categorizations which raise more questions than they answer.

Two groups are going to be deeply disappointed in the future of radio and TV evangelism—the skeptics and the true believers. The skeptics are proclaiming that the Bakker scandal will prove to be the funeral dirge of TV evangelism, that the contributors will realize at long last that they have been taken to the cleaners, and that all TV evangelists skim money the way Bakker did. They fail to see that American electronic evangelism will continue for the simple reason that it does meet audience members' needs and that some of the ministers are sincere.

On the other side, the American public as a whole can endure only so much TV evangelism. The true believer's dream of the day when TV evangelists become the instruments of a revival wave sweeping across America from sea to shining sea will remain a dream and little more. Since 1977 there has been a stable core of 14 million viewers who loyally support these programs. And in the past ten years, seven of the top-ten TV ministries have suffered a major decline in ratings.[15] In marketing terms, there is a finite market in North America for which TV ministers are forced to compete. The evangelicals and Charismatics dominate the field. They are the Coke and Pepsi of the electronic ministries. And those TV ministers who are already established as front-runners in the race have definite plans to keep their hard-earned positions.

One way the major TV ministers have prepared for numerical stability in the future is by having a family member waiting in the wings to take over. Robert Schuller makes sure his son, Robert A. Schuller, is seen each week on the "Hour of Prayer." The younger Schuller reads the scripture and says a short prayer. Occasionally he is allowed to preach and has begun a successful writing career by penning positive-thinking books, thus following in his father's footsteps.

Oral Roberts has been honing son Richard for almost twenty years to the point that Richard now has a daily one-hour show and hosts his father's weekly Sunday program. Richard's messy divorce from his former on-screen singing partner Patti was glossed over. Now his current wife Lindsay is placed at Richard's side for each show. He will naturally take over for his father when the time comes for Oral to retire.

Pat Robertson made thirty-one-year-old son Tim president of CBN while Pat concentrated on becoming president of the United States. Tim now co-hosts the daily "700 Club" and, although he has no camera presence and has been inept even at simple introductions of guests, he may eventually become sufficiently comfortable to take over permanently.

Jimmy Swaggart's only child Donnie is seen on his dad's daily and weekly programs. Although Jimmy has not allowed his son to preach on camera, there is no doubt that Donnie has been seriously considered as Jimmy Lee's eventual successor.

Jerry Falwell recently announced that his son Jonathan will study to be a preacher. Falwell's other children, a son who is a lawyer and a daughter in medicine, have stayed away from the ministry. By the time Falwell is ready to retire, Jonathan should be a well-practiced preacher.

Billy Graham's son, Franklin, formerly a wayward who gave his parents sleepless nights, has been appearing on his father's telecasts to promote mission work in Africa. He is a good speaker, comfortable in front of the crowd, and like his father visually pleasing before the camera. Both he and Graham's preacher son-in-law Leighton Ford are near the front of the line of potential heirs to the Billy Graham Evangelistic Association.

Each of these top televangelists hopes to carry on his successful ministry with a son. By gradually working the son into the telecast, the preacher is cultivating that essential ingredient of familiarity and trust between the offspring and the viewers—understanding how crucial this special relationship is in determining the future of the program.

Because of their inability to use television to develop such a relationship, mainline churches have failed in attempts to win back "fallen away" members. Catholics, Lutherans, Methodists, and others have had disappointing results after committing millions of dollars to develop programs to counter the success of the televangelists. The traditional denominations, insisting on not using the same tactics as the evangelicals, have failed to put forth a central compelling personality, have steered away from entertainment, and have resisted asking viewers to contribute to the program. The well-intentioned mainliners (whom Falwell now calls sideliners) do not understand that the success of any TV preacher is a result of a well-cultivated relationship between the sheep and the shepherd. The viewers are attracted to an individual who entertains and inspires, and they want to express their appreciation through letters and donations. The evangelical TV preachers will continue their success as long as the mainline churches are unwilling to use the devices necessary to implement a binding relationship between viewer and television minister.

Epilogue

If 1987 was problematic for Pentecostals and Charismatics, the early part of 1988 appeared disastrous. While Pat Robertson campaigned to move into the White House, Jim Bakker fought to stay out of prison. Five days after Valentine's Day, the news broke that Assemblies of God superstar Jimmy Swaggart had made several calls on a New Orleans prostitute with the intention of leaving with her more than a gospel tract. Insisting that he had not committed adultery (technically), Swaggart confessed to watching the prostitute perform what some of his Pentecostal brethren called pornographic acts.

In the spring of 1987 Swaggart had graphically described Jim Bakker's illicit sexual behavior as a cancer in the body of Christ that ought to be cut out. When the story of his own misadventures emerged in the news, there was disagreement among the brethren as to whether the evangelist's interest in pornography was a temporary delirium of only four months or was a major thread of his life that could be traced back over the years. In perhaps the greatest of his many theatrical performances, the Pentecostal superstar not only confessed his moral failure on TV, but labeled it a sin and refused to call it merely a moral mistake. Among Pentecostals, weeping publicly is often considered as a mark of sincerity, just as speaking in tongues is considered as the manifestation of baptism in the Spirit. But Swaggart appears quite aware that both crying and speaking in tongues can be a part of an act. Swaggart has been denounced as insincere or hypocritical for confessing his sin publicly only after he was photographed with the prostitute. But while the adjective "sanctimonious" might well apply to the man in this context, the label "hypocrite" need not.

245

A serious limitation in the worldview of Pentecostals and Fundamentalists makes it exceedingly difficult for them to gain profound
insight into human sexuality, both in its positive and negative aspects.
One of Swaggart's most devoted followers and best financial supporters
explained his hero's moral failure by saying that Satan had "tricked"
him. The same explanation was given by some of Bakker's followers
to explain their hero's downfall. What Pentecostals and Fundamentalists appear unable to see is that the Satan hypothesis not only
fails to help explain human immorality but often hinders their ministers from understanding some of the more subtle aspects of morality
and immorality. Like the hypothesis of original sin, the devil hypothesis
leads the mind into a blind alley. For example, if a Satan figure
is required before temptation can come into being, then Lucifer would
originally have required a satanic tempter. And that satanic tempter
would have required still another, leading to an infinite number of
satanic tempters in an endless past.

One American theologian referred to human beings as the only
species in "perpetual heat." This suggestion roots human sexuality
more firmly in biology, a fruitful field of study that makes Pentecostal
and Fundamentalist preachers grow nervous. While far more than
biology alone, human sexuality cannot be profoundly understood apart
from our polygamous genes. Strictly speaking, human beings are not
by nature (that is, biologically) monogamous. Social and moral regulations that restrict marriage to a monogamous bond would be unnecessary if it were entirely natural for one man and one woman to join
with each other in an enduring and exclusive union. Pentecostal and
Fundamentalist preachers are at a serious disadvantage in trying to
come to terms with their own bodies. They know from personal experience that bodily passions do not spontaneously regulate themselves
to adapt to the ideal of monogamy. This fact often confuses the
minister by giving him a double message. On the one hand, he looks
upon his body as a part of God's wondrous handiwork. On the other
hand, his body behaves like a team of horses, each threatening to
chase after the object of its own passion.

Since the monogamous ideal of marriage is regarded by the
preacher as a God-given law, he cannot help wondering why God
would provide him with a body that seems at times to generate sexual
passion for more than one member of the opposite sex. The minister
often feels caught in a trap. His own body is both a blessing and

Sometimes he seeks to escape from the trap by dissociating himself from his body and treating it as if it were a tool of either the Holy Spirit or Satan. As a result, he becomes painfully ambivalent about his body because he does not know whether he can or should identify with it. He becomes deeply troubled—sometimes resentful—that his God-given body is not perfectly fitted to the monogamous ideal.

Pentecostal theology has never successfully come to terms with the biological condition of the human species. If it had, it might now be able to accept the fact that in itself alone, sexual passion for more than one other person has a positive side. If over the centuries the human species had lacked all versatility in its sexuality, no widow or widower would have become sexually interested in a second marriage partner. Biologists today understand that sexual versatility has survival value.

On the other hand, the propensity toward igniting flames of passion for more than one person has its negative side, making sexuality indeed a mixed blessing. The truth seems to be that the human species is a rich and highly complicated synthesis of biological and socio-cultural ingredients. These two sets of ingredients do not in fact fit together neatly, though they can make an imperfect and wondrous compromise.

Far from being natural, therefore, monogamy is an astounding sociocultural achievement. Monogamy takes the ingredients of biology and combines them into sometimes bewilderingly complex social patterns and relationships. This entails that some biological ingredients must be controlled in deference to others. Polygamous passions have been restrained in virtually every society to varying degrees. If Jimmy Swaggart's sexual passion or curiosity ventured off in more than one direction, it was not because he was a freak of nature but because he was biologically normal. What he violated was not his nature but the "norms" and standards that both he and his denomination have set up as guidelines for reconstructing human nature.

The whole point of having a norm, guideline, or model is to use it as an ideal to strive for. It is not a description of what individuals are biologically, but what they believe they *ought* to be in their relationships with others. In some societies, people are prone to project onto their gods their own cultural norms and standards. When they violate these norms, they believe they have violated a covenant with the gods. They may call on the gods in the belief that they can assist

them in upholding the norms. Sometimes a severe crisis develops
when a god, preacher, or priest fails to measure up to the standard.
When Jim Bakker and Jimmy Swaggart violated the sexual standard
to which they themselves subscribed, they were not necessarily hypocritical. Their own biblical tradition uses the expression "weakness
of the flesh" to explain their failure. Translated into contemporary
language, their biological nature was too weak to allow them to
completely live up to the monogamous ideal. Or, stated in another
way, their polygamous genes were too strong and the sociocultural
controls too weak.

TV evangelist James Robison confessed that he had experienced
a moral problem similar to those of Swaggart and Bakker without
stepping as far as they into overtly unacceptable sexual behavior.
On ABC's "Nightline" on February 22, 1988, he made the following
extremely revealing comment:

> I know that in my own life, when I began to have difficulties,
> I began to fight sin and cry out against sin and literally shout
> at sin as though I could scare it out of my own life. [It was]
> as though I could somehow deliver myself by powerful
> preaching or by a rigid system of rules and laws that would
> somehow protect me rather than going for help. And I just
> simply want to say thank God I did go for help, because
> the fact is I myself, just as many others, would have fallen
> had I not gotten help. . . . I was headed for destruction. Thank
> God I found deliverance before it was too late. . . . The attacks
> of Satan, the powers of Darkness, are real. And they are
> assaulting our preachers!

Swaggart has been accused of hypocrisy because he waited until
he was caught before publicly confessing that he had frequently called
on a prostitute. Those who make this accusation might ask themselves
what the evangelist's realistic alternatives were. One alternative, of
course, was to make a public confession *before* he was caught and
photographed. But that would have served no good purpose and
would have hastened the arrival of the public scandal. His desperate
hope all along was to find a way to resolve his personal "moral problem"
and thereby avoid creating a scandal. Apparently, his prayers, tears,
and savage preaching against prostitutes and pornography did little

to scare off the devil (or, in less supernatural terms, to quell his own polygamous genes). This raises the question of why he could find no counselor or moral coach to help him better measure up to his moral standard. In dealing with this practical question, James Robison pointed out that many preachers harbor a deep fear of going to someone for help in sexual matters. This turns out to be a realistic and practical fear. If a minister who has trouble controlling himself sexually were to go to another minister for counseling, he might publicly expose him or reveal the secret to others. Swaggart himself acknowledged that it would have been better had he gone to someone for help, someone within his Pentecostal circle. Had he gone, the open publication of his sexual deviance might have been avoided. It must not be forgotten, however, that it was a fellow Pentecostal minister who blew the whistle on him. The Reverend Marvin Gorman of New Orleans hired a private investigator to follow Swaggart until he collected damaging evidence against him. By letting the air out of the tire of Swaggart's car, the private eye gave himself time for taking several pictures of the evangelist outside the prostitute's motel room.

It might be asked why Swaggart did not go to a professional psychologist or counselor outside his Pentecostal circle. Louisiana has hundreds of such counselors who are required by the ethics of their profession to reveal nothing about their clients. But even if he had become convinced that he could find a counselor who would not leak details of his confession, Swaggart would not have gone to any of them for the simple reason that he did not believe in what they were doing. In fact, he often mocked psychologists and therapists from the pulpit. Many Pentecostal preachers only three decades ago did not believe in going to physicians for help with physical maladies, insisting that Jesus could cure all diseases without the assistance of physicians. Swaggart seemed to hold that Jesus could solve all emotional and behavioral problems without the assistance of professional counselors or psychologists.

Ironically, only a few days after the scandal became public, Swaggart appeared on a taped TV sermon in which he denounced prostitutes. Perhaps like James Robison, Swaggart hoped to rid himself of temptation by preaching forcefully against prostitutes. In another sermon Swaggart had even told the moving story of a prostitute who came to him for help.

It appears that the Pentecostal superstar had been unduly sanctimonious in hounding fellow Pentecostal preacher Marvin Gorman,
who had had an affair. It seems probable that Swaggart felt he could
somehow control his own flame of passion by attacking Gorman's.
But can Swaggart therefore be passed off in this case as simply a
hypocrite who preached one thing and practiced another? The news
media and televangelists have in common a tendency to oversimplify
the causes of the behavior of individuals. Swaggart's tragic case
provides an opportunity for those who claim to be students of human
nature to gain insight into just how complicated the human species
can be. Doubtless some preachers who find it difficult to bring their
sexual behavior in line with their own monogamous ideal have simply
left off preaching the ideal. This was, of course, an option for Swaggart.
But he seemed unwilling to adopt it because it would have been
for him a double betrayal of the ideal. This point can be made with
a gentle touch of irony: his preaching remained faithful to the moral
ideal of strict monogamy even when his behavior at the motel revealed
him to be less than faithful to Frances. He was inconsistent, but
hypocrisy is more than being merely inconsistent.

Swaggart's hounding of Marvin Gorman and Jim Bakker seemed
to one critic of TV evangelists to resemble corporate raiding or even
to be an attempt to expand his empire by ruining his competitors.
One evangelist observed that far from showing mercy to wayward
preachers over the years, Swaggart had "ground them to dust." Now
that the shoe was on the other foot, Swaggart was said to have wept
and begged for mercy for two hours in Gorman's car outside the
motel. Gorman added that Swaggart promised to seek help and to
confess his moral failure to church authorities.

It is almost as if there were two Jimmy Swaggarts, just as there
sometimes seemed to be two Jim Bakkers. Swaggart did not readily
acknowledge his fascination with pornography (since childhood) as
a part of himself. This alien side of Swaggart was like a satellite
self, or like a rebellious "son" determined to go his own way even
if it meant stabbing the evangelist in the back by destroying his
reputation. Still the question remains: Why would the most successful
televangelist in the world sabotage his own success and turn against
himself? There are at least two ways to approach this question.

The first is to assume that Swaggart felt a need to punish himself.
In his book *Man Against Himself,* Karl Menninger, the founder of

the noted Menninger Clinic, observed, "By far the most prevalent method of relieving the unconscious sense of guilt is by atonement. As we already have seen, this is sometimes accomplished by sacrifice. Such sacrifices may be organic [i.e., mutilating or damaging the body] or they may be expressed in behavior."[1] But for what evil would Swaggart need to atone? What sin would have created a sense of guilt in him? The answer, according to this approach, lies paradoxically in Swaggart's astounding success. The religion of Swaggart's youth tended to identify wealth and worldly success with wickedness. Success in the world meant compromise with iniquity and therefore betrayal of Christ and his people.

A careful study of Swaggart's recent sermons reveals that he devoted considerable time to raging against worldliness. Yet he soared to the heights of success, becoming the most listened-to preacher in the world. Swaggart had in the name of Jesus acquired a personal jet, three spacious homes, and the use of a luxurious ministry "retreat" in California.[2] He wore expensive suits that cost several times more than those of the humble Pentecostal pastors in his home town of Ferriday, Louisiana. His denunciation of Jim Bakker's Prosperity Theology might be interpreted as his own Pentecostal conscience crying out in anger and bitterness against his own conspicuous prosperity. The incredibly successful Swaggart had insulted and enraged the Pentecostal conscience of his youth. He therefore began to engage in the sinful behavior of those whom he identified as worldly. In his own mind he joined the ranks of the lascivious against whom he had railed with righteous scorn, perhaps subconsciously knowing all along that in the end he would be caught in the lewd act and be savagely punished. This punishment, serving as an atoning sacrifice to his stern and fierce Pentecostal conscience, served of course to pull him down from the heights of success and humiliate him before the world.

There is a quite different way of approaching the evangelist's apparent attempt to sabotage himself and his entire ministry. It can be stated briefly. As a biologically vital and virile man, Jimmy Swaggart was simply unable to keep in full harness his polygamous tendencies and his desire to seek pleasure in a variety of ways. When he put on his sunglasses, pulled the hat down, and met the prostitute on the Air Line Highway pick-up strip on the outskirts of New Orleans, Swaggart acted not so much out of a need to punish himself as to satisfy some of the genetic sexual endowment bred into him by perhaps a million years of evolution and natural selection.

Early in his life, Billy Graham observed that several preachers had ruined their careers by sexual waywardness. He also came to believe that there were women out there who would try to lead a successful evangelist astray.

Evangelist James Robison of Texas went so far as to reveal how he became aware of women watching him and offering their bodies to him. "If I returned her gaze," he honestly confessed, "a powerful force-field between us seemed to draw her to me and me to her." He adds that while sitting on the platform at evangelistic crusades or in churches he became "filled with lustful thoughts and desires." Insisting that his imagination was not working overtime, Robison acknowledged that after the services, the women often sought him out before he could leave the platform. Some came to his hotel. "They might have appeared to be high-class, attractive women, even wives of spiritual men, but they had felt what I felt." This became a pattern that soon terrified the evangelist. His wife, Betty, began to feel inadequate as a wife and to imagine that God would take her off the earth so that James could find a more outgoing wife. This was so real to Betty that she became convinced she would die in her early thirties.[3]

In the meantime, James was so overwhelmed by sexual arousal that he feared he might succumb if an attractive woman were to approach him when he was alone and weak. One of his friends, the Reverend Peter Lord, admitted to James that lust had been one of his problems, too. Today, both preachers profess to have been freed from lust. James claims to have had a fight with demonic powers, which suggests that he is still unable to acknowledge and come to terms with his natural libidinous endowment.

Billy Graham resolved to be exceedingly cautious regarding women by always traveling in the company of at least one male member of his team or a member of his family. Perhaps without fully realizing it, Graham's escorts may be protecting him not only against conniving women but against his own unpredictable libido. Instead of shouting at a make-believe demon of sex, however, Graham wisely invented a social mechanism to help him monitor his biological endowment and guide him toward the monogamous ideal.

The news media have recently become preoccupied with the

question of Pentecostalism's survival, now that the moral imperfections of television evangelists have been shouted from the housetops. A few critical points can be made regarding this question. First, most evangelicals have had little practice in thinking within a framework other than their own. If their framework seems to them to offer a plausible sketch of the world in general, they will remain with it even when many of its details come under severe and perhaps unanswerable criticism. People everywhere are understandably reluctant to give up their worldview even when it does not serve them well, and this is doubly true when their preachers have severely warned against trying to understand any worldview other than their own. In the 1840s thousands of American evangelicals waited impatiently for the Second Coming of Christ and his establishment of a millennium on earth. When the appointed time came and passed, the disappointed believers generally did not give up expecting the impending return of Christ. Instead of shrinking, the expectation swelled into a movement that helped generate the emergence of the Fundamentalism and Pentecostalism of the present century. Pentecostals like Swaggart and Bakker are heirs of the nineteenth-century belief in the impending Second Coming and millennium.

The fact is that even though the numerous predictions about the millennium have failed repeatedly, the millenarian movement continues to flourish among evangelicals. In their new book *Television, Power, and Politics,*[4] Jeffrey Hadden and Anson Shupe contend that the evangelical movement is well on the way toward becoming a major political force in the United States. If this forecast comes true, the question will remain: Did it come about *because* of TV evangelists or *despite* them? It might very well turn out that the big-time televangelists, including Pat Robertson, will have done the evangelical cause more long-term harm than good. None of the top five televangelists has provided significant intellectual leadership for evangelicals. The top five are one and all intellectual featherweights, and it is becoming increasingly clear that turning to TV evangelists for moral leadership was misconceived from the start. In a January 1988 article sociologist Anson Shupe pointed out that evangelicals are still unable to come together as a solid moral front. This is a strange turn of events in light of the fact that many evangelicals have come to see themselves as the force that will turn the nation "back to righteousness and morality."

The power of televangelists to wield political influence has been explored by a number of social scientists. A careful study of the Bakkers, Swaggart, Robertson, and Roberts suggests that televangelists can do considerable damage to the evangelicals' attempt to create a solid political coalition. A recent movement in the United States called Christian Reconstructionism (Dominion Theology or Kingdom Theology) has set up a long-term political agenda to turn America into a Christian nation. Under such a government, Jim Bakker's sins would have made him the victim of capital punishment carried out by the Christian state. Jimmy Swaggart would have been either imprisoned or put to death, depending on how adultery was defined. Thousands of doctors and nurses would have been executed for participating in abortions. Numerous ministers would be sent to prison if, after listening to women confess to having had abortions, they failed to report the women to the police. Christian Reconstructionists demand that the Bible be the basis of all civil law and that every institution in America be brought under what appears to be a version of Christian American Zionism.

Critics charge that Christian Reconstructionists threaten to become the Red Guard of the religious right in their zeal to ignore the U.S. Constitution whenever it fails to implement the edicts of the Book of Deuteronomy. Reconstructionist James Jordan goes so far as to say that "the notion of human rights was introduced by Satan in the Garden of Eden."[5] Other Christians to the far right, however, contend that the Constitution is rooted in the Bible and that there would be no concept of human rights if the biblical religion had not given birth to them. Reconstructionist Joseph Morecraft claims that under a government controlled by Dominion Theology or Kingdom Theology the level of freedom would rise for everyone. By contrast, evangelical philosopher Norman Geisler told Bill Moyers that the ultimate result of Reconstructionism would be the abolition of freedom. He described the movement as a danger to America, democracy, and freedom.

Christian Reconstructionism has made significant inroads into Pentecostalism and Fundamentalism. Along with Jerry Falwell, the Reconstructionists have embraced the belief that America, like ancient Israel, could gain international supremacy only if it follows the God of Israel. Both Jim Bakker's television ministry and Swaggart's ministry have been essentially in agreement with this religiopolitical doctrine.

Pat Robertson has been teaching it for years. In reality, the TV ministries of these evangelists have long been highly political and have used television as a base for advancing a political agenda. If Robertson's CBN and the PTL Network eventually unite as a single organization, it will become an exceedingly powerful voice of the political far right. The fact that each uses many of the emotion-laden symbols of traditional Christianity will only add to its clout in the world of politics.

Today's televangelists have gained much of their success by convincing their viewers that their brand of religion is the foundation of the family and of morality. I suggest that their interpretation of their own importance in this regard is not rooted in reality. The success of televangelists lies largely in their being *parasites* on family culture and morality. Far from providing a foundation for morality, they have gained for their religion a free ride on the back of the family culture that most Americans embrace. In their latest book, Professors Hadden and Shupe show that Falwell did not create the morality of the majority, but simply presupposed its existence. I suggest that he and the televangelists are not the leaders of the moral majority but at best the followers. Had there been no TV evangelists at all, the moral rules and ideals of family culture would have continued as they have for centuries. Indeed, often despite the voice of many far-right preachers, human rights for women and children have recently emerged more clearly and gained a more secure position.

Some of the Reconstructionists are therefore partially correct when they say that the concepts of democracy and inalienable human rights are not unequivocally and clearly taught in the Bible. Christians in past centuries frequently quoted Scripture in defense of slavery, and since the Bible is rooted in the traditions of the ancient Middle East, many of its passages demean women. The principle of religious and philosophical freedom is not taught unequivocally in the Bible. Nor is the principle of freedom of speech. When the televangelists imply that the founding fathers were all evangelical Christians and that the nation was founded on the Bible, they rewrite history to serve their own purposes.

Thomas Jefferson saw that a large portion of the Bible failed to measure up to the highest moral ideal. While George Washington was an evangelical Episcopalian, he did not regard the United States to be a Christian nation but a nation where a variety of religions could thrive in peace. To "the Hebrew Congregation" of Newport, Rhode Island, he spoke of "inherent natural rights" and "an enlarged and liberal policy." To all America's Roman Catholics he offered reassuring words: "As mankind becomes more liberal, they will be more apt to allow that all those who conduct themselves as worthy members of the community are equally entitled to the protection of civil government." The second American president, John Adams, became a Unitarian as he grew increasingly skeptical of the orthodox doctrine of the Trinity and other creedal niceties. Skeptical also of prophecies, Adams believed that human reason could be trusted to explore nature without appealing to miracles. When Thomas Jefferson became president, he abandoned the precedent of proclaiming days of fasting and praying. "Fasting and prayer are religious exercises," he said, explaining that they do not as such belong to the province of government.[6] Thomas Paine, like Jefferson, was openly critical of orthodoxy. Abraham Lincoln began as an evangelical Christian but after many years of theological anguish became a Universalist who could no longer believe in everlasting hell.

The truth seems to be that from its beginning, the United States has been a nation where both religion and secular philosophies could thrive openly precisely because no one religious movement had succeeded in entrenching itself as the nation's orthodoxy. Jim Bakker, Pat Robertson, and other televangelists seemed to have overlooked this fact in their zeal to promote the myth of America as the divinely ordained New (Christian) Israel.

Notes

(**Note:** Within the text, biblical references may refer to the following versions: *KJV*–King James Version; *NEB*–New English Bible; *RSV*–Revised Standard Version.)

CHAPTER 1

1. Tammy Bakker with Cliff Dudley, *I Gotta Be Me* (Harrison, AR: New Leaf Press, 1978), 55.

2. Jim Bakker, *You Can Make It,* (Charlotte, NC: PTL Television Network, 1983), 113.

3. Tammy Bakker with Cliff Dudley, *Run to the Roar: The Way to Overcome Fear* (Charlotte, NC: PTL Television Network, 1980), 79.

4. *Ibid.,* 84.

5. Tammy Bakker, *I Gotta Be Me,* 108.

CHAPTER 2

1. Jim Bakker with Robert Paul Lamb, *Move That Mountain* (Charlotte, NC: PTL Television Network, 1976), 130.

2. Tammy Bakker, *I Gotta Be Me,* 104.

3. Jim Bakker, *Move That Mountain,* 152.

4. Tammy Bakker, *I Gotta Be Me,* 104.

5. Jim Bakker, *Move That Mountain,* 155.

6. Oral Roberts, *The Call, Oral Roberts' Autobiography* (New York: Avon Books, 1973), 38.

CHAPTER 3

1. E. E. Evans-Pritchard, *Witchcraft, Oracles and Magic Among the Azande*

(Oxford: Oxford University Press, 1937), 194.

2. Tammy Bakker, *Run to the Roar,* 36.

3. Jim Bakker, *You Can Make It,* 12.

4. Tammy Bakker, *Run to the Roar,* 36.

5. Tammy Bakker, *I Gotta Be Me,* 27.

6. See Nick Tosches, *Hellfire: The Jerry Lee Lewis Story* (New York: Dell Publishing Co., Inc., 1982), 40–45, 49.

7. Acts 2:17–18 (Revised Standard Version).

8. Pat Robertson with William Proctor, *Beyond Reason: How Miracles Can Change Your Life* (New York: Bantam Books, 1984), 80.

9. Tammy Bakker, *Run to the Roar,* 66.

10. See Pat Robertson, *Beyond Reason,* 1.

CHAPTER 4

1. Straub, *Salvation for Sale: An Insider's View of Pat Robertson's Ministry* (Buffalo, New York: Prometheus Books, 1986), 62.

2. See *ibid.,* 63f.

3. See Jim Bakker, *Move That Mountain,* 61.

4. Tammy Bakker, *I Gotta Be Me,* 69.

5. Gerard Straub, *Salvation for Sale,* 161.

6. See *ibid.,* 162.

7. Tammy Bakker, *I Gotta Be Me,* 90.

CHAPTER 5

1. See Kenneth L. Woodward and Frank Gibney Jr., "Saving Souls—Or a Ministry?" *Newsweek* (July 13, 1987), 52.

CHAPTER 6

1. Cited in Frye Gaillard's article, "The Rise and Fall of Jim Bakker," *Charlotte Observer* (March 29, 1987), 1B.

2. "An Interview with Barbara Cartland," in Kathryn Falk, ed., *How to Write Romance and Get It Published* (New York: Crown Publishers, 1983), 313.

3. See Henry Eichel, "Bakker Knew 'Kevin's House' Didn't Meet Codes," *Charlotte Observer* (August 11, 1987), 1A, 4A.

4. Dan Huntley and Henry Eichel, "Kevin, Family Forced Out of Kevin's House," *Charlotte Observer* (August 12, 1987), 2E.

CHAPTER 7

1. See Elizabeth Leland, "PTL Mementos," *Charlotte Observer* (May 24, 1987), 1C–2C.

2. See "Bakkers's Years of Luxury," *Charlotte Observer* (May 22, 1987), 8A.

3. See Charles Shepard, "Bakker Says He Wants PTL Back," the *Charlotte Observer* (May 29, 1987), 8A.

4. See Charles E. Shepard, "'PTL Dealings Defied All Business Practices,' Official Says," *Charlotte Observer* (May 23, 1987), 1A, 13A.

5. See John Wildman and Charles E. Shepard, "Highly Paid Bakker Aide Unknown to PTL Viewers," *Charlotte Observer* (April 28, 1987), 8A.

6. *Ibid.*

7. See Charles E. Shepard, "PTL Board Minutes Include No Bonus Figures," *Charlotte Observer* (May 29, 1987), 7A.

8. See Henry Eichel, "PTL Seeks To Oust Goodmans," the *Charlotte Observer* (September 19, 1987), 1C, 4C.

9. Cited in Charles E. Shepard, "3 PTL Directors Didn't Know What Bakker Was Paid," *Charlotte Observer* (April 22, 1987), 9A.

10. Associated Press, "Dortch Disputes PTL Dismissal Reason," *Charlotte Observer* (July 29, 1987), 6B.

11. Associated Press, "Fla. County Charges Dortches With Fraud In Land Tax Case," *Charlotte Observer* (August 2, 1987), 6B.

12. Michael Crook, "Polk to Prosecute Ex-PTL Official's Wife," *Tampa Tribune* (June 19, 1987), 1A, 14A.

13. See Charles E. Shepard, "2 Lawyers Left PTL Over Concern About Who Controlled Ministry," *Charlotte Observer* (May 29, 1987), 7A.

14. See Ed Martin and Charles E. Shepard, "PTL Dismisses 200 Employees To Cut Costs," *Charlotte Observer* (May 9, 1987), 10A. Staff writer Linda Brown contributed to this article.

15. The figures are taken from Charles E. Shepard, "PTL '86 Payments to Bakkers: $1.6 Million," *Charlotte Observer* (April 18, 1987), 1A. The figure on Jim and Tammy's compensation was updated from $1.6 million to $1.9 million by Charles Shepard in "2 Lawyers Left PTL Over Concern About Who Controlled Ministry."

16. Elizabeth Leland, "PTL Wants Bonuses Returned," *Charlotte Observer* (May 23, 1987), 1B.

17. Cited in Charles E. Shepard and Elizabeth Leland, "PTL Dug Itself Into a Hole With Burgeoning Partnerships," the *Charlotte Observer* (July 5, 1987), 5A.

18. *Ibid.*

19. Henry Eichel (Columbia Bureau), "Falwell Says PTL Rebounds," *Charlotte Observer* (August 5, 1987), 1B, 6B.

20. Jon D. Hull, "The Rise and Fall of 'Holy Joe,'" *Time* (August 3, 1987), 54.

21. Henry Eichel and Elizabeth Leland, "Bakker Allies Heat Up PTL Creditor Meeting," *Charlotte Observer* (July 23, 1987), 1B, 2B.

22. See Charles E. Shepard and Elizabeth Leland, "PTL Dug Itself . . . ," 1A, 4A, 5A.

23. See Associated Press, "Bankruptcy Judge Foresees Successful PTL Reorganization," *Charlotte Observer* (August 8, 1987), 3B. Roe Messner submitted in early September 1987 itemized bills, payment schedules, and correspondence from him and his associates to Bakker and Dortch. Messner's suit against PTL totals $14.9

million. See Henry Eichel, "Messner Details Claim of $14.9 million at PTL," *Charlotte Observer* (September 15, 1987), 1A, 6A.

24. Hull, "The Rise and Fall of 'Holy Joe,' " 55.

25. See *The Washington Post National Weekly Edition* 4:36 (July 6, 1987), 23.

26. Gary Wright, "Lawyer: PTL Focus Ended Job," *Charlotte Observer* (August 8, 1987), 1B.

CHAPTER 8

1. *Jim and Tammy Bakker: The Story of People That Love* (Toronto: Boulton Publishing Services, Inc., 1986), 203.

2. See Joe E. Barnhart, *The Billy Graham Religion* (Philadelphia: Pilgrim Press, 1972); Jeffrey K. Hadden and Anson Shupe, *Televangelism, Money, and Power* (New York: Holt, 1987).

3. *Jim and Tammy Bakker,* 192.

CHAPTER 9

1. See "Behind the Scenes at PTL: Building Heritage USA," *Charlotte Observer* (January 27, 1986), 5A.

2. *Jim and Tammy Bakker,* 26.

3. Cited in "Behind the Scenes at PTL."

4. See *ibid.*

5. Letter to the editor, *The West Coast Review of Books* 12:6 (1987), 19.

6. Gerard Straub, *Salvation for Sale,* 18.

7. See Edmund D. Cohen, *The Mind of the Bible-Believer* (Buffalo, New York: Prometheus Books, 1986), 398n.

8. "TV Evangelists (2)" program on Ted Koppel's "Nightline," ABC News, show 1521 (March 24, 1987), 7.

9. See Bruce Henderson, "Tammy Bakker Says, 'We're Very Sad Now,' " *Charlotte Observer* (April 29, 1987), 9A.

10. Frye Gaillard, "The Rise and Fall of Jim Bakker," *Charlotte Observer* (March 29, 1987), 1B.

11. Jim Bakker, *You Can Make It,* 90.

12. "Falwell: Case Could Lead to Criminal Investigation," *Charlotte Observer* (March 29, 1987).

13. Jim Bakker, *You Can Make It,* 91.

14. *Ibid.*

CHAPTER 10

1. See "Susan Rotolo, Bob Dylan," in Victoria Balfour, ed., *Rock Wives* (New York: Beech Tree Books, 1986), 58.

2. Buffalo, New York: Prometheus Books, 1987.

3. Tammy Bakker, *I Gotta Be Me*, 33.

4. See David E. Harrell, Jr., *All Things Are Possible*, 197–200.

5. A. A. Allen, *Power to Get Wealth* (Miracle Valley, AZ: A. A. Allen Revivals, [1963]), i–viii. Italics added.

6. Cited in Harrell, *All Things Are Possible*, 200.

7. See "Dallas—New Site of TVH Headquarters," *The Voice of Healing* (January 1953), 12.

8. Jim Bakker, *You Can Make It*, 87f.

9. *Ibid.*, 88.

10. *Ibid.*, 88f.

11. *Ibid.*, 86.

12. Richard L. Rubenstein, "Japan and Biblical Religion," *Free Inquiry* 7:3 (Summer 1987), 19.

13. Jim Bakker, *Move That Mountain*, 55f.

14. *Ibid.*

15. Jim Bakker, *You Can Make It*, 37.

CHAPTER 11

1. See David A. Yallop, *In God's Name: An Investigation into the Murder of Pope John Paul I* (New York: Bantam Books, 1984), 1–7, 117–127.

2. *Ibid.*, 216.

3. Andrew Greeley, *Confessions of a Parish Priest: An Autobiography* (New York: Simon and Schuster, 1986), 396.

4. *Ibid.*, 395f.

5. See "Catholics Give Less Than Prots," *Inside the American Religious Scene* 2:12 (July 3, 1987), 3.

6. "TV Evangelists Drop in Poll," *Inside . . .*, 3.

7. See "Evangelist Offers Job To Bakkers," *Charlotte Observer* (May 24, 1987), 2C.

8. Eve Simson, *The Faith Healers: Deliverance Evangelism in North America* (St. Louis: Concordia Publishing House, 1977), 106.

9. See Charles Shepard, "3 PTL Directors Didn't Know What Bakker Was Paid," 1A, 9A.

10. *Ibid.*

11. Cited in Frye Gaillard, "The Rise and Fall of Jim Bakker," 1B.

12. Melvin Richter, *The Politics of Conscience: T. H. Green and His Age* (Cambridge, MA: Harvard University, 1964), 23.

13. See Frye Gaillard, "The Child Who Would Be King," *Southern Magazine* 1:10 (July 1987), 32, 34.

CHAPTER 12

1. Rebecca West, *Living Philosophies* (New York: Simon and Schuster, 1940), cited in Karl Menninger, *Love Against Hate* (New York: Harcourt, Brace, & World,

Inc., 1942), 293.

2. Jim Bakker, *You Can Make It,* 38.
3. See Frye Gaillard, "The Child Who Would Be King," 37.
4. "News in Brief," *Inside the American Religious Scene* 2:15 (August 21, 1987), 4.

CHAPTER 13

1. See Joyce Wadler, "Breaking Faith, Two TV Idols Fall," *People Weekly* 27:20 (May 18, 1980), 85.
2. Cited in Karl Menninger, *Love Against Hate,* 281n.
3. See David Yallop, *In God's Name,* 26–31.
4. See Andrew Greeley, *Confessions of a Parish Priest,* 119.
5. Jim Bakker, *You Can Make It,* 28.
6. *Ibid.,* 29.
7. *Ibid.,* 94.
8. See *Inside the Religious Scene* 2:11 (June 19, 1987), 4.
9. See Jerry Falwell, "Future Word: An Agenda For the Eighties," *The Fundamentalist Phenomenon: The Resurgence of Conservative Christianity,* Jerry Falwell, Ed Dobson, and Ed Hindson, eds. (Garden City, NY: Doubleday, 1981), 203.
10. Cited in Charles Shepard, "National Church to Push For Answers," *Charlotte Observer* (March 25, 1987), 11A.
11. *Ibid.*
12. *Ibid.,* 1A.
13. See Charles E. Shepard, "John Wesley Fletcher Speaks Out," *Charlotte Observer* (March 29, 1987), 1A.
14. See Hebrews 6:4–6.
15. See Matthew 26:31–35, 69–75.

CHAPTER 14

1. See Joyce Wadler, "Breaking Faith," 86.
2. Frye Gaillard, "The Child Who Would Be King," 36.
3. Tammy Bakker, *I Gotta Be Me,* 77.
4. See *ibid.,* 76–82.
5. See *ibid.,* 79.
6. See Hans Sebald, *Witchcraft: The Heritage of a Heresy* (New York: Elsevier North Holland, Inc., 1978), 233.
7. New York: Harcourt, Brace, Jovanovich, 1938.
8. Tammy Bakker, *I Gotta Be Me,* 58f.
9. See Charles Shepard, "Bakker Treated for Drug Dependency," *Charlotte Observer* (March 7, 1987), 1A, 17A.
10. See Gaillard, "The Child Who Would Be King," 78.
11. Cited in Linda Brown, "Counselor Says Writhing, Retching Bakker Confessed," *Charlotte Observer* (March 25, 1987), 11A.

12. Cited in Wadler, "Breaking Faith," 86.

13. See Charles Shepard, "John Wesley Fletcher Speaks Out," 1A.

14. See Gaillard, "The Child Who Would Be King," 78.

15. Cited in John Wildman, "Fletcher: From Ambulance Driver to Faith Healer," *Charlotte Observer* (September 26, 1987), 1A.

16. See *ibid.,* 12A.

17. *Ibid.*

18. *Ibid.*

19. *Desert News,* Church Section (May 26, 1945), 5.

20. Cited in Jerald and Sandra Tanner, "Hofman Talks!" *Salt Lake City Messenger* 64 (September 1987), 6, 16. Italics added.

21. I have drawn from such released material as Frye Gaillard, "The Child Who Would Be King," 78; Charles Shepard, "John Wesley Fletcher Speaks Out," 11A; Jody Jaffe, "Jessica Hahn: The Woman Behind the Headlines," *Charlotte Observer* (May 21, 1987), 1A, 1C-2C; Joyce Wadler, "Breaking Faith," 86; *Star* (April 14, 1987), 5-7; Robert Scheer and Barry Golson, "The Jessica Hahn Story, Part One" (an interview with Hahn), *Playboy* 34:11 (November 1987), 82-99; "Bearing Body and Soul," *People Weekly* 28:14 (October 15, 1987), 32-37; Leon Freilich, "Why Jessica Hahn Said 'Yes' To Posing For Skin Magazine Photos," *Star* (September 29, 1987), 22-23. Jessica's affidavit has become a primary source. She gave her taped testimony to her legal representative Paul Roper in 1985. Bakker's lawyer heard the testimony and agreed to pay Jessica $265,000. In the thirty-one-page statement, Jessica told how Bakker "did everything he could to a woman."

22. See George Hackett and Peter McKillop, "Hahn Bares Her Soul, Etc.," *Newsweek* (October 12, 1987), 43.

23. See Ellen Goodman, "Jessica Hahn—The Victim Learns To Victimize Herself," *Charlotte Observer* (September 29, 1987), 19A.

24. See Jeffrey M. Masson, *The Assault on Truth: Freud's Suppression of the Seduction Theory* (New York: Farrar, Straus, and Giroux, 1984).

25. See Joyce Brothers, "Date Rape," *Parade* (September 27, 1987), 4-6.

26. See *ibid.*

27. *Ibid.,* 6.

CHAPTER 15

1. Henry Eichel, "Audit Shows Path of Money to Bakkers, Closest Aides," *Charlotte Observer* (July 25, 1987), 4B.

2. Cited in Flo Conway and Jim Siegelman, *Holy Terror: The Fundamentalist War on America's Freedoms in Religion, Politics, and Our Private Lives.* (Garden City, NY: Doubleday and Co., 1982), 50.

3. Henry Eichel, "A 2nd Heritage USA? PTL Plan Says Maybe," *Charlotte Observer* (August 12, 1987), 2E.

4. Jim Bakker, *Move That Mountain,* 127f.

CHAPTER 16

1. See Patti Roberts with Sherry Andrews, *Ashes to Gold* (Waco, TX: Word Books Publisher, 1987), 69.

2. Tammy Bakker, *I Gotta Be Me*, 87.

3. Andrew M. Greeley, *Confessions of a Parish Priest*, 133.

4. *Ibid.*, 134.

5. *Ibid.*, 135f.

6. *Ibid.*, 401.

7. Jerry Sholes, *Give Me That Prime-Time Religion: An Insiders Report On the Oral Roberts Evangelistic Association* (New York: Hawthorn Books, 1979), 192.

8. Bloomington: Indiana University Press, 1985, 431.

9. Old Tappan, NJ: Fleming H. Revell Co., 1980.

10. Falwell's sermon cited by Frances Fitzgerald, "A Disciplined, Charging Army," *The New Yorker* (May 18, 1981), 107f.

11. *Ibid.*, 138.

12. *Ibid.*

13. Tammy Bakker, *I Gotta Be Me*, 34.

CHAPTER 17

1. Arthur Koestler, "The Initiates," in *The God That Failed*, Richard Crossman, ed. (New York: Bantam Books, 1959), 39.

2. See Kenneth L. Woodward with Andrew Nagorski, "Visitations of the Virgin," *Newsweek* (July 20, 1987), 54f.

3. See Don Jacobson, *The Story of the Stories: The Chosen People and Its God* (New York: Harper and Row, 1982).

4. See John Calvin, *Institutes of the Christian Religion*, III: xxiii, 8, and II: iv, 3.

5. Gordon Clark, *Religion, Reason, and Revelation* (Philadelphia: Presbyterian and Reformed Publishing Co., 1961), 221.

6. *Ibid.*, 238.

7. John Emory, ed., *The Works of the Reverend John Wesley, A.M.*, 7 vols.; vol. 5 (New York: J. Emory and B. Waugh, 1831), 488.

8. New York: Schocken Books, 1981.

9. Jim Bakker, *You Can Make It*, 37.

10. See Oral Roberts, *3 Most Important Steps to Your Better Health and Miracle Living*, 209–213.

11. Jim Bakker, *You Can Make It*, 38.

12. *Ibid.*

13. *Inside the American Religion Scene: News and Analysis By Religious News Service* 2:13 (July 17, 1987), 4.

14. See Gerard Straub, *Salvation for Sale*, 159.

15. See David E. Harrell, Jr., *All Things Are Possible*, 142.

16. G. H. Montgomery, "A Lying Spirit in the Mouth of the Prophets,"

International Healing Magazine (April 1962), 6.

17. Cited in Harrell, *All Things Are Possible*, 58–63.

18. *Ibid.*, 63.

19. Jim Bakker, *You Can Make It*, 41. The italics are Bakker's.

20. Cited in Jerry Sholes, *Give Me That Prime-Time Religion*, 38.

21. See Jim Bakker, *Move That Mountain*, 95f.

22. Richard Kern, "Child Strangled in Exorcism Try," *The Iberian* (January 11, 1987).

23. Arno Clemens Gaebelein, *The Healing Question* (New York: Our Hope Publications Office, 1925), 93, cited in Eve Simson, *The Faith Healers: Deliverance Evangelism in North America* (St. Louis: Concordia Publishing House, 1977), 170.

24. Jim Bakker, *Move That Mountain*, 51.

25. *Ibid.*, 39.

CHAPTER 18

1. See John Wildman and Charles E. Shepard, "Highly Paid Bakker Aide Unknown to PTL Viewers," 8A.

2. Ken Hoyt and Frances Spatz Leighton, *Drunk Before Noon: The Behind-the-Scenes Story of the Washington Press Corps* (Englewood Cliffs, NJ: Prentice-Hall, Inc., 1979), 284.

CHAPTER 19

1. Ben Armstrong, *The Electric Church* (Nashville: Thomas Nelson, Inc., 1979), 20.

2. *Ibid.*, 43.

3. Jack Gould, "Video Departure," *New York Times*, October 26, 1952.

4. A. William Bluem, *Religious Television Programs* (New York: Hastings House Publishers, 1969), 37.

5. James Morris, *The Preachers* (New York: St. Martin's Press, 1973), 94.

6. Bluem, *Religious Television Programs*.

7. Allan Sloan, "The Electronic Pulpit," *Forbes*, July 7, 1980, 118. Also see Jeffrey Hadden and Charles Swanson, *Prime Time Preachers: The Rising Power of Televangelism* (Reading, MA: Addison-Wesley, 1981), 80.

8. "Critics, Electronic Church Try Two-Way Communication," *Christianity Today*, March 7, 1980, 66; Peter G. Horsfield, *Religious Television* (New York: Longman, Inc., 1984), 89.

9. Jimmy Swaggart, "Daily Word" broadcast, June 22, 1987.

10. Robert Schuller, "Hour of Power" broadcast, June 21, 1987.

11. Art Linkletter and Robert Schuller, "Hour of Power" broadcast, June 28, 1987.

12. Robert Schuller, "Hour of Power" broadcast, June 21, 1987.

13. Pat Robertson, "700 Club," May 12, 1987.

14. Jerry Falwell, "PTL Club," June 22, 1987.

15. Horsfield, *Religious Television,* 105.

EPILOGUE

1. Karl Menninger, *Man Against Himself* (New York: Harcourt, Brace and World, Inc./Harvest Book, 1938), p. 378.

2. See Joanne Kaufman, "The Fall of Jimmy Swaggart," *People Weekly,* 29:9 (March 7, 1988), 35.

3. See James Robison, *Thank God, I'm Free: The James Robison Story* (Nashville: Thomas Nelson Publishers, 1988), p. 115.

4. New York: Henry Holt and Co., 1988.

5. Cited in Tom McIver, "Christian Reconstructionism, Post-Millennialism, and Creationism," *Creation/Evolution Newsletter,* 8:1 (January/February 1988), 15.

6. See Edwin Scott Gaustad, *A Religious History of America* (New York: Harper and Row, 1966), pp. 125-131.